D0061488

Awakening the Energies of Love

Discovering Fire for the Second Time

Someday, after mastering the winds, the waves, the tides, and gravity, we shall harness for God the energies of love, and then, for a second time in the history of the world, humanity will have discovered fire.

Pierre Teilhard de Chardin

Awakening
the Energies of Love

Discovering Fire for the Second Time

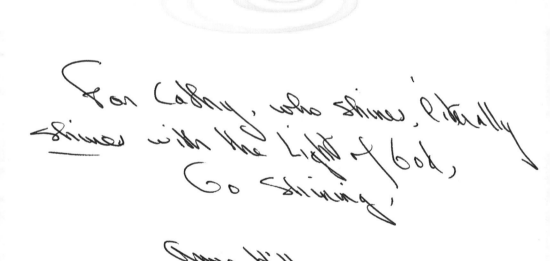

For Cathy, who shines, literally
shines with the Light of God,
Go Shining,

Anne Hillman

Anne Hillman

www.annehillman.net

Copyright ©2008 by Anne Hillman
All rights reserved. No part of this book may be reproduced in any manner
whatever, including information storage, or retrieval, in whole or in part
(except for brief quotations in critical articles or reviews),
without written permission from the publisher.

For information please contact:
Bramble Books
E-mail address: info@bramblebooks.com

The Library of Congress Cataloging-in-Publication Data:

Hillman, Anne.
Awakening the energies of love : discovering fire for the second time / Anne Hillman.
    p. cm.
ISBN 978-1-883647-16-2 (alk. paper)
1. Love--Religious aspects. 2. Spirituality. 3. Spiritual life. I. Title.

BL626.4.H55 2008
205'.677--dc22

2008026937

1   3   5   7   9   10   8   6   4   2
08 10 12 13 11 09

Printed in United States of America

The paper used in this publication meets the minimum requirements of
American National Standard for Information Sciences—
Permanence of Paper for Printed Library Materials, ANSI Z39.48-1984

Acknowledgements

The author gratefully acknowledges the generosity of the following poets, translators, publishers, and museum coordinator who freely gave permission to reprint selections from their works:

Coleman Barks, for three selections from Jalal al-Din Rumi, *The Essential Rumi*, translated by Coleman Barks, HarperCollins.

Wendell Berry, for an excerpt from "The Clear Days," in *The Selected Poems of Wendell Berry*, Counterpoint Press.

Daniel Ladinsky for an excerpt from *The Gift: Poems by Hafiz*, translated by Daniel Ladinsky, Penguin Group, Inc.

Robin Begbie for "Connecting," ©2007 by Robin Begbie.

Colin Oliver for "In The Vast Sweep Of Heaven," ©2004 by Colin Oliver.

Jennifer Paine Welwood, for an excerpt from "Unconditional," from *Poems for the Path*, ©1998 by Jennifer Welwood.

George Quasha and Susan Quasha and Barrytown/Station Hill Press, Inc. for Mary Caroline Richards, "Poet," from *Imagine Inventing Yellow: New and Selected Poems*, Barrytown, New York: Barrytown/Station Hill Press, ©1991 by Mary Caroline Richards. All rights reserved. Reprinted by permission of the Publishers.

Ruth Janson, Coordinator of Rights and Reproductions, Brooklyn Museum for permission to reproduce Pablo Picasso's "Minotauromachia."

Grateful acknowledgment is also made for permission to reprint excerpts from the following works:

"For the Time Being," ©1944 and renewed 1972 by W. H. Auden, from *Collected Poems* by W. H. Auden. Used by permission of Random House, Inc.

"let it go – the," Copyright 1944, ©1972, 1991, by the Trustees for the E. E. Cummings Trust, from *Complete Poems: 1904-1962* by E. E. Cummings, edited by George Firmage. Used by permission of Liveright Publishing Corporation.

Excerpt from "Little Gidding" in *Four Quartets*, copyright 1942 by T. S. Eliot and renewed 1970 by Esme Valerie Eliot, reprinted by permission of Harcourt, Inc.

Excerpt from "The Dry Salvages" in *Four Quartets*, copyright 1941 by T. S. Eliot and renewed 1969 by Esme Valerie Eliot, reprinted by permission of Harcourt, Inc.

Excerpt from "East Coker" in *Four Quartets*, ©1940 by T. S. Eliot and renewed 1968 by Esme Valerie Eliot, reprinted by permission of Harcourt, Inc.

Excerpt from "I Came Into the Unknown," edited by Willis Barnestone, from *The Poems of Saint John of the Cross*, copyright ©1972 by Willis Barnestone. Reprinted by permission of New Directions Publishing Corp. Sales Territory: World rights.

My gratitude also for permission to reproduce the following art works:

The reconstruction painting of "Homo habilis" ©1989 by Jay H. Matternes.

Authorization to reproduce Pablo Picasso's "Minotauromachia," ©2007 Estate of Pablo Picasso / Artists Right Society (ARS), New York.

"Schematic of the brain" image and excerpt. Copyright ©1977 by Carl Sagan. Originally published in *The Dragons of Eden* by Random House. Reprinted with permission from Democritus Properties, LLC. All rights reserved. This material cannot be further circulated without written permission of Democritus Properties, LLC.

"In the Wilderness," was previously published in *Heron Dance Journal*, North Ferrisburg, VT: Heron Dance Publishers, 2004.

"Green" was previously published in somewhat different forms in *The Salt Literary Journal*, Santa Fe, NM: Salt Publishing Co., January, 2000 and in *The Almanac*, Menlo Park, CA: Embarcadero Publishing Co., January, 2000.

'Love is Born of Grief ' and the story entitled "Grief" in which it appears were previously published in different form in *The Almanac*, Menlo Park, CA: Embarcadero Publishing Co., October, 1998.

"The Snake—1" was previously published in slightly different form in *The Almanac*, Menlo Park, CA, June, 2003.

For our children, our grandchildren,
and their great-grandchildren's great-grandchildren

All of them

o

With deepest gratitude for

Richard Moss
Joyce Schmid
Brenda Morgan

You have lit the Way

Table of Contents

Foreword
by Richard Moss

All of us know something of love: we fall in love, love our children, love those who love us, fall out of love and from our
emotional emptiness yearn for it obsessively. Few of us know
what it is to be claimed by love, not claimed as in an obsession
with another, but claimed as in taken hold of, shaken, brought
to our knees in awe and gratitude, and eventually strengthened.
This is love as fire, and the core of what this book is about.
We test metal in fire; heat it red and plunge it into cold water
to temper it and give it extra strength. Love, in the way Anne
Hillman experienced it and discusses it here, is a spiritual fire
that awakens us to a new consciousness; one that instructs us
and makes us strong for a new purpose.

   This book challenges us to answer whether we, as individuals and as a society, are meeting the imperative of evolution.
That imperative, our new—even essential—purpose, Anne tells
us, is to realize a sense of ourselves, individually and collec-
tively, that goes beyond the divisions created in our minds by
allegiance to different faiths or ideologies. Welcoming all faith
and philosophies, she invites us, instead, to see the deeper,
more essential reality that is the source of all of these views. It
is an evolutionary leap beyond separateness to a fundamental
sense of connectedness and inclusiveness. This profound new

understanding rests upon a direct experience of a transcendental dimension of love. Quoting paleontologist and philosopher, Teilhard de Chardin, she calls this realization of love "Fire for the second time."

Human evolution took a giant leap when our early ancestors tamed fire, accelerating the development of language and marking the beginning of mankind's unconsciously grandiose project to control the planet for its own ends. Now that original survival project has created such material abundance that it threatens the health of the natural world and thus, our future survival. We are at the threshold of another evolutionary step, this time not achieved through physical fire (or its modern equivalents in the form of the latest weapons, medicines and technologies), but instead in the form of a transcendental fire, a spiritual awakening of love that burns away our ego-centeredness and opens our hearts to our essential unity.

This book is about that spiritual transformation. Anne Hillman might not admit it, but she was compelled to write about this because it is the kind of experience one cannot keep to oneself. That fire claimed her and showed her that the evolution of consciousness has not reached its apex with our current mental capacities; it is very much alive and working in us, calling us to a more than reasonable love. What she tells us, in retrospect, is that long before that experience became concrete and immediate, she was being called toward it, that her whole life was readying her for this potential, although she had no way to know that this was the case. The point she is making is that this is true of all of us. And by telling her own and others' stories, and drawing upon imagery and insight from traditional and non-traditional spiritual sources as well as from science, she makes that path accessible to others.

As her long time friend, I can tell you that Anne is a wise woman. She is also a mother and a wife, has suffered the death of a husband, forged several careers, and is a musician. Now, as an elder, she shares a broad vision of our spiritual potential and richness through her writings and with small groups of individuals who gather at her home. Some years ago while she was sitting quietly in the predawn stillness as she does most days, Anne noticed an almost imperceptible sensation in her upper abdomen—something unfamiliar, not pain, not even discomfort—that she hadn't noticed before. Although apparently in perfect health, she nonetheless listened to this new information from her body and went to see her doctor. The MRI showed two tumors in her pancreas. Listening to something so vague she couldn't even describe what she was sensing may have saved her life.

This isn't a story Anne would choose to tell you about herself as a way of introducing her, but I choose it because it testifies to how deeply she lives the path about which she writes. How many of us appreciate that we can notice and potentially avert an incipient disease simply by becoming still in ourselves and open to the moment of being? When do we make space for this in our lives?

How can we imagine, in the urgency that propels our lives, that we could ever obey something that calls us beyond survival, and which awakens us to the necessity of transcendence? We are all constantly tested in the tension between these two fundamental necessities: survival and transcendence. Our bodies demand survival; our souls yearn for transcendence. What reconciles these seemingly opposing needs is the fire of transcendent love. Without being tested in this love, our fears for our own survival forever lead us into the illusory pursuit of control—and thus, into endless competition and conflict with others. And without being tempered in the fire of love, transcendence can become merely a form of flight from the pain and paradox of daily life. This kind of flight cannot make us strong enough to resist fear, let alone, instill a passion that insists upon the moral vision and behavioral changes necessary to heal ourselves and our world.

This is an important book about the human spirit eloquently expressed in prose and poetic imagery so that we can see ourselves with new eyes, recognize steps we may already be taking, and find assistance to take further steps toward a new heart. Drawing on the accounts of others who have been graced by this fire, Anne explains how our current human consciousness is but a stage in a continuum of consciousness evolution, and how the next step, forged in the cauldron of love, is our birthright and our destiny. What does that next level look like? How can you awaken to it in your life? This book will inspire you to answer those questions for yourself.

Richard Moss, MD
Author of *The Mandala of Being*
http://www.richardmoss.com

The Known

Homo habilis painting ©1989 Jay H. Matternes

Fire for the Second Time

At a national professional conference almost thirty years ago, the walls of the huge hotel ballroom were hung with hand-painted posters. One of them so captivated me that I wanted it the way a child wants to keep a treasure found in the sand at the beach. I asked someone on the committee if I might have the poster when the meetings were over and later, when I learned it was mine, eased it off the wall as carefully as if I were unwrapping a beautiful gift. Since then, this unframed sheet of newsprint has hung where I see it every day. The paper is faded and worn but the poster paint is still radiant, a message emblazed in cobalt blue over a bright red and yellow campfire:

> When man discovers Love,
> He will have discovered Fire for the Second Time.
> Pierre Teilhard de Chardin

I will always be grateful to that unknown artist. I didn't know the quote or realize it had been distilled from a longer one, but the power of the single phrase that called Love *"Fire for the Second Time"* never left me.

I recognized in its simplicity something I had always intuited—that Love was more than a feeling; more than consolation, companionship, or goodness. It was not the romantic love I'd sought as an adolescent, nor was it the love of a young woman for her husband, or a mother for her child. It was something more—something at root, seminal, and forever indefinable.

Teilhard's original words gave voice to a much larger vision—one that spanned the journey of the whole human race:

Someday, after mastering the winds, the waves, the tides, and gravity, we shall harness for God the energies of Love, and then, for a second time in the history of the world, humanity will have discovered Fire.

It was then I understood: The awakening of Love in the human heart was the spiritual journey of our Time. It heralded a transformation that would be as life-changing for each one of us—and for all those we subsequently touched—as the taming of fire had been for our ancestors in the wild. Deep within me, I knew that this Love called Fire had wooed me from the earliest days of my childhood—I had been its disciple all my life.

The Call to Awaken

1 Invitation to Awakening

> Someday, after mastering the winds, the waves, the tides, and gravity, we shall harness for God the energies of Love, and then, for a second time in the history of the world, humanity will have discovered Fire.
>
> Pierre Teilhard de Chardin[1]

We stand at an evolutionary juncture, called to awaken to a new kind of Love.[2] This Love is not a feeling; it is a great power. Awakening to this radically different Love may be gradual or it may come in a flash—an explosion that rocks you to your core. Either way, it will shatter your perception of who you think you are. The power of Love initiates a complete change of mind— the fundamental transformation that Teilhard de Chardin calls *Fire for the second time.*

Hidden behind the beauty and simplicity of Teilhard's words, lies the *first fire.* He doesn't mention that fire,[3] but its flames illuminate his every line and shine through these pages, as well. It was fire that opened wide the doors of possibility, fire that brought us from strange, upright creatures on the forest floor to our humanity. Carried from the wild and harnessed in the cave, fire offered its warmth, light, and a center for the human circle—a safe place to gather for the long cold night, and there, attempt to voice our awe.

Our ancestors' longing—their passion for fire—led to an act that drove evolution. They harnessed fire and language blossomed.[4] Out of the confluence of fire and language emerged an immense creativity, one that evolved into thought, reflection, story, and an ongoing search for meaning. It was a radical transformation of the human mind.

Transformation is born at the great hinges of Time—one like ours in which everything about us is fundamentally changing. Those who carried fire home in their hands lived at a Time in the great cosmic unfolding when the combined forces of nature and psyche invited them to act in a new way. Propelled by a yearning that ran counter to their bodies' counsel and to the time-tested wisdom of their clan, they took an enormous risk: Instead of running away from fire, they engaged it. Our ancient progenitors were following something other than what they knew. Call it a vision or a dream; *something* led them to step off the threshold of the known into the darkness of the unknown.

We, too, stand at an evolutionary juncture, led by an unspoken yearning we've felt in our bones since childhood: a longing to be somehow more than we are. This deep human desire—whether to love more completely, to be more whole, to live in peace, or to come face to face with the divine—propels us on an inward path toward an unknown. Long proclaimed by philosophers and religious traditions of east and west, this unknown marks the conscious emergence of a Love that is qualitatively different from the one that we think we know. To engage its energies is a collision, a radical break in continuity with the familiar. Such a Love conflicts with old structures of mind, old beliefs, and old behaviors; it entails a new orientation, new ways of seeing and hearing, and an entirely different way of relating—to everything.

Before embarking on such a journey, you may be asking certain questions:

What is a call and how do we answer it?

What is the Love of which Teilhard sings,
  the Fire of transformation?

Why does awakening matter?

How does one awaken?

I invite you to live into these questions with me and to circle them in an ever-deepening way as we walk the path of awakening together.

What Is a Call and How Do We Answer It?

Our call takes place underground, far beneath our awareness. Like a soundless song, it sings to us all our lives, whispering in a wordless way, *"Follow!"* The aboriginal names this indwelling call her[5] songline. It is her soul path; her potential. Listening to it, following it, she is intimately connected to the place where she was born and to the mysterious Beginnings from which her ancestors came. I call it the song of the soul.

I became aware of my own songline one spring morning when out of the blue, my husband, George, asked me at the breakfast table, "What's the most memorable last line in a movie you've ever heard?" "Last line!" I was still in my bathrobe and barely able to think. "I can't even remember the title of the movie we saw last night, much less, the last line!" Yet even as I spoke, as clearly as if it were yesterday, there stood the figure of Jean Valjean in a grainy black and white film I'd seen in high school—*Les Miserables*. Summing up his philosophy of life, his last words were, *"Aimez-vous bien. C'est tout."*

"Love well. That is everything."

With that memory, arose another, more painful one. Years before, I had been abruptly widowed when my first husband, Milton, was killed in a plane crash.[6] He was thirty-four. As Valjean's words echoed in my mind, I remembered the tiny home in the woods we'd shared with our son and daughter—

the way the New Hampshire sky, the trees, and the deep spring afloat with aspen leaves had held us.

The tall trees had not protected us from our pain. They'd stood as silent in our anguish as in our joy, blessing our fierce efforts at love as they blessed our children's soft childhood. That little family still lies at the heart of me. At the breakfast table that spring morning, as I relived the devastation and the rupture of his death, I remembered our subsequent departure from the woods' embrace, the struggle to start over in the city— its parched streets, its noise, the absence of trees—and the long dry walk that followed.

Milton and I had been musicians in those early years, but I could no longer sing. I needed a different kind of work. Stirred by the social upheavals of the sixties, I decided to enter a new field: the dynamics of change. In class one day, a professor asked us to write an epitaph for our own tombstones. Having just been through the heartbreaking process of choosing one for my young husband, I knew how significant a question it was. Without a pause, a phrase presented itself: *She loved well.* As the professor waited for us to complete our task, I stared at the epitaph I'd lettered across the newsprint before me. It felt like a very high standard for a young widow who was still grieving her husband and wishing she'd known how to love him better while he was alive.

I became a consultant in the field of Organizational Development. Moving from state to state and from east coast to west, I worked to help the management in hospitals and other organizations plan and design their own change. I had never been so lonely. Moving, working, dating, raising my children to maturity, I was trying to do everything—but I had no idea who I was. Ten years after Milton's death, I stumbled and fell. Exhausted, lonely, and too proud to admit I was afraid, it became clear that change agent or not, I needed to change myself. It was the defining moment of my life and the turning point that foreshadowed a long and difficult journey ahead.

More than twenty years after that midlife reversal, and remarried for almost as long, I sat at the breakfast table with George and pondered his question about last lines. Along with the memories it unleashed—Jean Valjean's words, Milton's ragged death, and the epitaph, *she loved well*—came a revelation: Hidden beneath the countless changes of direction in my outer life, there had been an inner constancy. No matter how many professions I'd had or states I'd lived in, no matter how many failures or wrong turns made, I had followed only one path: The yearning to love and to love well had been my songline. I had kept a commitment to my self.

I also recognized, from this longer perspective, that it was a commitment to something more. At midlife, I hadn't yet understood that the yearning I felt for connection and love was not just my own, but part of a longing for meaning and for community that was pervasive. We *all* lived—as we do now—in a fractured culture and a suffering world, and most of us were searching for new ways of relationship. By now, however, I knew that even though my earlier response had been to something deep within me, the whispered song that had drawn me through life like a magnet was a call that rang throughout the human race.

> *The desire to love is not just a personal consecration but one sourced in the depths of life itself. This longing and the need of the earth and its peoples are one and the same.*[7]

Our longing—our yearning—is part and parcel of the song of the soul, and it has always beckoned us toward a future that is not ours alone. We may choose to follow it by ourselves, but *that* we follow it matters to generations; for just as the embers of the first fire ignited the power of language, those of the second will ignite the power in our hearts.

We belong to an awakening species. Human consciousness[8] literally exploded after man snatched fire from the wilderness. From that Time on, other transformations ever so gradually led countless generations driven purely by instinct to awaken to deeper feeling, and later, to the mystery of thought. In our own lives, we each relive these ancestral awakenings: We evolve quite literally from animal-creatures in the womb who are initially guided by sensations, to young children who are also influenced by deep feelings, and who then cross the threshold of thought. The call of *Fire for the Second Time* now bids us seek beyond our reliance on thought in order to become wise in love.

The call to awaken is an invitation to adventure—one lived on life's frontier. Like all frontiers, it can be exhilarating at times, frightening at times, daring always. I believe this ongoing inquiry into life is the song we are here to learn. Each one of us has our own part to sing, and I am still learning mine. We are all pioneers, and in our yearning and our questioning, we have already set forth—particularly in our uncertainty, particularly when we ask the deeper questions people have always asked.

Who am I?

What is love?

What is God?

I think that as we ask these fundamental questions of identity *and cannot answer them*, we step past a culture's intellectual, social, or psychological responses—and start to turn toward the unknown. As we do, Love whispers to us that we are not the small-hearted persons often portrayed by the media, not the brittle public selves donned by television anchors with strident, stylized voices. It says we are far more than consumers wooed by the advertising world; more than our jobs or our achievements; more than what we know, what we do, or what we own. It tells us we belong to life and are already far more than we *think*—and that we will find both Love and *who we really are* by following a different path—one that takes us to our root.

The path to our root is not linear. It is a deepening: deeply thought, deeply engaged, and deeply felt. As a human community, we've lost track of the depth that binds us to a context larger than ourselves—to the community, to the planet, to the universe—to the greater Life itself. We have been focusing on more immediate goals. We've gone to the moon and back, to

Mars and the depths of the ocean; we've sought to heal the sick and solve the great mathematical puzzles of all time. The tools we've invented—telescopes, microscopes, space ships, and drills that probe the earth's crust—have been our guides to many magnificent discoveries in the outer world. But few have found the inner compass that *orients us* to these vast regions of existence—and to the unknown vastness of our selves. To follow a soul path like this is the quest of a lifetime and relates us to the great mysteries of the outer/inner life. By engaging its practices, we awaken to a larger personhood—one that is infinitely more aware, infinitely more empathic.

What is the Love of Which Teilhard Sings, the Fire of Transformation?

It may seem that the Love that calls us is not the love we thought. It isn't.

This Love called *Fire* is *charged*: with the numinous, with light, with aliveness—and also with danger. If you seek what it means to harness the energies of Love for God, you will need to prepare yourself for its power. Teilhard's phrase—*for God*—sets the call to love squarely in the domain of religion and spirituality,[9] but for many of us, words like God—or Brahman, the Tao, the Mystery, and many others—can be hard to swallow. For some, such language seems incompatible with their worldviews. Others may feel disappointed with the version of God they absorbed as children. Still other seekers feel spiritually homeless. If you have any of these concerns, I invite you to turn to Appendix I, "The Issue of God." Words like God, *divine, sacred, holy*—are loaded, encrusted by centuries of misunderstanding and misuse. To me, they are but hints and whispers, intimations of the unknown.

How many ways there are to connect with the mystery of life! One person sits in a garden contemplating a flower and sees in it the divine. Another dances or drums, paints or meditates, or wonders at the night sky. John Adams is an example:

> I find my imagination . . . roaming in the Milky Way, among those mighty . . . orbits of suns, planets, satellites, and comets, which compose the incomprehensible universe; and if I do not sink into nothing in my own estimation, I feel an irresistible impulse to fall on my knees. . . .[10]

Whatever our way, if we follow it deeply enough, it will bring us to the same place. All well-honed spiritual paths point to a root experience of awakening that transcends what we may have heard in our religions. Such an awakening cannot be taught in sermons or books, workshops, 'weekends,' or university classes. We can learn a lot *about* a path but the reality is, we have to live it.

Ellen Grace O'Brian writes:

> A spiritual path must present both philosophy and practice. . . . Study without practice can be likened to going into a fine restaurant, studying the menu, and departing before ordering or even tasting a meal. . . . Without a practice . . . spiritual aspirants are left with a set of beliefs and dictates they must struggle to follow without having a way to access the inner resources to do so . . . . Philosophy provides a foundation. . . . Practice will build upon that foundation a knowledge that is unshakable. . . .[11]

Along with a philosophy, a mature spiritual practice demonstrates experientially that what the soul knows is not about being good or bad. It is not about the heroic journey or having the power to fix our lives. Nor is it following glib rules for spiritual success. If you are serious about your soul's quest, you will need to go deeper than this.

Whoever carried fire home in his hands, first had to question every belief he had about fire—and those beliefs lay at his core. At our core, we have to question our beliefs about life, about love, and about who we are.

Life is deep.

What the soul knows is about the depth of love and fear, of creativity and destruction, joy and defeat; about human courage and self-giving and an entirely different kind of faith. It doesn't pander to those in the pews who want their religion neat—a quick shot on Friday or Sunday to last the week.

If you yearn for this kind of depth, you may, like me, have found yourself more than once at the boundary of a religious or spiritual tradition, wondering on the one hand, if you should enter or on the other, if you should leave! You may be inside the boundary, yet feel perplexed—thinking you don't understand or that something is missing. You may be outside the boundary, having thought you'd long since put religion behind you. You may have years of spiritual inquiry behind you; you may have none. But if you are seeking greater depth, it is you whom I am addressing—whatever side of the door you are on, whatever your experience or tradition, if any. Our different perspectives require an embrace that can hold *all* of our individual stories, along with the many sacred and secular narratives that make our heritage rich. We find that embrace at our core.

Love is deep.

From the perspective of the greater Love, one is not *right* or *wrong* to be either inside or outside a particular boundary! A boundary is only a concept, a convenience used to define an organization's identity. Its social function is to interpret who 'belongs' and who 'does not.' So doing, it obscures the deepest intent of religion and creates conflict. These conflicts are tearing our social fabric and our world apart.

> "What a sad thing," laments British poet Colin Oliver, "to be part of institutions which wind up dousing the very thing that began them: *Fire*."[12]

It can be helpful to think of a boundary, not as a wall, but as a process, a permeable membrane. In the search for a compelling context for your life, you might feel undecided, and move back and forth across invisible boundaries for a long time. As you do, you may be surprised to discover that there are countless ways of understanding sacred texts and stories, some of which have long been misused and misunderstood. If you are seeking Love, a mature path is likely to instill in you a deep appreciation for diversity of all kinds, and you may find, as I have, that there is much to learn from the lives and teachings of those who've walked the many Ways different from your own.

Why Does Awakening Matter?

If we are to embrace our differences, our spiritual journey needs to show us how to hold them in a way that unifies, rather than separates; a way that frees us from judgment, fear, and prejudice—and the suffering and violence that grow out of them. The fruit of a mature spiritual path helps to heal the divisions and the pain that our boundaries have created. That is why awakening matters to all of us.

How Does One Awaken?

The common experience of awakening lies at the root of every tradition, every authentic spiritual teaching. The consciousness that emerges from such an awakening embraces every point of view, yet takes us beyond all of them. To sustain such a consciousness, however—to live an awakened life—requires that we do more than think about it. *We need to inhabit ourselves—* to redeem realms that have been lost to intellect but still reside in our hearts and bodies.

We are deep.

When we awaken, we know in every cell that we are far more than separate individuals: We are one human family that has always belonged to life. Our awakening is part of life's continuous unfolding and we will retrace its path. On our journey, we'll make a gradual descent from the familiar realm of the mind into a way of being in our hearts and bodies that offers a different means of perception.

My intent is to offer an interior experience that will give you the flavor of the awakening process and a glimmer of its living truth. While no book can replicate the spiritual journey, it is my hope that this one may offer you something more than thought; and that our passage together might provide the taste and feel of a hallowed world—a hallowed quality of being— and the wonder that rises with it.

We are all haunted by a song we scarcely know how to hear.

We awaken as we open to Life and learn to 'hear' differently. What we seek is profoundly primal—far deeper than thought. And while the mind's straightforward tone will establish the themes of our journey at the start, *it is the other voices—of the heart, the body, and the soul*—that will lead you from what you *know* in the first half of the book into the realm of the *unknown* in the second. The familiar voice of the mind may give you some ideas, but it is the other voices that actually convey the experience. Each chapter will lead you deeper into the song of the soul, deeper into your own awareness. If you'd like to come with me, I invite you to let go of the day's tasks, the constant effort to understand, and settle back in a comfortable chair or a quiet corner—in order to hear the subtler voices that lie within you:

> *The soul's whisper:* The whisper that breathes through 'The Song of the Soul' that follows hints at a primal belonging you once knew when you were very young. Something in you may recognize it, but it will not be your thinking mind. You'll hear that soundless whisper again as the child begins to tell her story; but sadly, it vanishes as she becomes an adult.

> *The heart's cry:* When the heart starts to tell its stories, no matter whose voice is speaking, it may begin to tap memories and feelings of your own. And though you may not hear the whisper yet, it is an opportunity to notice where your own heart takes you.

> *The voice of the mind:* You may lose the whisper temporarily when the intellect weaves its way into your life and heart; but once it has traced a path through the realms of the known, it steps aside to make room for a voice that leads us gently into the unknown.

The voice of the Storyteller: In the Interlude, the ancient voice of the Storyteller rises and begins to sing with a poet's cadence. She invites your body's remembrance of what it felt like to lie on the ground and fall in love with the mystery of light:

> There is a shade of green, a shade of wrinkled, barely unfolded leaves that I heard whisper long ago. It is a green that has light shining through it . . . light of light, light reflecting itself . . .

The body's chant: As she tells of rare encounters with creatures from land and sea, the Storyteller introduces the voice of the body and you may begin to feel its pulse as your own. The body's silent chant is an energy that rides on the subtlest of tones, the language of a new and radical intimacy with life.

It is the turning point of our journey.
We enter the unknown.

The voices of an awakening humanity: Only then, when you've listened in your bones to the stirrings of your body's wisdom, does the Storyteller gather her many singers to give voice to the experience of Mystery. Because we are awakening to this Mystery as a group, they are a chorus—of mystics and poets, philosophers and scientists, friends, strangers, and many ordinary people—all taking soundings, all seeking the depths of Life. Their songs, their stories and poetry are a calling out; a yearning winged from soul to soul, a leaning into God.

Then there is silence—and a kind of peace and understanding that knows no explanation. Out of the silence comes the soul, singing poetry. Singing Love.

I invite you to listen for the current beneath the words:

Notice what is evoked in you by the different voices—the intellect's weaving, the heart's cry, the body's chanted memories, and the poetry of the soul. The sound of each voice will induct the feeling of a different quality of consciousness in you. As each one metamorphoses to the next, ask yourself which voice you prefer—for it will shine a light into the depths of your soul.

Listen, too, for the hints and whispers of your own song:

If you find yourself sparked by feelings, memories, or images, I encourage you to jot them in the margins. When you've finished, go back and look them over—for it is there you will find your own creativity, your beauty, and your own path to the holy. Follow that path—not mine—for it traces the melody of your songline, the soul's guide toward your own awakening to the fullness of Love.

Then you will know that the mystery you've been seeking has also been seeking you; and that the questions you've asked have been answered by Love itself.

Listen! The sound of the whisper—do you hear it?—the song . . .

Invitation

The Song of the Soul

The inhabitant or soul of the universe is never
seen; its voice alone is heard. All we know is
that it has a gentle voice . . . a voice so fine
. . . that even children cannot become afraid.

Inuit teaching[13]

Something like a breeze whispered to me when I was very
small—something of such sweetness, a quality of realness and
truth like light shining on green leaves, the feel of a cat's soft
fur, or the scent of my mother's skin. And inside my body where
there are no words, I knew what it meant . . . but I couldn't say
what it was or even hold onto a hint of it. It was like the way
I can hear a song so clearly in a dream, yet cannot bring it to
mind once I awake. Still, it was of such importance that I spent
a lifetime following this sound that was not a sound, nor light,
nor touch—seeking its source.

Later, something about the way the church spoke to my
very young self with its rhythms and pageantry and light shining through colored glass invited me to look for it there. I sought
it in church for decades—that almost tangible hint of love and

rightness and belonging that the whisper had once conveyed—but it was gone; or at least *I* couldn't find it there. So I gave up in despair and walked away. Over the years, I returned to the church in hope and left, returned and left again . . .

The whisper continued, though, like a secret promise. I never made out its source. All I knew was that it seemed to have something to do with love, something to do with God, and something to do with who I was. It felt like the song of my soul.

The whisper was the starting point of a sacred journey, one that eventually brought me home. For a long time, I didn't know this home existed or that it was inside me, the path was so circuitous. Sometimes, you have to stray far outside the familiar and follow the events of your life no matter how far they take you—all the turns in the road, the hints, the chances, the failures; the hard work of inquiry and practice and change—and then, if life will have it, there comes a gift you could not have imagined or even sought, *for you could not have had the slightest idea in advance of what this gift would consist.* Afterwards, when you review your life, *everything* that had mattered to you—that to which the church, the poets, and philosophers had given expression in word and song and ritual—you know to be true. Just not the way you had thought. So it was that I sought love and found *Fire.*

As you read these words, if you listen, not with your ears but with your whole body, you may feel that current of living *Fire* radiating through you. No matter if it isn't apparent. You can, if you wish, trust that it is carried anyway, in ways that can neither be explained nor understood. This is the dilemma of the religions and the poets: To address a mystery—to name or describe something *so real*, yet which cannot be perceived by the five senses—is impossible. We are at a loss to describe such 'senseless' experience, awaiting words yet to be invented. Still, there are moments when each of us catches a glimpse of what the saints were blinded by. We never forget them.

Marilyn Veltrop[14] writes of being on a mountain in Maine:

I stood in a strong wind that was blowing clouds up the mountain-
side and gasped! A huge surge of energy rose through my body. . . .
What exhilaration! I took off my clothes and flew like an eagle on
the mountaintop, then stood with my arms raised and vowed to have
more of that ecstasy in my life.

You know this place. Think of an instant when you knew you
were at one with life; when you stood at the edge of the reality you knew—and saw you'd been given a taste of the infinite.
Maybe, as a child, you sat in your yard in the middle of a thun-
derstorm and felt each crash, your eyes wide open with wonder
as lightning flashed all around you. Or you lay in a warm field of
pungent grass watching clouds shape-shift overhead and your
body felt the earth turn on its axis for the first time. Perhaps you
fell in love with the sweet mystery of your newborn early one
morning and at the same moment, came to love the dawn. Or
you stood, terrified and exalted on a mountain top—a novice on
borrowed skis—and the sunlight pierced your terror and made
a feast of frost and ice on the trees. The glory of life rushed at
you and ran over you like a train.

Or you read a poet like T. S. Eliot, whose meaning you don't
quite understand; and even as he, too, struggles to give voice
to the ineffable, something reaches out from behind your mind
and beyond the obvious, and whispers, *"Yes!"*

With the drawing of this Love and the voice of this Calling

We shall not cease from our exploration
And the end of all our exploring
Will be to arrive where we started
And know the place for the first time . . .
Not known, because not looked for
But heard, half-heard, in the stillness
Between two waves of the sea . . .[15]

So it is that the whispered song of the soul calls to awaken
us all our lives. No matter what our experience, our minds do
not—cannot—understand. Still we yearn for it. Still we grope
together in that darkness—which is God.[16]

Endnotes for Chapter 1

1 I have chosen to use the better-known version of this quote from Teilhard, although I do not have its source. The original is from Pierre Teilhard de Chardin, SJ, *Toward the Future*, tr. Rene Hague, New York: Harcourt Brace Jovanovich, 1975, 87. "The day will come when, after harnessing the ether, the winds, the tides, gravitation, we shall harness for God the energies of love. And on that day, for the second time in the history of the world, man will have discovered fire." (Dated by Teilhard: "Peking, February 1934.") Translator Hague provides this comment on the word ether: "Writing today, Teilhard would say 'space.'" *Author's note*: In the same vein, I have replaced the word man with *humanity*.

Teilhard was a renowned scientist, paleontologist, and Jesuit theologian. According to his biographer Ursula King, PhD, Teilhard expanded "the dialogue between religion, science and mysticism . . ." and his "views put him on a collision course with his Jesuit superiors and church authorities in Rome. . . . His powerful vision and life-affirming spirituality speak . . . vitally to the concerns of our time." Ursula King, *Spirit of Fire* (Maryknoll, NY: Orbis Books, 1996, back cover.) Born in France in 1881, Teilhard served at the front during World War I after spending three years in Egypt, teaching and collecting fossils. After receiving his doctorate, he taught in Paris where King says he was considered a "brilliant research scientist and much sought after lecturer." The author of over two dozen books and numerous papers, he lived and worked in many other cities, particularly Peking and New York where he died in 1955.

2 I am using capital letters to differentiate between *love* as we know it and the larger *Love* to which the soul calls us; between life and the vast unknown—the Life behind the life we see; between the *fire* tamed by archaic humanity and *Fire* for the second time; between *way* and the *Way* that denotes the spiritual path or journey; between *time* and *Time* as an epoch; between *beginnings* and the *Beginnings* that denote both our childhood, and in history, predate the emergence of human intellect.

3 However, his biographer, Ursula King, PhD, describes the important role Teilhard played in the excavations of Peking man near hearths that may have been "the earliest evidence for the use of fire anywhere else in the world." (Ursula King, *Spirit of Fire*, Maryknoll, NY: Orbis Books, 1996, 130.) She notes that these hearths filled with ash, cinders, and charred animal bones "were a landmark in human cultural history," and that at the time, the fossils dated most likely from 450,000-500,000 years ago. *Author's note:* The dating of fire is a moving horizon. For further detail, see Chapter 3, endnote 2.

4 There are differences among experts as to which came first, fire or language. Whichever came first, they tend to agree that the two are inextricably interwoven in terms of evolutionary development.

5 To resolve the language of gender, I have generally alternated between references to male and female. I have also given some words gender where there is none, such as soul (F) and others, like God, none at all.

6 Milton Gill was a concert organist, composer, and Chair of the music department at Dartmouth College. Just after his *Processional for Organ* (New York: G. Schirmer) won the prestigious American Guild of Organists' national first prize, he was killed in an airline crash returning from his first major concert tour.

7 Italicized, indented statements like these are my own. They are often phrases that were not "thought" but rather, emerged spontaneously from the *soundless sound*—the whispered song of the soul.

8   The word *consciousness* has many interpretations and I refer to it as *that aspect of ourselves that underlies our awareness.* I also use related words such as *awakening, realization, opening, and illumination* interchangeably, although some traditions may assign specific meanings to each of them.

9   The words *religion* and *spirituality* are difficult to define and any part of a definition may often pertain to both. *Religion* tends to refer to organizations that, at some point, have given form to their experiences by coming to an agreement about beliefs, doctrine, moral suasion, and the nature of group activities such as ritual, worship, etc. The word *spiritual* relates to the search for the sacred, or for ultimate meaning, higher consciousness, or transcendence. It usually implies a personal relationship with something larger than oneself; of perceiving and internalizing one's own relationship to the rest of existence (or God, creation, the universe, or life, etc.) It also usually implies experiential elements of the sacred and therefore, most spiritual traditions include a particular *path,* or *work,* or *practice* that frees one from ego's demands. Most religions also have a spiritual wing, and these are richly expressed in the mystical traditions of East and West. I include, here, native and women's spiritualities. In addition to these examples, there are also many people who regard their spirituality as an active and vital connection to a force, energy, or spirit, or sense of a deep self and which is unrelated to any tradition.

10 *The Works of John Adams, Second President of the United States: with a Life of the Author,* 10 vols., Charles Francis Adams ed., Boston: Little, Brown and Company, 1850-1856, volume 10, 389. Cited in Kees De Mooy, John Adams, *The Wisdom of John Adams,* New York: Citadel Press, 2003, 108.

11 The Rev. Ellen Grace O'Brian, *Living the Eternal Way: Spiritual Meaning and Practice for Everyday Life,* San Jose, CA: CSE Press, 1998, 39-40. Rev. O'Brian is the founder of The Center for Spiritual Enlightenment in San Jose, which focuses on the essential truth and harmony found in all the world's religions. See *http://www.csecenter.org*

12 Colin Oliver, a British poet and educator, has offered much insight and wisdom for this manuscript. He is the first of several colleagues, readers, friends, and group participants whose voices add depth to my own perspective. All of them have given me permission to quote their unpublished remarks. Rather than footnote each one, I've gratefully noted each person in the acknowledgment pages.

13 Quoted in M. J. Ryan, *Attitudes of Gratitude: How to Give and Receive Joy Every Day of Your Life,* Berkeley: Conari Press, 1999, 56.

14 Those whose unpublished remarks I have quoted are listed under "Gratitude" at the end of the book.

15 T. S. Eliot, "Little Gidding," Four Quartets, *Collected Poems 1909-1962,* New York: Harcourt Brace and Co., 208-9. Eliot alludes to the immense inadequacy of words in "East Coker" of the same collection: "Leaving one still with the intolerable wrestle / With words and meanings. . . ."

16 See T. S. Eliot, "East Coker," Four Quartets, *Collected Poems 1909-1962,* 186: "I said to my soul, be still, and let the dark come upon you / Which shall be the darkness of God."

2 The Call, the Yearning, and the Journey

Nothing that knowledge can grasp,
or desire can want, is God.
Where knowledge and desire end,
there is darkness, and there God shines.

Meister Eckhart[1]

There is only one ancient and forever work of art: the slow fashioning of life and the gradual awakening of Love. The invitation to participate in Love's measured emergence is our call. Our yearning is to meet that Love face to face.

We are often hardly aware of either the call or our yearning, yet they are like two poles of a magnet, drawing us into the unknown. In that darkness, says Eckhart, *God shines*. It is a long journey into the shining.

The journey of awakening often has its beginning in a long-ago whisper heard by a little child. The child still belongs to the fullness of life, is intimate with it in all of its glory. Spontaneous, imaginative, living more in her[2] body than in her intellect, she is closer to the Mystery; closer still, to her own heart. More immediate in the way she attends to Life, she finds her way by listening to the soundless sound of the whisper. It is a sure guide to what kindles and nourishes her spirit—what brings her joy.

The day comes, however, when the child discovers the whisper can no longer be heard. It is simply—gone. A friend's 11-year-old son cried out to his parents in dismay, "Mom! Dad! Guess what? Billy and I just realized—we've lost our imagination!" It isn't only imagination, of course—no word can encompass what has been lost. You probably have your own remembered glimpse, or a mysterious 'place' that let you know you belonged to Life, and you know how hard it is to describe it. It hints of something more, something not yet, and at the same time so real, it must have once been true.

Thomas Berry, who was Teilhard de Chardin's student, once observed,

> We cannot tell the story of anything without telling the story of everything.[3]

Perhaps a brief personal story can trace the call and our yearning in a way that is closer to a child's way of knowing—one that's simple and concrete. Many narratives of the soul's journey are closely intertwined with loss. Mine was, for I began to lose the sound of the whisper when I was very small, and have spent most of my life trying to find it again.

If I had not almost died when I was four and found myself when I awoke from a long coma in a strange, bare room with needles in my arms and legs; and if I had not been immobilized by splints and left alone for hours—except for broad nurses with bedpans who came and went and didn't smell like my mother—then perhaps I'd have had less time and reason to wonder. I lay for weeks in a big white hospital bed, trying to make sense of what was happening to me. I remembered I'd been in my father's arms, but I didn't understand. Why did he leave me there? He'd carried me down a long curved corridor and given me away to strange men who stared at me over white masks. I remembered bright ceiling lights that hurt my eyes and a tray full of shiny knives. The men put me on a table and grabbed my legs. When I tried to kick them away, they tied me down, and then put a bad-smelling strainer over my nose.

The hospital was a terrifying place. It left deep scars on my soul. I can still feel the shame of the bedpan, my horror of the needles, and the painful tear of adhesive ripped off my belly. I can see the red gash that was underneath it and smell the iodine. Medicine saved my life, but a child is too tender for the brutality of hospitals.

As I lay in the white iron bed, I looked down at the red and purple petunias around the flagpole below my window and listened hard for the whisper. *What had I done wrong?* I needed to know so my father would never take me to this place again. But the whisper was gone, and with it, my ability to walk. When I got home, I had to learn all over again. All I could do was crawl.

How mysterious the connection between one life-altering event and another! Only a month before these strange people surrounded me in their white masks and clothes that crackled when they walked, my parents had decided to join a church. If going to church hadn't collided with the terrors of the hospital, perhaps I wouldn't have begun so young to respond to an insistent tug, something that seemed to be calling me forward. Though it made no sense, it was like a spark inside me that at St. Thomas' Episcopal Church in Malverne, L. I., was lovingly nurtured.

My parents didn't go to church very often, but I did. It seemed a magical place to me. I used to stare at the big front door and wonder at the way it came to a point at the top like the castle arches in my storybooks. It was a pretty fancy doorway for a church that was only a cellar. Half-built in 1939, the foundation had been hastily roofed over with planks and tarpaper when the War came and stopped all construction. But I paid no attention to the black tar dripping down its walls. It was my church underground.

I walked there every Sunday, pulling my little sister in our red Radio Flyer wagon. Each week, I climbed down the church's seven steps into a concrete foundation. It became the template for what I later called the foundations of the soul.

My sister and I sneaked down the cement steps on our way home from school one day and explored the men's bathroom. It had a strange-looking fountain that you couldn't drink from or wash your hands in. While we were there, I crossed the red carpet and stepped through the double oak doors into the sanctuary. Inside, I was in a different world—one that smelled of candle wax, sweet smoke, and leftover lilies. It was *my* world.

On Sundays, I loved to look at the stained glass pictures on the transoms, and watch processions of people march down the aisle in embroidered robes. I stared, fascinated, at the long pole one of them carried, topped with a golden cross. Two of the big boys used other poles with curved hooks and pixie caps that sometimes, mysteriously lit candles, and at other times, snuffed them out. I loved the sound of the chant rising and falling on the breath of the congregation. I didn't understand what any of it meant, but that didn't seem to matter. Something else in my body did.

Week after week I listened, wide-eyed, to stories about a snake in a Garden, a giant felled by a boy named David, and a man named Moses who talked with a bush that burned. My favorite was a story about a baby born under a star so bright, it drew kings from the far corners of the earth. For years, I tried to draw it. My Nana had given me a big picture book filled with pastel drawings of children and angels, all shining with light. The book's glossy paper glittered with gold paint that streamed from haloes and stars and the centers of flowers. Over and over, I copied the picture of the baby in the manger until those pages were worn and smudged with crayon and small fingerprints. I never could get the Virgin Mary's face right. I thought it was the loveliest face I'd ever seen.

I practiced being the Virgin Mary and sat for hours with a bath towel over my head on our front porch steps. I just sat, and looked lovingly at the life-sized doll they'd given me in the hospital, and waited. My sister, only ten months younger, cried, "*I want to be Mary! How come I always have to be Joseph or the donkey?*" She didn't understand. To me, it wasn't just a game. It seemed, instead, a way to enact what had captivated me: something important that I'd found down in a basement church. I saw it in the beauty of colored glass, the gleaming gold cup, and the heavily brocaded vestments that swished past candles and made them flicker. I felt it when I stepped inside, put on my own white cassock, and processed down the soft red carpet, singing. And when I crouched on a green painted stool and listened to stories, I knew that here was a place for me—one that offered itself in ways that were beautiful to my senses and to something deep inside me that aspired to wonder. From the beginning, these were the clues to what I was seeking—the source of the whisper I'd heard in a language not of words.

I didn't understand what they read in church, but the rituals spoke *more than the words*. Sometimes—when they sprinkled a baby with water and held him high for us to see—they tapped a longing deep inside me. Other times, they spoke to my fear. When they raised a golden cup and said it was full of blood, I felt a fist of uncertainty slam in my belly. That same fear and uncertainty came with the wail of air raid sirens in the night, talk of my father going to war, memories of the hospital, and my near-acquaintance with death.

Perhaps, I thought, I would learn more about the rituals' meaning, someday. In the meantime, it seemed of great significance that I enact the one drama I did understand—that of the Virgin Mary holding the baby. In my heart, I wasn't sitting on a cold brick stoop on Long Island. I was on the hay in a manger with stars overhead, and shepherds and kings and cattle all around . . .

They say that the soul listens; that it waits and when it hears what it needs, stirs mightily and begins to call us out of our locked places. Surely, *something* in me was wide-awake and prompting me to keep hoping, to keep following my yearning. Something wanted to be fed. And the things my body heard in church and which made no sense to my mind, spoke to the interior one who watched and listened and seemed to know that what was occurring was important. So, I kept walking—first to my underground Sunday School on Long Island, and later, to choir practice and teen groups in Vermont and Connecticut—asking my questions about what it all meant.

When I became an adolescent, filled with desires not only physical but also a passion to seek and find what mattered for my life, I began to reason as young people do. I delighted in abstract concepts, in geometry and algebra and the world of ideas. For the first time, I began to question the lessons I'd learned in the church of my childhood. Once I was in college, I held them up to the scrutiny of many minds. I took courses like *Myth, Metaphor and Symbol* and read Tillich and Buber and William James. And when I opened Joseph Campbell's *The Hero with a Thousand Faces*, I was shocked to discover how many stories there were of scapegoats dying nailed to trees. My professors drew arrows and Greek words on blackboards. They helped me begin to translate the concrete religious beliefs of my childhood into the more abstract spirituality my mind needed at the time.

But they never spoke of the whisper I'd heard as a child. Nor did they teach me how to develop a firm foundation underneath my intellect—or to ground what I'd learned in the deeper nature of *who I was*.

And so, after years of academic study, I set aside my search for the mysterious and developed a great respect for reason. I decided that the unseen had no value, for science had taught me to trust what could be defined and measured. There seemed no reason, any longer, to believe or to explore what had called me for so long. Instead, I viewed intellect as the ultimate in human development and came to rely on the power of logic to inform my life.

I had made up my mind.

Together with a large part of my culture, I had found a new belief system and lost my bearings—the whispered song of the soul. 'Grown up' now, focused on cerebral activity and demanding work in the outer world, it was left to art, drama, literature, and music to fill the huge gap that remained in my soul—an unspoken yearning for what was true, and a deep need for feeling, for beauty, and for mystery.

During my adult years, I went to church for long periods of time. I still yearned for the sense of meaning and the feeling of belonging that the whisper had intimated—the mysterious presence, the felt connection to a larger reality—but the actual experience of what had been promised seemed to be absent. It did not meet my longing.

It wasn't until my mid-forties that I mentioned my dilemma with the church to a colleague who'd once been a Dominican priest. He told me a story of a beautiful tree in the center of a garden, surrounded by a high stone wall. He likened the tree to a person searching for the sacred, and the wall, to the boundaries defined by her religion. He concluded by saying:

> The tree needs to grow out of the garden. Its branches need room to expand and spread wide. They need to reach far outside the garden's walls, for they cannot be contained by the walls' limits. But the tree always remains rooted in the garden.[4]

His story helped to reconcile my hope and my grave disappointment in the religion of my childhood. I had done everything I could to stay within the garden's walls, but letting my branches expand had become a mounting demand. Once more, I left the church but the church never left me. It remained inside like the tree's roots in the garden, guiding me not so much morally (for my family had provided that structure), as in my human passage. Its stories and teachings gave direction in ever-deeper waters, reminding me how to navigate and integrate a life at every turn. I have been continuously fed by that heritage. Since early childhood, it has been my foundation and formed a large part of who I am. Like the tree's branches, however, I had to seek far outside its walls before I could return and listen again—but this time, not with my ears.

When I heard the story of the tree in the garden, I was just beginning—for the second time—to start my life over again. The first was when my husband, Milton, had died in 1968. In the ten years that followed his death, however, everything in our culture was turned upside down. I was completely unprepared for the upheaval. We women—along with people of color— were beginning to see ourselves differently, and demanding to have our value confirmed. A new generation was looking at war with different eyes and confronting authorities on every side. Everything was up for question, and all the rules—whether for sex, or for war, or for all that our parents and culture had taught us—were discarded. *What we thought we knew* was in shambles.

In this new environment, I struggled to navigate the complexities of parenting alone in a couple's world with no cultural structures for support; to find companionship in an era confused by new roles and a new sexual ethic; and to negotiate the conflicting demands of a workplace unused to the presence of professional women and wanting me to make coffee. It was impossible.

During those ten years, the structures that had held my life together crumbled. The tools I'd learned for coping with challenges—and with feelings that disturbed me—no longer worked. Overwhelmed and exhausted, I stumbled and fell. I felt like a failure on every front. It was like being broken. I didn't know that brokenness was the beginning of the Way of Love. I only knew that I was lost and lonely and felt deeply known by no one—least of all, myself.

Half way through my life, I had not yet matured. Driven, riding on willpower, with an apparently bright future and a challenging job, I was outwardly competent, even 'successful' in society's view, but I hid the truth of a deeper self behind the drive for incessant activity. I had no idea what I felt or needed, and no sense of who I was—other than the role my culture had taught me. It had bestowed, as I later discovered, a very shallow identity.

Facing that identity put me at a threshold, and at that threshold, my past and future were in collision. To navigate the change, I had to let go of what I'd always relied on: *what I thought I knew* and *who I thought I was.*

It eventually became clear that making up my mind, such as I'd begun to do in adolescence, needed a complementary action on my part. If I were to have balance in my outer life, I would need to look inward. If I were to move forward, I'd also have to look back to see where I had been.

Something else also became very apparent: that if I were to be authentic and more whole, I would have a great deal of *un*learning to do. Reader Colin Oliver again responded,

> Unlearning comes in steps I think, putting our weight on floors that give way like trapdoors. With each fall we shed something. As E. E. Cummings says:
>
> ... let all go
> dear
> so comes love[5]

I had no idea, at the time, what letting go entailed or that it had to do with love. Thoroughly trained to live almost entirely in my intellect, it was terrifying to admit I *did not know*. But *not knowing* was the only way I was going to leave this threshold of conflict and it felt like walking into the dark.

It was at this point I found a spiritual path that taught me how to slow down, and how to begin all over again, one step at a time. I tried to follow it, but I also resisted it every step of the way. I didn't like being a beginner. It felt to me like crawling had felt when I came home from the hospital at four. I wanted to race ahead, to learn *as I knew how to learn*: by reading and discussing things intellectually. Eventually, I found that I had to walk this kind of path differently—and the going was slow and emotionally painful: It was humiliating to admit my failures; demeaning to have to ask for help. Little did I realize that letting myself be a beginner like this was, itself, the beginning of the path of awakening.

It was a steep path, and by following it, I was going against the grain of my culture, for my culture had also made up its mind. Speeded up and out of control, it couldn't teach me a thing about being a beginner, about feeling, or about not knowing. It had no use for vulnerability or weakness or need; indeed, it branded them 'childish.'

'Childish' was the last way I wanted to appear to other people! My culture had taught me the importance of being independent, and I had bought it wholesale. I propped myself up with a false self-sufficiency that was as brittle as an eggshell. My reliance on that kind of 'strength' buckled under me at midlife. It was a long time before I understood that real strength included an ability to be vulnerable.

The path I found, like any genuine spiritual Way, offered a series of deliberate practices that helped to create a foundation for a mature and authentic identity. It changed my life and I shall always be grateful for it.

Since then, I have learned that there are many spiritual paths, and recognized that all authentic paths are rigorous. They require far more than an hour on a cushion, a bench on Friday night, or a pew on Sunday morning. The Yoga path entails more than philosophy or postures, just as the serious study of Aikido or Tai Chi is a far deeper journey than a self-defense or exercise class. The discipline of a Twelve-Step program is considerably more arduous than quitting an addiction; and the commitment to therapy, a greater consecration than entering counseling to adjust to current circumstance. My own choices have taught me that any spiritual practice is slow and lifelong—measured in progress, not perfection.

After a fitful year of struggling to learn how to navigate my new path, I occasionally seemed to 'hear' the fleeting suggestion of a long-forgotten whisper that came as if on the wind. The whisper first came in images, and when I paid attention to them, it was as if something inside me were weaving new connections: Scenes of early childhood floated into my awareness along with imaginations about archaic humanity; and every time I stumbled and failed at my chosen path, ancient images of the Garden of Eden became braided with my own feelings of shame. These images and associations helped me to make rudimentary connections between the evolution of the human race and the mind of a little child. I also wondered if there were a relationship between my own painful experience of being a beginner and the sacred stories of my youth. Bare intimations, I had no words at all to express what was inwardly gestating. All I had were images and flashes of insight that were so fleeting, I almost didn't notice them.

During that period, my professional organization asked me to be a presenter at their national meeting in Colorado. They wanted a workshop on stress. I'd taught stress management for burned-out executives for some time but clearly, the real student had been me—stress was my middle name! By the time the Organizational Development Network called, however, I'd made enough inner changes that I had little interest in giving the kind of workshop I'd done before. Instead, my fascination was with the images that were now emerging into my awareness. With no idea of what I might offer at the conference, I was utterly shocked to hear these words come out of my mouth: "I'd like to try something new. If you're willing to let me experiment with a silent presentation using slides of art and photography, I'll give it a try."

What am I saying?! I asked myself. I'd never worked with art or even used a slide projector! Moreover, it would soon be my children's summer vacation and I wanted to spend my time with them! That left little room for trying to learn a new way of life and to work at the most stressful job I'd ever had. *How will I ever fulfill such a commitment?*

But the call of the images that were flowing through my mind enticed me, and as I proceeded to follow their lead, everything I needed to create the project was proffered—often without my asking. The school's art teacher lent slides; neighbors gave me magazines filled with pictures; and my company's photographer offered technical assistance. I worked on the wordless presentation for months. Eventually, a satisfying visual sequence evolved that portrayed a person's spiritual journey woven with the long story of humanity. I called it *The Evolution of Stress.*[6] My hope was that whoever watched the images go by, one after the other, would have a visceral experience of ever-increasing tension, time pressure and alienation . . . and then a turning, followed by an emerging sense of peace.

The first slide in the sequence was a photograph of a coiled snake. Little did I know that the snake in its many manifestations would figure mightily in my own journey. Then came drawings of human evolution, paired with an infant held high after birth and the words: *"The universe resounds with the joyful cry, 'I AM!'"*[7] There followed the faces of little children filled with fear and anger and sadness. . . . Masaccio's frescoes of Adam and Eve preceded many other artists' views of the slow progression of humanity, and its gradual movement out of a deep communion with life and into the modern world: Images of naked children in Africa leapt into the air. Whole families scythed grain by hand in Europe. Paintings by Picasso and Hopper and Bosch exposed the dissolution of the culture I saw around me: the distancing of people from one another, the loneliness, and the stark poverty of human relationships. Their art mirrored the fragmentation of my own soul. Mid-way through the presentation, New York City's horse-drawn carriages in 1900 morphed into collages of today's clock-and profit-driven tensions. The series of slides then climaxed in the agony of Charles Munch's painting, *The Scream*.

The second half of the presentation began with a caption, "The Turning Point" and a photograph of a narrow wooden gate that stood half-open on a path. The last lines from Robert Frost's poem, "The Road Not Taken," signaled a change, and the images that followed reflected a growing awareness, and a renunciation of old ways. There were photographs of meditators in saffron robes sitting by the sea, and paintings by Miro and Klee that hinted at spirit and the dream world. Gradually, the tensions resolved and the production ended with Matisse's joyful painting of a circle of dancers and two final photographs—the serenity of a mountain stream and the mysterious beauty of the galaxies.

The Evolution of Stress expressed my own early experience of the spiritual journey. It also depicted, from a stance I was barely beginning to trust, the development of a relationship to what had gone before, to the present, and to what was yet to come. I had yet to take the second half of the journey, and its images were mostly intuited. But putting the sequence together seemed to satisfy the silent one who was watching from inside me.

At the national meeting, the conference room was packed. I gave the slide presentation in near silence—and it was received in the same way. There was no applause. As my colleagues left the room, they hugged or thanked me nonverbally, but without their words to tell me how they really felt about my work, I wondered: Had the images affected them? Had they been moved at all? More than a little disappointed and thinking I was alone, I turned to pack up my equipment. I hadn't noticed the man standing alone at the back of the darkened room.

He came forward, took both my hands in his own and spoke in a husky voice,

"Thank you." He took a deep breath and let it out slowly.

"I want you to know that I'd been planning to go back to New York when this conference was over and commit suicide. After seeing your presentation, I'm going to call a therapist. I need to change my life."

The man's gut-wrenching response was startling. But it gave me the first glimpse of a new perspective—one that was a 180-degree turn from my driven ways. By simply responding to my inner promptings and having no idea where I was going, I had been offered something of importance to give to another person. It was a stunning discovery.

There was more to me than I thought—some other faculty had been giving coherence to my fragmented world and at the same time, pointing a way to offer myself to others. Only then, did I understand that by stepping off the cultural treadmill and taking time to notice the nascent hints drifting past my mind, I had indeed begun to hear the whisper again. And without even thinking, I'd followed its lead.

From the beginning, the whispered call of my childhood—*something to do with love, something to do with God, and something to do with who I was*—had fueled a deep yearning, and both the call and the yearning had set my direction. Together, they had brought me to a threshold of conflict where I knew I had to change my life. And I did.

The mysterious whisper was more than intuition, though. It came not only from inside me, but simultaneously from the outer world: At this same conference, I saw the poster with Teilhard's caption that called Love *"Fire for the Second Time."* His evolutionary vision not only mirrored the same trajectory as the slide presentation; it also gave it language. At the time, though

I didn't yet understand that these inner and outer promptings were somehow bound, I was nonetheless, deeply affected. I hardly knew that I was being pulled by the call toward a potential that was dormant in my soul; nor did I understand that I'd been invited—along with every other human being—to participate in a widespread human transformation. I only knew that Teilhard had offered me a vision for my life, and that I wanted to follow it.

How I longed to express what I was discovering! But I was just setting out on this spiritual journey: I had no words—only images. It would take thirty years for words to come and be given form in the book you are holding. In the meantime, however, I was nourished by the voices of countless others[8] who had followed the whispered song of the soul before me: poets and philosophers, sages and saints, mystics and psychologists and ordinary people like you and me. They were my guides and my companions—and their wisdom enlivens every one of these pages.

The root yearning hidden beneath all human desires is for a Love that has long been calling us. Love's whispered call is not only personal; it breathes through the soul of every human being. We are all being carried on the same tide, drawn by both the call and our yearning as inexorably as the moon draws the movement of the waters. This two-way tide joins 'the story of anything,' as Berry said, with 'the story of everything.'

Our part is to listen for the whisper and then to cooperate with it. What good is awakening to a consciousness of Love if it does not affect how we live? If it does not motivate the changes in thought and attitude, feeling and behavior that will help to heal the conflicts among us? While Teilhard's vision ends with a Love he calls *Fire*, our own awakening begins when we find ourselves at a threshold of conflict and dare to take the first step beyond it.

It is at this threshold that we make the choice, alone and together, to change our lives. And we are at the threshold now . . .

Endnotes for Chapter 2

1 Generally attributed to Johannes Eckhart, OP (c. 1260-c. 1328), also known as Eckhart von Hochheim and widely referred to as Meister Eckhart. Eckhart was a German theologian, philosopher, and mystic. Unknown Eckhart document.

2 On language: As previously noted in a footnote to Chapter 1, in order to resolve the language of gender, I have generally alternated between the masculine and the feminine. I have also given some words gender where there is none, such as *soul* (F) and others, like *God*, none at all.

3 Thomas Berry, SJ, in a lecture at Santa Sabina Center, San Rafael, CA, February, 1988. Berry is my inspiration and a mentor. He is a linguist, an historian of cultures, a philosopher, and an author.

4 Luis Janssen, PhD, a colleague and transpersonal psychologist who had been a Catholic Dominican for 25 years, told me this story in the early '80s.

5 E. E. Cummings, "let it go—the," *Complete Poems*: 1904-1962, edited by George J. Firmage, New York: Liveright Publishing Corporation; 1994, 569. *Author's note:* The poet's publisher states that the commonly held belief that Cummings preferred his name to be written in lowercase letters is erroneous and that it should be noted in this manner. Although the use of lower case by an earlier publisher caught fire, Cummings did not have his name legally changed to "e e cummings" and wrote his French translator that he preferred the capitalized version.

6 Patricia-Anne Hillman Gill, *The Evolution of Stress*, presented at the Organizational Development Network National Conference, Snowmass, CO, 1979. ©1979.

7 These are the words of Russian composer and pianist Alexander Nikolayevich Scriabin, 1871-1915.

8 *The Daybook,* published by the Rev. Marvin Hiles and Nancy Hiles, was my richest source of this kind of encouragement for many years. Selections from the years 1976- 2000 have been compiled in *An Almanac for the Soul*, P.O. Box 1528, Healdsburg, CA 95448: Iona Press, 2008.

3 The World in Conflict— A Threshold for Transformation

We look with uncertainty
Beyond the old choices for
Clear-cut answers
To a softer, more permeable aliveness
Which is every moment at the brink of death . . .[1]

We stand right now at a threshold where past and future are in conflict. This conflict takes place between the kinds of perceptions we've held—about ourselves, about life and reality—and the new kind of perception that is needed. We may experience the threshold as a crisis—and it is. For though we want to step beyond it, what we may have to *do* to leave goes against the grain of everything we've believed to be true.

The crisis we experience at a threshold is often painful but it also holds the seeds of possibility. The Chinese symbol for the word *crisis* contains two characters: one for 'danger' and the other, for 'opportunity.' To hold the conflicts we face in this way is an opportunity to see everything differently—and ultimately, the change in *how we see* characterizes an awakening.

The single act of taming fire catalyzed the first human awakening. More than a million years[2] have passed since a few red-hot coals glowed in a hastily dug fire pit and then burst into flame. Fanned, nurtured, then carried from hearth to hearth, that fire became a way to cook food, fire pots, forge metal—and then to transport us over the face of the earth and even into space! One daring act by a single person who saw fire differently—as both opportunity and danger—unleashed an enduring creative power that gave humankind an ever-increasing sense of control over the forces of nature.[3]

The outcome of this feeling of control eventually led to a fundamental change of identity: Much of humanity began to see itself as powerful—and quite separate from the earth and the community of life from which it arose. We came to believe that we could tame anything—and that the earth was ours to control, along with everything in it. This identity has now become well seated in us. We do, indeed, tend to experience ourselves as powerful. We've exploited the winds, the waves, the tides, and gravity just as Teilhard's words had predicted! We've peered into the distant past of the universe with our instruments and pierced the origins of living cells. Now, however, this concept of self is at the root of the conflict between the ways of our past and the way of the future. The very forces we've unleashed—be they from atoms or engines, military weapons or religious convictions—endanger us.

Our inventiveness has been a tremendous boon, but it has also put us in grave danger of extinction. This is the paradoxical nature of the threshold, whether it is personal, as mine was at midlife, or communal, like the one on which we now stand. This threshold doesn't feel like an opportunity! As we continue to struggle with both sides of many conflicts, it feels more as if we have lost our bearings. We find ourselves plunged into shifting currents that break completely with the past, a planet convulsed in a wave of revolutions: social, political, scientific, and economic. We are beset by ecological disasters and by local and international conflicts—all of them traumas on which our mass media feed. We can't help but notice the suffering: the strange autoimmune diseases . . . the violence . . . the homelessness . . . Wherever people gather—in backyards and in pubs, on park benches and around kitchen tables—there is a pervasive, underlying unease: *"Something is wrong! Things are unraveling . . . What is happening to our families? . . . on the playgrounds? . . . in the workplace? . . . the schools . . . our government . . . our world?"*

Many of us struggle between an immense concern about these upheavals and an almost unconscious need to push them away—yet they haunt us, for they create profound moral dilemmas, personal and collective. How, we ask, do we resolve the interactions between world hunger and world health? How do we grapple with the ethics of stem cell research and capital punishment? Can we balance our need for fuel and its depletion? Or for new construction with the habitats of other creatures? We try to weigh the benefits of economic globalization with the desperate needs of the third world. But we find it impossible to resolve the countless differences between cultures and countries, much less entire species! These dilemmas leave us in conflict—inner and outer. Mired in conflict, one thing becomes clear: It signals change.

We live in a period of massive change—and an extraordinarily rapid *rate* of change. Quite recently, a friend told me that his grandfather had once said: "My life is defined by how far I can travel and return in one day on a mule!" Yet now, only two generations later, my friend travels by jet—and at the same time, multitasks in cyberspace. Consider the number of major social upheavals you've encountered in the last 30 years! Our bodies and minds, however, are slow to adapt. Evolution's strategies for change are infinitesimal, slow and deliberate. Our bodies were magnificently designed for stalking prey on the jungle floor, but today's technology is thrusting us ahead at warp speed. No wonder the world feels out of control!

Change involves loss—and while that loss may involve places and things and people we love, it invariably includes the loss of *what we thought we knew*. As these losses accumulate, it can feel like the failure of everything we've thought to be true.

When it seems we are losing everything that matters, our minds fight to take back control. The losses we are experiencing now, however, are beyond anyone's capacities to control, beyond any nation's governing structures, and beyond any religion's moral frameworks. Yet despite this unsettling reality, there is a massive exertion of control by the world's institutions: notably, our governments, businesses, and religions. These forces competing for control also heighten the ways we polarize each other—sexes, races, religions, and nations. People take sides and every clash is fought out of fear. This deep-seated need for control keeps us pointing our fingers at others. In extreme cases, the powerful take control in acts of war, the powerless in acts of terrorism.

The Rev. Martin Luther King summed up our condition:

> Our scientific power has outrun our spiritual power. We have guided missiles and misguided men. Our hope for creative living lies in our ability to reestablish the spiritual needs of our lives. . . . Without this spiritual and moral reawakening we shall destroy ourselves in the misuse of our own instruments.[4]

If we need such an awakening as he describes, what keeps us entrenched in our positions? Our inheritance from the mind of the snake—not the snake in the Garden of Eden, but a snake like the one I met face to face in the shed behind my vegetable garden.

The Snake (1)

It was dark in the garden shed when I slid open the deadbolt on the door, and something made me look down before I stepped in. A large brown gopher snake, easily four feet long, lay on the cement floor just inside the door. A majestic creature, he was completely entangled in a mound of fallen bird netting.

The snake stared at me fiercely, his tongue darting. He was utterly entwined. Helpless. I felt helpless too. As I looked at him, his skin seemed shrunken and dry and I wondered: *Is he thirsty? Do snakes drink?* I'd never even thought about snakes drinking, but I went around the shed to the vegetable garden and filled a shallow plastic cup with water. *How will I give it to him?* Bound or not, I had no stomach for holding his head over the cup with my bare hands. I poured a little water on the cement floor in front of him. He was startled and his pink tongue darted furiously. Then, he bowed his head. Touching the forked tips of his tongue to the scant pool, he dipped them delicately again and again into the water until the floor was dry. I shall never forget it.

When George came home, we headed for the shed, he with blunt-ended scissors, and I in long asbestos gloves that had seen better days at the grill. I bent down to the creature and held him as carefully as I could, my right hand just below his head and my left, half way down his body. His jaws and upper body were immobilized, tightly wound by several strands of sharp black mesh, but his tail was free and undulating. Suddenly, he knotted it around the handle of a rake that hung on the wall and whipped his upper body furiously against my grip. Leveraged, he was as strong as I was. George knelt and loosened the snake's tail, then clamped it between his knees while he worked to free him from the tightly bound net. But the snake had other strategies: He lengthened and narrowed his long body in my hands, then shortened and swelled up again. Depending on his mode of defense, I had to keep changing my grip and at the same time, keep an eye on his head! As he struggled, he stared at me with one unblinking eye. I was scared, but I looked right back and kept talking to him, soothing him. *It's all right. We're not going to hurt you.* I was also scared for *him*: While George carefully snipped at each filament that cut into the snake's flesh, I was asking inside, *Where are his organs under that snakeskin? Where is his heart?*

After an hour's work, we were both stiff and tired. George cut all but the last strand and pulled me up from the cold cement. I held the snake tightly in both hands until we got outside, then bent down. As George snipped the netting wrapped around the snake's jaws, I let him go. The creature turned toward the shed. For a moment, we thought he was going back inside. Then he changed direction. Graceful, regal, he sailed across the field.

The next day, a freshly shed snakeskin lay on our doormat.

The mind of a gopher snake is programmed to enter openings. It is a fine program for catching gophers in their holes—but not for finding the way out of a maze of netting! Despite the different situation, the snake had continued to follow his program with certitude, weaving his way into every opening he saw. Going from bad to worse, he bound himself tighter and tighter with every choice, until dozens of sharp filaments strangled him. He was trapped in a net of his own convictions.

We are trapped too. Like the snake, we are programmed, caught in an ever-tightening stranglehold of our own beliefs. Many of us hold deeply seated convictions about others and ourselves that do both great disservice. At times, we believe we're insufficient—that we're not good enough, perhaps, or smart enough or loving enough. At other times, we are convinced about what we think is true, what is right, and what does or doesn't work. Our conviction fuels our certainty, our passions and our aggression. It rests on the gut-level program we inherited from the mind of the snake. This same program evolved to fuel an ever-growing sense of power in human beings—once we discovered how to tame fire. That power defined the nature of *Homo sapiens—people who know.*

This self-concept has increasingly separated us from others and from the rest of the living planet. Our knowing depends on making distinctions and these distinctions divide us whenever we look at conflicting realities in either/or ways. We often maintain beliefs and judgments about others whose take on issues are different from our own—on politics or religion, for example. In those difficult situations, we tend to choose one point of view as the 'right answer' and make the other wrong. *We take sides because this is how our minds work.* It is also the way our culture works. We are encouraged to pick one point of view and then stick with it. We're taught emphatically: "You can't get what you want if you waffle between one choice and another!" And so, we learn to stand firm in our convictions, like wooden soldiers holding their positions on the board. This is how culture is created—how it is taught and then, kept stable.

Someone once said that insanity is doing the same thing over and over again but expecting different results. Surely, we want to have a tried and true set of instructions to follow. We'd like to be right, to believe that we've chosen the most honorable point of view. But this can mean that when others disagree with our positions, we will make them wrong. The way we reinforce our positions with judgment and blame lies at the heart of the personal and global conflicts that tear at our lives. Instead of creating a world that is moving in the direction of healing and peace, we find ourselves sliding further and further away from each other, divided by the strongly held beliefs that give us a sense of control.

But we have found, to our chagrin, that the control we sought with our judgments has not solved any of our predicaments in our relationships or in our lives. Still, we may nevertheless crawl like the snake though endless repetitions of the same beliefs year after year—and seldom question them. Almost 400 years ago, Francis Bacon wrote:

> The human understanding when it has once adopted an opinion . . . draws all things else to support and agree with it. And though there be a greater number and weight of instances to be found on the other side, yet these it neglects and despises . . . in order that . . . its former conclusions may remain inviolate.[5]

Science has only recently given a name to this tendency to hold onto our beliefs: *confirmation bias*. Using a brain-imaging technology, researchers at Emory University have defined exactly where in the brain this bias is seated. They've also demonstrated that it is both unconscious and driven by emotions.[6] Their findings confirm Bacon's opinion: that we are programmed to reinforce our given positions, thereby keeping our world polarized.

Polarization—this way of taking sides and hanging on to our point of view—is a driving force at any threshold of transformation, a collision between what we know and what we do not. (As we shall see, there are many other kinds of conflicts that characterize the threshold. They include conflicts between what we want/don't want; believe/don't believe; feel/deny, and so on.) What a bind we're in! If we are used to knowing, what does it mean for us to trust unknowing? This kind of precipice is likely to feel dangerous, for the mind that knows is afraid. Will it fall into darkness and be lost?

Here we remind ourselves once more of the Chinese characters for 'crisis': danger and opportunity. Without a doubt, those early animal-men were threatened when they imagined carrying embers from a fire in the wild. They were in awe of the colossal power of fire, but they were also desperately in need. The catastrophic global changes that had forced their long migration[7] had brought them to the cold steppes of Asia, and fire offered warmth. To survive—and dare to carry it home—they had to change their minds.

Catastrophic change, whether personal, social, or global, holds the potential for boon as well as danger. The changes we face today can throw us into denial and paralysis—or catalyze a transformation of consciousness—one that begins with *not knowing*. It is difficult in our Time to trust such an idea or to think of it as anything but a chasm—a bottomless pit. However, this mind of ours which sets up polarities in order to think, is only the mind that has evolved, *so far*. It has no awareness of the depths of love, wisdom, and healing that lie in the abyss, the Unknown.

This Depth—with all the energies it contains—is the frontier that awaits us—*and intellect cannot access it*. It represents a different kind of intelligence, one far greater than our own; far greater, still, than the one we imagine we'll create on the Internet. At depth, we live in a dynamic state of relationship—with everything. Such a communion is different from communication. It is the deepest kind of intimacy there is—with all the fire and vulnerability that intimacy involves.

The spiritual journey leads us from the loneliness of our separate points of view toward this larger perspective. Some of you may be quite familiar with disciplines that have long carried you in this direction. Others may just be learning. Still others may be saying, "Wait! Those of us who live our lives and judge our progress by what we *do* find it hard to understand this change of direction. It makes no sense." Still others may add, "It's not that we don't want to leave the threshold. We don't know how! Besides, we're confused and so overwhelmed with one crisis after another, that all our time goes into putting out brush fires. There are so many problems to solve! If there will be nothing to show for the time we'll spend, no real worldly accomplishment, maybe not even a 'solution', isn't it just self-indulgent and lazy?"

If we, in our diversity, are to travel together, how can we walk holding hands? Some of us are scientists; others steeped in psychology or one of the professions. Some are familiar with the physiology of the human brain. Still others have spent years as parents and are deeply conversant with a child's development. Some have made religion their context; others, business or technology. Some are in theater or music; some write poetry or paint or dance. It is most important to me to honor every perspective so that we start with a shared understanding of *who we are*, *where we have been*, and *where we are hoping to go*.

> *The hardest things to change in a person or a culture are the beliefs and values held at our core.*

We are programmed to know. *The work of spiritual practice is to override the program.*[8] In Chapter 1, Ellen Grace O'Brian observed that a spiritual practice is necessary to help us access inner resources that can guide us toward change. A practice helps us to reorient ourselves to something different from knowing. We have long been problem-solvers, and that program keeps us firmly anchored in our old identity and behaviors. Like the snake in the garden shed, we have already tried what we know. We've put our hope in social programs and in education, and sought help from economics, law, and technological wizardry. We've looked for solutions in medicine, or in victories; in romantic love or the promise of an afterlife. But as Einstein noted, "Our solutions at the level of the problem only create more problems to solve!"[9]

We will always need to use our problem-solving minds. At the same time, the very nature of thinking blinds us to a much more comprehensive way of dealing with our lives—one that can empower and relieve us. Transcending the "level of the problem" entails more than out-of-the-box thinking, however. It implies getting beyond thinking, altogether. That awareness puts us right at the trailhead of the Way of awakening.

Evolution begins with a whisper. In our Time, that whisper may call us toward a spiritual path. There is no path, of course, and no journey. Our life is the path to awakening, so there is really no other place to go! Perhaps, it is better to say that a path or Way spans the distance between who we know ourselves to be and *who we really are*.

For those who may be closer to the beginning of your journey, I offer this encouragement. If you are sensitive to what energizes you and what gives you joy, you will find your Way. You may choose yoga or meditation, a martial art, or a practice within a tradition. Any well-trod path can help to free us from the strangling net of our convictions. A path and its practices help us all to trust that transformation is possible:

We can enter a period of preparation.

We can risk dangers, physical, emotional, and social.

We can change our minds.

We can develop a different kind of faith.

We can consent to a new kind of identity.

We Can Enter a Period of Preparation

Teilhard offered us an ennobling vision of Love: *Fire for the second time.* If we are goal-oriented, it can be tempting to roll up our sleeves and try to head straight for that new *Fire.* The whisper that calls us, however, lies outside our normal thinking process; it is not a message we can hear with a mind full of thoughts. To develop the necessary quality of awareness takes preparation, and much of it is interior. Although in rare instances, a person might walk in off the street with his yearning and suddenly 'wake up,' most often, our access to awakening is eased by a practice that helps us develop new ways of 'seeing' and of 'hearing.' Before I ever started a formal practice, I had already begun to open the lens of perception in several simple ways. I'll call them: *dusk, being, seeing, and meditation.* Though they are mentioned here only briefly, their meaning will grow as we repeatedly circle our questions on a spiral path that broadens and deepens throughout the book. If you use your imagination and are willing to try out some of the experiences described, you'll start to understand what I mean by hearing, feeling, and knowing *in your body. This* kind of 'doing' is how your understanding will grow.

Dusk

We can begin to see and hear anew by learning to nurture an *inner* dusk. In the western world, we're accustomed to a daylight mind. We are used to a sharp mental focus, and thanks to the way language creates distinctions, we're also used to seeking clear-cut answers. It seems strange to contemplate the idea of using our minds differently, to be more open and receptive, and 'not thinking.' Not thinking entails a way of perceiving that does not respond to constant stimulation. Instead, we learn to *be*.

Being

Shirley Holley writes about how she develops this inner perspective:

> I have to let all these tasks fade into the background so I can get myself to *being*.

Being is not a concept. It is a doorway—a way of being fully present in both your outer and inner life. In your outer life, it's like feeling the water on your hands as you wash each dish, or the way your foot sometimes senses the soft give of the ground with every step; it's noticing the wind, the sound of the birds, or being present in conversation with a friend. In your inner life, you learn to be by simply paying attention to the silence inside, moment by moment. Few caught up in a world careening out of control want to take the time to cross that abyss. To do something so different—to stop, to be quiet and listen, to orient consciously to our own interior spaces—seems not only strange, but somehow self-indulgent, empty, and uncomfortable.

Seeing

Maria,[10] a 43-year-old executive, had entered therapy. She wanted to change, yet when she began to make the transition to this new way of being, she was scared. At least, the pain of her old way of life had been familiar! In a *Mining Your Life for Meaning* group, she learned to use writing to *see* herself better, and in the process, saw clearly how her old self was in conflict with the new one that was emerging:

> Moving fast, driven, not thinking, not feeling, not breathing. Fast, fast. Keep moving, don't stop. All will be fine as long as I'm in motion,

fixing something. Feeling? I can't feel anything right now, I have work to do. Chop, chop, keep moving. Cross one thing off and add four more—after they're done, write them on the list anyway just so they can be crossed off. But why is there no sense of accomplishment? Never mind. Do, do, next, next. How can there be this much to do? I'm so tired. I'm not accomplishing anything of real value.

As she wrote, Maria began to see things she hadn't known about herself before:

I've abandoned *myself*. It is so sad! How much of me I've missed! 'There is value in cleaning that garage,' the old part of me is saying. 'Not the kind of value I want right now,' the new is saying. But right now it feels like more effort to be still and quiet and calm and reflective and feeling than it does to tackle another closet. The closet I can do without crying. . . .

Meditation

A year later, Maria learned to meditate. After months of sitting quietly and simply watching her breath go in and out, she had moments when she let go of 'doing.'

I am seeing now that breathing is connection. To myself. To how I really feel about things. To my own center of calmness and best decision making. It pulls my mind back from inconsequential wanderings, excessive complaining or operating completely blind. I'm not in a habit of checking in with myself—I just react like a little bulldozer most of the time; but when I breathe, things are different. My heart opens up. I can see more clearly. I feel connected to God and to others. . . .

At midlife, I had also learned to meditate, and after the first evening's instruction, slept through the night for the first time in many years. That did not go unnoticed! Sometimes, a person might scoff at the idea of meditation or see it as 'fuzzy thinking.' I found that to understand such a practice required my willingness to give it a try before I made a judgment. Meditation is an art. It asks only that we temporarily set aside our intellect and learn, like Shirley and Maria, to *be*. In time, rather than finding that our minds are fuzzy, we discover we've developed, instead, a capacity for *acute attention*.

When I started to meditate, however, I didn't understand what I was doing, or why. This strange way of letting go of thought felt like going into the dark. At the same time, I was surprised, for it seemed to offer a quality of rest—an ebb-time—that balanced the kind of urgency that characterized my life. After a little over a year of taking time each day to simply be here, alert and present, I began, like Maria, to see—and I was seeing myself. It was then I knew I had to change my life. A decade later, the story of that transition became a book, *The Dancing Animal Woman*.

Meditation wasn't always a peaceful practice. Sometimes I felt intense emotion and other times, quite empty. I suspect that most of us would rather avoid such uncomfortable feelings. It would seem easier to respond to life in the old way: to gain control by getting active again, seeking answers and making decisions. But whenever I took that more familiar route in my life circumstances, I found to my chagrin, that it didn't solve my predicaments. I tried, but I couldn't encompass *with my thinking* both sides of the many conflicting feelings and situations I faced. Instead, I remained caught—in a net of opposing convictions. To me, the task seemed mind-breaking.

It is hard to believe that the potential for transformation lies within the very 'mind-breaking' we fear.

Shall we fight the new or cooperate with it? We fight, unwittingly, as long as we try to make work what is no longer working. To cooperate, we need to find a different way. The movement toward the Unknown is like standing on a precipice and seeing only darkness ahead—but not the light in it. It is not for the faint-hearted. Surely, when archaic man encountered fire in the wild, his body must have contracted in terror—an unequivocal "*No!*" to the dangers long held in cellular memory. But one by one, each person who dared to go forward was heeding a call from *outside what he knew.* Each one responded by whispering, "*Yes!*" We can do the same.

All along the human trajectory, there have been people who felt called by something they couldn't explain—a whisper, a yearning, a burning—something outside of the ordinary. Little did they realize when they left the threshold of the known and entered new territory that they were participating in the creativity of the universe. When we leave *what we know* at the threshold of conflict, what lies beyond it can be radically creative. Cosmologist Brian Swimme[11] celebrates this kind of creativity by asking, *"What Time is it?"* With his question, he reminds us that only once in the earth's unfolding story was there a Time for the emergence of flowers; only once for the emergence of dinosaurs, of birds, of mammals—and of that particular mammal, *Homo sapiens*. He repeats: "There is only one Time for each one of us. And because of the urgency of the period in which we live, your own unique creativity is desperately needed—no matter how dangerous the unknown may seem."

We Can Risk Dangers, Physical, Emotional, and Social

In a way, all creativity can be dangerous. No one prepares to enter the unknown without recognizing that reality. The relationship between creativity and danger—be it physical, psychological, or social—is a theme that runs throughout history: From the first *Homo erectus* who tamed fire to Socrates, Jesus, Gandhi, and Martin Luther King—all had to face dire consequences for threatening the deeply held beliefs *of the group*. A group tends to believe it knows, and that what it knows is right. Every community has long since *made up its mind*. It resists change because it is certain, and its certainty is based on its stories.

Thousands of years ago, the Greeks told a tale of a man named Prometheus who "snatched fire from the gods" and carried it home as a gift to his people. Prometheus was following his own deeply felt yearning: He saw fire's potential, but by stealing it, broke tradition's rules. For his troubles, the Greek god, Zeus, had him chained alive to a cliff where an eagle pecked at his liver, forever. But is it the perceived 'gods out there' who punish someone who dares to change the *status quo*—or is it the people themselves? In this story, even though the group may have perceived fire as a great gift, when we listen beneath the surface, we recognize that claiming fire was also one of the group's most ancient terrors. Obviously, it is not only the archaic community's disapproval we're concerned with here. The myth also dramatizes the potential danger to anyone who has dreams that reach past what the group believes is *true*.

We have witnessed the world over reenactments of the Prometheus story: the community's promise of swift retribution for tampering with the powers of the gods. In our Time, there was violence for two centuries as women tried to change the rules. There was violence again at Selma when a black child walked into a school for whites. There were gunshots at Ohio State and more at abortion clinics. And there is probably no better example of violence perpetrated on all sides than what we are witnessing today, in the Middle East.

It is easy to form judgments of those who were the initiators of these events that were so disturbing to their communities. It is just as easy to judge those who resisted what they were trying to change. But if I label a group as people 'like me,' or 'not like me,' 'liberal' or 'conservative,' 'destructive' or 'creative'—and let it go at that—do I see how slotting people like this lets me off the hook?

I discovered that it did *me* harm to take sides: It was a way of avoiding the larger self I was seeking. Better I learn to heed the adage: *"Take no enemies!"* If I were to begin to address my programming, I needed to try something different.

In our Time, we can embrace both sides of our own 'Prometheus stories.' Perhaps a way to begin is to look at the community's role from the broader perspective of nature. Nature is conservative. She doesn't take potential danger to her handiwork lightly. Any change—a mutation in a plant or an animal—needs to be tested for years against existing conditions. When a new plant is introduced to a region, it is not merely a question of *its* survival. There is a long negotiation between all the life forms there: the surrounding plant and animal community. To serve the goal of maintaining life, nature takes its time.

If we look at human prehistory, the span of time between *Homo habilis'* emergence and the kind of animal-men who later tamed fire was two million years![12]

Surely, we are a part of nature. From this larger point of view, it is easier to see that the function of our communities surrounding any new 'event' in human culture—a medical breakthrough like gene therapy, for example—is to be a necessary stabilizing force. Its role is to maintain life. As with nature, its point of view conserves the *status quo*. I have come to honor it by naming it the 'conserving community.' Because a community looks to the past for guidance, it tends to resist change, particularly anything that threatens its deeply held beliefs about what is *right*. This slow working-out of conflict between a culture and the succession of individuals who seek change is no different from nature's adaptation to a new plant.[13] If the attempt at making change moves too swiftly—the culture will crumble. We have seen what happens in the hasty effort at change played out on the bitter stage of Iraq.

In our Time, there are many, who in their very real fear, clamor to strengthen society's rules, and to enforce them with stricter punishment. Their fears need to be heard. We cannot deny the importance of rules to a culture. The great tragedy since the sixties has been the dismantling of many of society's traditional views—about authority, for example, or accepted sexual behavior—without enough people in place who were mature enough to navigate the change. People who are mature have an internal capacity to monitor their own behavior wisely: It doesn't change when there's no outside authority around to reward or punish them. Our culture does not encourage this kind of maturity. As a result, we've become polarized on many issues such as these.

Real stability, however, is energetic. It has movement—it's like a dance. This kind of dance has everything to do with the relationship between the dancers—their flexibility and sensitivity to others so that all move together as a whole. Then the system remains in balance. It is therefore, also very important to hear the voices of those who are seeking change, and at the same time, to recognize that their worldviews and head-on solutions can be just as entrenched as those in the conserving community!

If we are going to journey together, whatever our point of view, it will help us to take a 'step back' from *where we stand* on any issue, and to examine our approaches and solutions from a perspective that includes all of us. If we have *made up our minds*—if we believe what we know and know what we believe—we will not go forward. Like children in adult bodies, we will not have addressed the biased thinking that keeps us separate and programmed for conflict. In Swimme's words, that Time is over.

We Can Change Our Minds

If there is hope for us—man and woman, Arab and Jew, East and West—it does not lie in the rising up of a great leader to tell us what to do. The Time of the hero is past. No rescuer will come to fill the deep crevices of earth with oil again or season poisoned land with sweetness. If we hope to bless our children's and grandchildren's future lives, we need to do the hard work of challenging our own thinking—and hold one another gently and with mercy as we each untangle the limiting beliefs that hold us and our culture captive. With the willingness to cooperate and change our minds—to let go of our own certitude, be it religious *or* scientific—we can begin to *see* differently, and take a first step toward the radical kind of Love that holds both sides of that polarity in its embrace.

Teilhard's biographer Ursula King wrote:

> In Teilhard's understanding, it is the transforming power of love which alone can create a true human community . . . . The fire of love may be the only energy capable of extinguishing the threat of another fire, namely that of universal conflagration and destruction.[14]

This kind of Love unifies, and Teilhard addressed its evolutionary nature:

> Then, for a second time in the history of the world, humanity will have discovered Fire.

Like a Zen koan,[15] his vision can act in us to jump-start a new mode of inquiry, unanswerable by the problem-solving mind. This is the realm of the spiritual quest for truth. But the *Fire* kindled by awakening to this kind of truth is a gift we simply cannot imagine. Says Joseph Campbell, it

> cannot be communicated . . . only the way to [it.] Whereas truths of science are communicable . . . ritual, mythology, and metaphysics *are but guides to the brink of a transcendent illumination, the final steps to which must be taken by each in his own silent experience.*[16]

Both Teilhard and Campbell point us toward an entirely different kind of consciousness—one that has many centers because it is shared by all of us.[17] In Einstein's language, that makes our own individual, religious, or national perspectives quite *relative*! Such a consciousness is new territory.

Try as we might, many of us have not found what we yearn for, though we may have sought it in science, psychology, or philosophy, or in beliefs and persuasions of every kind. The nature of our search is reminiscent of an old Sufi tale from the Muslim tradition. In that story, a man named Nasrudin was searching on his hands and knees for a lost coin. But he wasn't looking for it where he'd dropped it on a dark roadway; he was looking under the light of a street lamp where he could see!

It is likely that we, too, have been looking in the same way— beneath the bright lamp of our intellect. But we won't find what we've lost there. We've probably passed by it many times but it is so ordinary, only a little child might notice it—or someone broken or in a wheelchair closer to the ground.

If there is hope of finding what we long for, it lies in the countless whispered suggestions that are *"heard, half-heard, in the stillness / Between two waves of the sea"*[18]—those we have not tried, not known how to put into practice, not half-noticed at all. We have heard them in many languages, such as this passage from the Hebrew:

> . . . and a little child shall lead them.[19]

What should we make of such a statement? Perhaps in our rush to grow up, we cast aside the clue to what we were seeking. Perhaps in our efforts to learn our ABCs or to ace the college boards or get a job, we lost the key to its meaning in the shadows outside the lamplight. But if we listen, we might hear a still small voice saying inside, *Wait! Maybe there's something we've left behind* . . .

And the same whisper comes through a poem and sets our direction:

> In my beginning is my end.
> T. S. Eliot[20]

Endnotes for Chapter 3

1   Anne Hillman, *The Dancing Animal Woman—A Celebration of Life*, Vermont: Bramble Books, 1994, 215. These last lines of the book were put into poetic form by Patricia Cane, PhD, Director of the organization, Capacitar, and published in the *Capacitar Newsletter* in 1994. Capacitar serves the world's traumatized peoples. I have abbreviated her poetic rendition of words that came to me on the breath of the whisper.

2   See article from BBC News Online retrieved April 29, 2004, which describes an excavation in Israel (dating from between 790,000 and 690,000 years ago), with earlier finds in Swartkrans, South Africa dating from 1.5 million years ago and Chesowanja, Kenya, pegged at 1.4 million years ago. *http://news.bbc.co.uk/1/hi/sci/tech/3670017.stm*.

3   Brian Swimme and Thomas Berry, *The Universe Story*, San Francisco: HarperCollins, 1992, 273-4. At this time, the authors suggested that it was most probably *Homo erectus* who tamed fire.

4   From 'Thought for the Day,' February 2006 at *http://www.wisdomatwork.com*

5   Francis Bacon, *Novum Organum*, 1620.

6   *Scientific American*, June 26, 2006. In 2006, scientists used brain imaging—functional magnetic imaging (fMRI) techniques—that confirmed the function of certain brain structures to support confirmation bias. Drew Westen, PhD, Emory University, conducted the study. See also *http://www.sciam.com*

7   Brian Swimme, PhD, Introduction to *The Powers of the Cosmos* (DVD), 2004. See also Appendix II at the end of this book, "Catastrophic Change and the Fundamental Transformation of Consciousness."

8   I make this statement based on my own experience. However, in order to respond to an inquiry that came after this book was completed, I found several articles on the Internet, retrieved September, 2007. In his original manuscript for the Buddhist journal, *Inquiring Mind*, Fall 1999 (Vol. 16 #1), entitled "Prehistoric Mind: Evolutionary Psychology for Meditators," Jourdan Arenson clarifies the need to override our programming: "According to the emerging science of evolutionary psychology, our minds are far from unconditioned at birth. We inherit a prehistoric mind . . . conditioned by two million years of human evolution . . . . To be sure, a lot has changed since our hunter-gather days. But a lot has not. We still need to recognize faces, learn a language, find our place in groups, keep up a reputation, earn praise and avoid blame, cooperate with others, detect cheaters, deter aggression, avoid disease, find mates, raise children. . . . These behaviors are guided by complex mental mechanisms which . . . are biologically based. . . . Science suggests that our most harmful tendencies—competitiveness, cruelty toward outsiders, social climbing, moral condemnation, revenge—are not learned or imposed from outside; they are latent in our genes. The fault is . . . deep within our biological nature.

      "Our biological nature is revealed by an *objective* inquiry into the mind. Our spiritual nature is revealed by a *subjective* inquiry into the mind. Evolutionary psychology looks at the mind as [an] 'it' [and] asks, 'how does it work?' [in order to discover] organic design and functional purpose. The cynics are right: no spiritual nature is revealed by objective inquiry. For such a revelation, we must experience the mind as 'I.' Only through subjective practices, such as meditation, do we discover faith, values, and insight into our spiritual nature—the Buddha-nature that transcends our biological nature but, at the same time, is not separate from [it.] . . . In meditation, we aim to experience the mind-body process without being deluded or trapped by it. We slow the mind's whirling in order to see the mind-body process clearly . . . and thereby gain a measure of freedom. But there is a paradox: if we want freedom we must first find acceptance. Evolutionary psychology helps the meditator by identifying particularly powerful patterns in the mind-body process that he or she must accept.

"The good news of Buddhism is that the process of evolution has not reached an end. It continues in our own lives, especially in our spiritual strivings. . . The findings of evolutionary psychology can help us in that spiritual quest . . . [to] accept and understand our biological nature, and thereby build the wisdom and compassion necessary to transcend it." *http://members.tripod.com/~dlane5/ evomed.html*

9   An undated selection from 'Thought for the Day,' http://www.wisdomatwork.com
10 Maria is a pseudonym and her unpublished contributions are used with her permission. Maria was a participant in one of the many *Mining Your Life for Meaning* groups I developed several years ago in which group members use a form of free-writing and other practices to help themselves make life decisions congruent with what really matters to them. (How the groups began is described in Chapter 14).
11 Brian Swimme, PhD, in a lecture, 1987.
12 These dates continue to change.
13 Thomas Berry calls the slow educational process by which any new pattern is instilled in a culture *cultural coding*.
14 Ursula King, PhD, "Rediscovering Fire," *Earthlight Magazine*, Fall 2000, 15.
15 A *koan* is offered by a Zen master to a student in order to jump-start a new mode of inquiry and resolution. It has a specific answer that is inaccessible to the problem-solving mind.
16 Joseph Campbell, *The Hero with a Thousand Faces*, Princeton: Princeton University Press, 1949, 33-34. Italics mine.
17 Thomas Berry calls this shared consciousness *multicentric*. Jung would have called it the *collective consciousness*.
18 T. S. Eliot, "Little Gidding," Four Quartets, *Collected Poems 1909-1962*, 208-9.
19 Isaiah 11:6.
20 T. S. Eliot, "East Coker," Four Quartets, *Collected Poems 1909-1962*, 182.

4 Embers From the Beginnings—
The Roots of Consciousness

[For the human species now to evolve] a new
descent into a more primitive state must come
about . . . [and] we must reach far back into
the genetic foundations . . . to the shamanic
dimension of the psyche itself.

Thomas Berry[1]

Philosopher Thomas Berry has long suggested that humanity
needs to let go of a self-concept based on power and reinvent
itself as a species. He reminds us that to do so, we have to go
back to our Beginnings for any genuine transformation of identity takes place *at our core.*

On my writing desk, I keep a small double picture frame
with a drawing of a *Homo habilis* woman striding across a savannah two-million-years ago, and behind her, a stand of plane
trees. She is naked, with a large head, and her hands hang
loose at her thighs. Her hair is short and matted, her breasts
erect, and there is a scattering of hair across her shoulders and
upper back. She is muscled, slim, kinetic. It is her expression,
though—eyes alert, eyebrows arched, short nose, and flared
nostrils—that compels me.

Homo habilis painting © 1989 Jay H. Matternes

2

In the other half of the frame is a photograph of our grand-son, Mike, when he was an infant. He lies on his belly, also naked, head erect. His alert expression is almost identical to hers: bright eyes, quizzical eyebrows, and a short little nose with flared nostrils. Both of them seem vitally alive, and completely attentive to what is happening in the moment. I framed the two pictures to represent my human lineage at the time—the ear-liest and the most recent of our human species' long line. And while the field of genetics has radically revised our understand-ing of the entire pattern of human evolution,[3] I use these two figures—in a broader sense—as metaphors for the two human Beginnings we all carry within us: that of the child and the child of the race. They are young in the scheme of things, this ancient grandmother and my infant grandson. He stands at the Beginning of his own story and she, at the Beginning of human evolution. All I can do is infer here, but I stand in good com-pany,[4] and my imagination tells me this: At these Beginnings, they are at-one with themselves and with life, not divided—as we are—between what is 'mind' and what is 'body.' They have not yet developed the capacity for intellect but have innate gifts—albeit unconscious—to guide them: a bodily trust in life and a kind of wisdom that doesn't depend on words. Bone of our bone, these children function primarily through instinct and feeling, gifts of the animal body we have inherited.

The Old Mind

The price of intellect is, in part, to be cut off from our bodies, and their redemption is crucial to our survival and that of our world. We need to be aware of the capacities that lie within them, some of which are boon and others, danger.

The Boon

The body's capacities for relatedness can contribute to an increased sensitivity to others, so needed in our Time. A way to explore that sense of relatedness is to reflect on a few of the qualities inherent in each person in the picture frame. My *Homo habilis* grandmother did not have an objective mind like ours. Hers was a subjective awareness. She saw the land, the plants, and animals around her along with the wind and the rain *as herself*. She didn't experience herself as separate from her tribe or from the world around her. She simply *was* whatever was going on—right then and there. Anthropologist Levi-Bruhl called this kind of consciousness that preceded ego development a *participation mystique*.[5] (The footnote defines these two kinds of minds.)

This way of being is also characteristic of the baby whose development repeats the experience of the human race. The baby primarily knows, wants, and responds *as a body*. His is a 'body-ego.'[6] Life in his mind is kaleidoscopic. People disappear. They dissolve, then reappear. His is a peek-a-boo world that exists only in the present. In a present-tense mind, the baby can't sustain a memory of someone who is absent until he is about eighteen months old.[7] Moreover, neither he nor the *Homo habilis* woman has yet developed a separate sense of 'me.' They have no point of view. Neither relies on the kind of thinking self—the 'subject/object' consciousness—with which we tend to identify. They simply *are*, that's all, where nothing is outside them. Everything perceived is a subject—and the entire subject, *who they are*. This characterizes the *participation mystique*.

These Beginnings lie underground in us: the child that we once were and the child of the race. They live, as Berry reminds us at the beginning of the chapter, in our genetic foundation, the deepest foundation of our souls. The foundations of buildings are soon covered over by a more visible structure—a house or a cathedral, for example—and we don't usually notice what lies beneath it. Likewise, our earliest foundations become covered over by a thinking self that uses words. But the wordless gifts from our Beginnings—the images, sensations, feelings and intuitive wisdom that are our birthright—all lie underneath that more familiar self, and are ordinarily hidden from awareness.

The Danger

These gifts beneath the surface of our minds also carry powers for destruction. In ways that have now become critical to all of our lives, these powers lead us to war. At war with each other over our convictions and our beliefs, we are also at war within ourselves: Our old and new minds are at war over what really matters to us, what success means and what we *think* we want. Even as we try to balance the choices we make, when we don't know what exists in our depths, we don't know who we are!

As long as we remain unaware of the power and presence of these two Beginnings in us, they have great bearing on the ills that plague our lives. But the closer we allow ourselves to come to see them, the greater possibility there is for transformation. If we can understand and embrace the powers that we find in our root selves, they can become part—but not all—of the emergent consciousness of Love: what Teilhard called *Fire*.

The Thinking Mind

We lost our connection with these powers in the process of learning *to know*. We can see in any toddler how much she wants to know. As she learns to follow this longing, she mentally 'steps back,' removes her sense of self from her surroundings, and begins to *see* differently. She sees that her surroundings are made of objects and solidifies her new perceptions by naming them. By this means, she develops a subject/object consciousness.

When our granddaughter, Callista, was sixteen months old, she pointed from within her parents' arms to each thing she noticed: "What's that?" she'd crow, and as soon as they'd named it, she'd point to something else across the room. When they carried her there, she'd exclaim again, "What's *that?!*" It was a game and she loved it. When Callista discovered the magical powers of language, she saw herself differently. She gradually realized that she was separate from other people and objects. In this process of differentiating herself from her surroundings, she was developing a single point of view—her own. In the very human work of naming, Callista was repeating the inner experience of *Homo sapiens* from the Time we discovered the power of words: *She was creating the world.* The creation story she told herself repeated the lived experience of all the children of the race—including the ancient ones who'd told stories like it around the fire:

> In the beginning, God created the heavens and the earth . . . divided light from darkness . . . divided the waters from the land. . . . He called the dry land 'earth' and the mass of water 'seas'. . . .[8]

As these elders had done before her, each child gradually creates her world: She sees it outside of herself as an object—and then divides it into parts. Formed from many experiences, those 'parts' include people, things, places, perceptions, feelings, sensations, and bodily memories—all defined by the power of language. Like bees creating a honeycomb, she builds a structure for an 'I'—a self distinct from the external world—out of all those mental divisions. Once this honeycomb of categories is constructed, the spiritual 'honey' is trapped—it no longer flows.

It is that flowing we have lost.

By naming—by using a subject/object language to define a self that is separate from others—the littlest child enters the kind of consciousness we now enjoy. A great gift, this consciousness also represents a great loss. As a body-ego, the littlest child had been an (albeit unconscious) member of a *participation mystique*. Now she identifies, instead, with a self her mind has created. 'Stepping back' from her body's orientation and into this newly constructed identity—an ego—she also makes an object of herself: She sees herself as separate, and loses the wholeness of the *contextual self* she once had been. All these losses are at the root of her very human loneliness.

Her loneliness is increased by the way her ego uses judgment. That capacity evolved from the *yes/no* of an animal's response to its environment. Since the first one-celled creature, every animal-body has asked itself of anything it met: Take it in? *Yes or no*. Spit it out? *Yes or no*. Turn to it? Run from it? Mate with it? *Yes or no?* The youngest child's animal-body operates in the same way. He is also influenced by his parents' reactions to their environment and absorbs their *yes* or *no* to life, as well. All these root judgments define for him whether or not something is safe, desirable, or life threatening. On this bodily foundation, his ego develops. Like its forerunner in the mind of the snake, his ego-mind's judgments are based on fear for his survival—regardless of the cost to others.

It follows quite naturally that we use the same *yes/no* mechanism to evaluate ourselves—the mental chatter some of my friends call 'the committee.' The next step is to judge others to the same degree we judge ourselves. To *know*, the child-in-us fabricates a reality out of all these little compartments—all created out of judgment and fear. But it is just a honeycomb of categories, a false reality, a way of feeling in control. Our ability to make distinctions tends to create in us a sense of knowing based on what we *think* we know—what ego knows by thinking, observing, comparing, and evaluating.

But what we think is only a small fraction of what the bodymind knows as a whole. Words can only describe a portion of *What Is*. In the process of learning how to know, the child has lost her connection to her body, along with its way of relating to others and to her surroundings. More than that, she has lost her deeply felt sense of communion with what cannot be named—the ineffable dimension of life—the sacred. With these losses, her sense of self has greatly contracted. Redeeming these dimensions is much of the work of the spiritual Way.

Those who are on a spiritual path therefore practice discernment. There is a huge difference between discernment and knowing. Discernment is not 'figuring something out' intellectually. It uses the powers of the body, heart, and mind, *together*. It brings the whole body's wisdom to bear on a concern—and the body *as a whole* resolves it. Joan Blackmon, a friend and companion on the Way, helped me to clarify the difference:

> Discernment is more contemplative than thinking. It is quiet. Reflective. You allow whatever it is you're questioning to work itself through you. You wait . . . and you listen . . . and at some point, you feel a sense of completion.

You can actually *feel* the resolution. There is a subtle shift inside as if something unsettling had settled down—like a billiard ball that had fallen into the right pocket.

The Mind of the Shaman

Ego is a great gift, and since its emergence, our species has accomplished extraordinary things. At the same time, the crises we face are—quite naturally—the products of this more recent form of consciousness: ego's view of the world. These crises have led people like Einstein and Berry to suggest that we need a different way to address the issues that beset us. Berry calls for us to reinvent ourselves by reaching "far back into the genetic foundations . . . to the shamanic dimension of the psyche itself." Why the shaman? Berry reminds us that in nature, the potential for the deepest change lies in origins— our 'Beginnings.' We are familiar with the amazing potential in stem cells. They are 'original cells,' and can be transformed into whatever kind of cell is needed by the body. The same creative potential lies in the shaman's more 'original mind.'

The shaman is one who has slipped through the crack between the *yes* and the *no* of making judgments. His mind—unlike that of the child or the child of the race—is not trapped in a single reality. Instead, he is said to *"walk between the worlds."*[9] So doing, he becomes a healer of mind, of body, and of circumstance. Philosopher Mercea Eliade explains that the true shaman received his unusual gifts because of an early wounding,

> repercussions, within the psyche, of the radical separation between profane and sacred and the resulting splitting of the world.[10]

The sacred and the profane are rejoined in the soul of the shaman.

It is not my intention to explore the Way of the shaman here, but one of its dimensions is important. In seeking what he has lost, the true shaman is not reversing evolution and going backwards; rather, he returns to the Beginnings to increase his conscious awareness. Just as we do when we attempt to enter a mind 'at dusk,' the shaman uses the sound of his drum to enter a quality of mental processing that is different from his ego-mind. Having once been torn from the sacred ground of his own being, he learns how to find that ground again and—like those who tamed the first fire—he does not run away. Staying, he gains access to several different realities in which to work. He is able to choose among them and makes his choices consciously. Moreover, depending on the needs of the situation at hand, he can function in more than one reality at a time—e.g., from within the mind of the *participation mystique* and the observing mind *at once*.

The Emergent Consciousness

Our everyday consciousness tends to operate within the single mind of intellect. Thus far, in these chapters, we've remained within that logical domain. But if we are on a quest for *Fire*, we'll need to go deeper than this! The consciousness we seek is one that embraces. In this sense, it is not unlike the mind of the shaman. But as we shall see, awakening implies an intellect that is able to cooperate with a wholly different kind of processing—one that is too vast to be called 'mental'. Such a consciousness is not split. This emergent consciousness does not judge. It includes. It is as real as Love is real; as immeasurable as Love is immeasurable. This consciousness of Love is a gift, but we can prepare for it by learning how to listen differently. We learn to become increasingly receptive to the more subtle aspects of our lives that our thinking mind might label primitive or even useless.

And so, we turn now toward our own Beginnings to redeem realms long lost to our intellects but still residing in our bodies, hearts, and cells. We will be listening for hints and whispers from many sources—in the words of others who have traveled/ *are traveling*[11] the Way, and in the 'soul language' of dreams, metaphor, poetry, and images. If you decide to accompany me on this journey into depth, we will let ourselves drop down into the mystery of our bodies like a rock plunging into a lake. Falling, letting go, we will drift into a mind 'at dusk.' The deeper we fall, the less familiar the territory and—like evening—the darker it grows. As we fall, we can imagine a pattern of concentric circles that appears on the shining surface of the water above us. This pattern can become a metaphor for our growing embrace—first of our selves, and then of others: The further we fall from the domain of thinking—the more we *see* of ourselves. The more we accept what we find—the wider our embrace spreads. Deeper, wider, more unknowing yet more compassionate, Love unfolds in us—at depth.

To deepen our sense of self, we will first enter the mind of the dream. Some dreams can shine a light into the dim world of wisdom and feeling that lies beneath our thoughts. In later chapters, we'll seek the creature's instinctual habitat, for the creature shows us what it is like to be seated *in the body*. Its perceptions may seem strange to us, but there, in our depths, we will have begun to approach our Beginnings. The closer we are to the Beginnings-in-ourselves, the less we *know*, and the more we are likely to doubt. To *not know* is a radical shift but it is the beginning of the Way of Love. The ancient teachings—Jesus' 'become like a little child,' the Buddha's 'beginner's mind,' and Thomas Berry's 'shamanic dimension of the psyche'—all echo the Beginnings. Spiritual masters like these are not idealizing the past. There is a crucial difference[12] between their three metaphors and a return to the mind of an infant. They call us not to regress into childhood, but to wake up to an emergent consciousness that both includes previous kinds of awareness *and transcends them*.

There comes a moment in the spiritual journey when the very nature of conflict—which to the ordinary mind appears destructive—is transformed. This transformation of conflict into peace marks the emergence of Love—*Fire for the Second Time*. The grace and the glory of such a moment leave us overflowing with gratitude and with joy. *Nothing* can compare with it. Shall we leave the threshold of conflict? We can, if we're willing to let go of the old ways we've relied on and open to a change of mind.

Some Different Ways of Preparing for the Path

Though the more experienced reader may be familiar with much of the following discussion, I include a brief summary here, so we may all start on the same page.

If we are to open to a consciousness that embraces differences, it is important to mention once again that there are countless paths of transformation, and each of us finds our own way. Suzanne found her center by walking a labyrinth. Janice practiced 'conscious dreaming.' Joan learned to pray and meditate. Although we do our inner work alone, we may eventually want the balance of companionship. Marcia went to a shamanic drumming group. Bill chose Alanon. John practiced Tai Chi. Al joined a church. Mike went to school and studied philosophy. There may also come a time when some may want the help of a more experienced person to guide them—perhaps in deep therapy or spiritual direction; in an ongoing meditation group that includes a regular 'check-in' with an experienced teacher; in individual work with a spiritual advisor; or with a sponsor in a twelve-step program. There are many more possibilities. Sometimes, one path unfolds into another. Sometimes, we choose it—and other times, the path chooses us! When I answered the whispered call, I learned to meditate. But the path that later chose me demanded that I become a beginner. Eventually, it led me further back to these other Beginnings—the child and the child of the race.

Not everyone will want or need to do the kind of work I did, but what I found in it was essential to my own healing and to wholeness. For those who are just beginning to inquire, I'd like to suggest that we often begin our spiritual work intuitively without even knowing it, then follow where it leads. I listened to my dreams long before I found a formal path—and over time, the path that unfolded looked like this:

Working with dreams

Meditating

Spending time in the wilderness

Being at dusk

Learning to listen in a new way

Excavating the Foundations of the Soul

We will explore the first five briefly in this chapter.

Working With Dreams

Ours is a story mind. Before words, before the taming of fire, the stories we first knew were embedded in dreams. Ever since those Beginnings, dreams have provided a universal path toward the sacred. The way some dreams express their truth is a language nearer to God, closer to poetry, richer than prose, and wiser than waking. Dreams have been my teachers for more than forty years and many of them have offered me an ongoing record of life's wisdom. Dreams like these were the first to demonstrate to me that there was a deeper, more comprehensive intelligence than thought.

To my more logical self, a dream's characters, places, and events can seem mixed up because they're not clearly defined: Animals turn into people; people morph into other people; scenes change and dissolve. Yet, precisely because so many of life's facets glitter in a dream at once, its picture-and-body language has a richness that my dissecting mind lacks. By presenting a collage of images and feelings, perspectives and stories, dreams offers nourishing food for the soul. I have named what creates them 'the dreamer.'

The dreamer's work of art is like a Picasso of the mind. On the surface, it seems fractured—until you take a closer look. Then you may be astonished at what it can show you about yourself and life from all kinds of different perspectives. When I'm willing to learn from the dreamer's multiple views of reality, there often seems to be more intelligence in the dusk of my dreams than in the bright daylight of my thoughts.

When we pay serial attention to our dreams, we may learn that this dreamer can sometimes be quite insistent, as if she has a specific message to deliver. If we don't understand a dream early in the night, she might provide the same message in a different guise before dawn. On subsequent nights, she may continue to spin story after story, layered with the same meaning. Over and over—sometimes for a period of years—she'll offer her teaching, until it is deeply understood.

In *The Dancing Animal Woman,* I described a dream at midlife about a simple road sign pointing "One Way"—back down the way I had come. It led me on a journey back into childhood. Many years later, the dreamer invited me to go deeper, by showing me the Way to my human Beginnings:

I dream that I unlock the door to my house, knowing the dog is on the other side. As I turn the key, I hear his excitement at my homecoming, and I think I also have to feed him. Then I dream of a primitive woman, so anxious to have a baby, but afraid that she won't be able to give birth because she has so few cycles left in her. I say to her that if worse comes to worse, I can get her a modern pill that would help her. She doesn't want that. She wants to do it in the old and natural way.

She is hungry and I go to feed her. There are leftovers from someone else's plate, spaghetti wagon wheels cooked with fiery red peppers. I don't like them but she is delighted and says, "Oh, they'll be hot and I love that!" I start to serve her this used, leftover food and put it on a dirty paper plate that still has other people's food stuck on it. I know she won't care because she doesn't know any better, but then I realize she deserves a clean plate and go to find one for her.

There are countless methods for working with one's dreams. One way that I've learned to interact with a dream is to imagine every aspect of it—each person, place, thing, action, setting—as a facet of my self. Often they represent things that I'm not aware of in my waking life or am too busy to notice. When I claim them, they enrich me and enlarge my sense of who I am. What I learned from this dream was not only that I had to change, but also that there were particular directions in which I needed to go. If I were to translate its whispered message to more linear language, it might sound something like this:

I am the house to be unlocked, the hungry animal-(body)-self on the other side of the door who needs to be fed. I am the two-million-year-old mother with very little time left to give birth—to something new. With such a short time, I am the one who needs to adapt for I am coming Home to who I am. This primitive woman in me needs to be nourished. What she likes is food that is hot, fiery, and spicy. She is pioneering (as the wagon wheels suggest), exploring new territory. But I am feeding her leftover food: My mind is full of old ideas, images, and memories from other people's plates. She wants heat. Fire. What I'm offering her is dried out. I realize I need to honor her by giving her a clean plate for something new—what she is wanting to bring to birth in me in the old and natural way.

This dream introduced me to my primitive self, and at the same time, also seemed to speak to collective concerns. In recent months, I'd been asking myself—a long-'liberated' woman with several careers behind me—questions like these about what was going on in my culture:

> *What are we doing,* we mothers, minds exhausted, bodies numb, racing from meeting to meeting with packed calendars? We men, competing for enormous amounts of money? We professors, teaching old, old facts? Where will the New come from? How will the young ever find the free time to be creative? At what personal and societal cost is this intensity? Our culture is so violent; we're constantly at war. Our children fall bloody on school playgrounds. Can we learn to live differently?

The dreamer's images seemed to answer my questions. They used paradox—a central quality of creativity—to bind the polarities of primitive and new, outer and inner, animal and human together. A paradox, as we know, is something that appears to be a contradiction—but at the same time, is true. Like the Chinese word for conflict, it is a way of *seeing* that makes space for a resolution. Real creativity often comes from the rubbing together of opposites we feel sure will never be reconciled—and then suddenly, an entirely new idea, or work of art, or even a baby explodes out of nowhere.

Dreams come out of 'nowhere!' They don't exist in the space and time framework we live in. When we listen to this dream from a threshold of conflict, all we seem to hear is contradiction—an assertion of opposites. But when we hear it paradoxically, the conflicts disappear. Instead of being a threshold of conflict, the threshold becomes an open space for transformation. To me, the dream suggests that if we want to heal our collective pain, perhaps we need to learn to walk like the shaman—between the worlds—and find a way to rejoin in ourselves the modern/*primitive,* human/*animal,* mind/*body,* old/*new,* dried-out/*and alive.*

Many of my dreams have provided reflections of just such different ways of being. They are like the spider's night webs in my garden, which reflect different views of reality. At dawn, the morning sun backlights these single filaments stretched between the lowest branches of the oak tree and the native iris beneath them, and as it rises above the horizon, they begin to stir. Each gossamer strand slants in the solar breeze like a shining silken thread. Some glint gold and reflect the sun; others take on the blue-green of their surroundings. Like Navajo sand paintings designed to blow away in the wind, these webs are fragile and last only a night. The next evening, the spider begins all over again.

The spider's work in the night inspires me. As the first light of my awareness begins to touch the many strands of the dream, I see how they reflect facets of the primitive woman in my soul. Then I ask her for help:

> How do I greet you, ancient presence in my soul, creature of the savannah? How I have misunderstood myself in this modern Time! Mother, you are woven into the landscape so completely, you are one person with it. Your nostrils know intimately the scents of moist earth, of ripe passion fruit, of prey and the smell of a stranger; you know the smell of desire and the smell of danger. Your eyes see the slightest variation on a path and even in the dark, your feet know how to find the way. Yours is the intelligence of life itself. You are not split from it. You don't divide it into parts. You're alive to every nuance of the aliveness around you. You have a natural trust in your own merit, simply because you are. The world rolls at your feet. I don't live my life like you do. I've long since forgotten how to *be*. Surely, the fruit of consciousness was a great gift . . . but how can I redeem your kind of understanding, as well?

That question lit my way.

Meditating

In meditation, I learned to let my awareness drop to deeper and deeper levels. I've found it to be the single most important practice for learning how *to be*. For years, I assumed there was something wrong with the way I was meditating: I couldn't stop my thoughts, or my feelings, or an itch I wanted to scratch! But I learned that it was the mind's *job* to think! *My job as I meditated was simply to sit there; to become aware of these natural events, and let them pass. It was a model for living my life without being so reactive. Meditation takes us into what poet Jane Hirschfield calls *liminal space*. She described it in a talk:

> All traditional cultures contain rites of passage in which each person may experience the liminal—a threshold state in which individual identity drops away and the initiate becomes permeable to all being. Certain writers, like monks, take on the threshold as a lifelong task. This role of rolelessness can be seen as a kind of Bodhisattva path: The artist begins to speak on behalf of everything and everyone, creating through art a way for a culture to recognize itself as whole in all its parts.[13]

Liminal space is where transformation occurs. It is not a dissociated state—we are not severed from ourselves. It is *a different orientation*. We are exquisitely alert and our attention is heightened and very receptive. As if standing in a doorway, we are neither on one side of the door or the other. It's a little like being the old Roman god, Janus, whose head faced both front and back at the same time. The regular practice of meditation (or its open-eyed equivalent, contemplation), can lead to the quality of incisive presence that Hirschfield describes. The poet Wordsworth sings about the same quality of experience:

> . . . And I have felt
> A presence that disturbs me with the joy
> Of elevated thoughts; a sense sublime
> Of something far more deeply interfused,
> Whose dwelling is the light of setting suns,
> And the round ocean and the living air,
> And the blue sky, and in the mind of man:

A motion and a spirit, that impels
All thinking things, all objects of all thought,
And rolls through all things . . . .[14]

On the Way of Love, it is this palpable Presence that we attend.

Spending Time in the Wilderness

Camping in the wilderness is another way of getting a feeling for the kind of liminal space which Hirschfield describes. The wild that was once our home is a living continuum. Nothing stops the eye or impedes our awareness of presence—no boundaries, no signs, no walls, or fences. When George and I canoed and camped in the Canadian wilderness, it took only a few days of living outdoors for words to dissolve. Listening to the immense silence, my mind relaxed—and nothing separated me from my self or from the life around me.

In the wilderness
my mind spreads out like water
    pools
        shines
            reflects green boughs
                and blue sky . . .
I listen to the trees whispering
and think no thoughts[15]

Being at Dusk

Liminal space is a way of *being* and of *seeing*. It is not unlike the twilight—literally, the 'between light'—that is neither night nor day, but both, and something more. Without definition, dusk is simply *what it is*. I love its softness, the waning light, the gradual cease of activity in nature. Tiny insects are backlit. They hang in the gold air as if suspended in honey. Then they stop flying. So do the birds. The wind drops. Everything is stilled.

In this stillness, dusk becomes a time to listen with my whole body to life—to be present—not in an unconscious way like my archaic grandmother of the savannah. But awake.

I once invited a small group of women to come to my home at dusk, to bring something of their creativity, and to watch the day die and a full moon rise. "Dusk?" each one of them asked, "Dusk? When is dusk?" Used to telling time by a clock, not one of them knew, but by the evening of our gathering, each woman had found out when dusk began and arrived precisely at sunset.

Since Edison invented the electric light, the word 'dusk' has gone out of our vocabulary. When it starts to get dark, we turn on the lights and rarely notice the slow changes between the setting of the sun and full darkness. My friend, Harriett Wright, who has lived in Africa, tells me that dusk there provides a respite from the heat of the day:

> At dusk, all the colors begin to change and the whole pace of life slows. You can feel it. It is healing.

We have lost dusk in the evening news, the commute hour, and the nightly traffic jam, but we can still nurture its healing qualities in our lives. I've learned to stop working when dusk comes, to become quiet and let myself go gradually into the night. It is my favorite time of day. I don't turn on the lights until it is quite dark, and the more I give myself to this timespace with no edges, the more I reenter the dusk of my mind. You might want to try it.

There is stillness to all these practices and an infinite perspective that we have lost. With focused activity let go, we find ourselves closer to reclaiming our inheritance from all the animal-human ancestors who lived at the dawn of time—and still live in our cells.

Sir Laurens van der Post, who was given a Bushman's education by his native nurse in South Africa, said, "I was brought up in a way that never separated me from my instincts and my instinctive self." He writes:

The Bushmen of the Kalahari personified an aspect of natural man which we all have, but with which we've increasingly lost contact. This has impoverished and endangered us. When I spoke to Jung about it, he said, "Oh, this is not an extravagant thought at all. *Every human being has a two-million-year-old man within himself, and if he loses contact with that two-million-year-old self, he loses his (her) real roots.*" So the question of why modern man is in search of himself and has lost his religious roots has a lot to do with the interest in the Bushmen, this naked little man in the desert, who owned nothing.[16]

The question Jung poses echoes the dream of the primitive woman. It hints at something that connects us with our Beginnings, the mystery of belonging, and the lost sacred. The bushman of the Kalahari knew that he belonged because he was at Home: in his body, in the vitality of the living community, and in the spiritual reality that encompassed him—Presence. It is no wonder our entire culture resonated with the movie character, E. T., when he moaned, *"Ho-o-o-ommmme! H-o-o-o-o-ommme!"* The loss of connection with our two-million-year-old self is the loss of our residence in the deepest foundations of our souls, and the Presence at the Beginnings that still lives at our core.

Learning to Listen in a New Way

To find our Home again, we turn inside to listen, then follow the soundless song of the soul. Sometimes, we may hear it whispered in a dream, other times, through the words of spiritual masters; yet others, through images or flashes of insight or in stories like van der Post's.

From an early age, the song of the soul called to me repeatedly: in dreams, in meditation, in the wilderness, and at dusk. It also whispered through the image of foundations—beginning with the underground church of my childhood. Each time I encountered a foundation in my life, I was enchanted. It was only afterwards, in reflection, as I listened in a different way, that I recognized these foundations were an invitation to greater depth. As the song continued to whisper through my images, it kept drawing me deeper into the mystery of my own life, deeper into humanity's journey of awakening, deeper into the Way of *Fire*.

The song of the soul may call you through scripture or poetry. You may find it in art or music, in nature or in the elegance of a mathematical equation. What matters is not how it arrives. What matters is that, by trusting our innate bodily wisdom enough to follow its lead, each of us learns what needs to be birthed in the old and natural way.

When the call to awaken comes, we may feel it
as sweetness, or as grief—it comes in many forms.
However we feel it, it is an indication that
the Teacher is near.[17]

Ellen Grace O'Brian

Endnotes for Chapter 4

1   Thomas Berry, *The Dream of the Earth*, San Francisco: Sierra Club Books, 1988. Condensed from pages 201, 210-212.

2   Jay Matternes, reconstruction painting of "Homo habilis," ©1989. All of Matternes' artwork work is scientifically correct. In this full color work (which has been cropped), he made a painstaking reconstruction of the fossil skull, skeleton, and musculature of a Homo habilis in order to flesh out the most accurate possible life appearance. See *http://www.jaymatternes.com*

3   The science of evolution is evolving radically in our time and more information about our human family tree is being generated at a rapid rate. Until the early 21ˢᵗ century, it was thought that *Homo erectus* was the descendent of an earlier form of human, *Homo habilis*, who appeared on earth some 2.6 million years ago. *Homo habilis* was a hunter-gatherer whose arrival was thought to mark the beginning of the stone ages. His descendent, *Homo erectus*, was believed to have been the first to leave Africa, beginning about 1.5 million years ago and the probable tamer of fire. *Erectus* migrated all over Eurasia, Australia, North and South America and the excavations of their shelters found in Asia show "extensive remains of ashes, charcoal, burnt bones and charred clays." Until recently, it was believed that 300,000 years after *Homo erectus* (200,000 years ago), an archaic *Homo sapiens* may have appeared, to be followed a mere 40,000 years ago by modern man, *Homo sapiens sapiens,* who had language.

Now, however, an article in *Newsweek*, March 19, 2007, 52-58 reports that the linear view of human development has been supplanted by one which describes countless variations of the species arising at the same time, then dying out, followed by more of the same pattern for millennia. The fields of genetics (the study of DNA) and paleoneurology (which examines the imprint of the brain on the insides of fossil skulls) show that neither *Homo habilis* nor *Homo erectus* left descendents. Rather, this more current (2007) version of our prehistory says that *Homo sapiens* seems to have its roots solely in the last group to have left Africa, a mere 66,000 years ago.

4   Steven Mithen, *The Prehistory of the Mind*, New York: Thames and Hudson, 1996. Mithen, PhD, a professor of archaeology, states in a discussion of his book: "[While] there are no clear answers about cognitive evolution in these records of the past, cognitive abilities can be inferred from reconstructions of past behavior, just as psychologists infer the cognitive abilities of children or apes from behavioral observations. But one can . . . reconstruct evolutionary histories for many of those aspects of human cognition that appear to be uniquely human (but not, the archaeological record suggests, necessarily unique *to Homo sapiens sapiens*.)" Retrieved September 2007 at *http://www.nybooks.com/articles/844*

Robert Cancro, MD, summarizes Mithen's book in the American Journal of Psychiatry 155:12, December 1998: "Mithen argues that the human mind is a product of undirected, selective evolution that has occurred over several million years . . . [and] that, in order to understand the mind of current humans, it is essential to study the early history of humans, humanoids, and great apes. As an archaeologist, he feels that one can study the behavior of these earlier creatures through the traces left at various archaeological sites. Through studying the skulls and artifacts of these creatures, he argues one can deduce their brain size, their behaviors, and perhaps even their beliefs. These inferences include an understanding of why and how religion developed as human activities." (Tense adapted for continuity.) Retrieved September 2007 at *http://ajp.psychiatryonline.org/cgi/reprint/155/12/1787.pdf*

5   I have tried to use little or no jargon in this book but have not been able to avoid the words *ego* or *participation mystique*. As I use them, they are basically defined as follows:

     Ego denotes that aspect of the individual which is self-aware; the part of the psyche which experiences the external world or reality through the senses, which organizes the thought processes rationally, and which governs action. In this book it does not refer to the more popular definition of the word: an inflated feeling of pride. Webster's Unabridged Dictionary defines *ego* as *"the self; the individual as aware of himself."* But this is a self as distinct from the external world. Ego is a product of a mind that thinks, observes, and judges. It does not take into account feelings, intuition, or ways of knowing other than those based on intellect's more logical point of view. Webster's dictionary also defines *intellect* as "the power of knowing as distinguished from the power to feel and to will." So these terms can be confusing! Bill Kueppers, PhD, clarified: "The difference between the intellect and the ego in making distinctions lies in the ego's instinct for survival. The ego needs (is instinctually invested in) constant reassurance of its very being and value by such distinctions, and this is where the oppositional element causes difficulty: anything that seemingly threatens my existence or my value is 'bad.'"

     Participation mystique describes the shared group mind of early human clans. The term was first coined in 1926 by anthropologist Lucien Levi-Bruhl who studied the thought processes of hunter-gatherers and the first agricultural peoples during Paleolithic and Neolithic times (400,00-10,000 BC). It denoted a primitive consciousness in which each person experienced him (her)self as the corporate body, a kin network that acted as one person. *This communal and collective entity spanned the historic continuum of the larger group.* Jung took up the phrase, as did Jean Houston, PhD, a teacher, philosopher, and researcher in mental potential. See Jean Houston, *The Possible Human*, Los Angeles: J.P. Tarcher, Inc., 1982. *Author's note:* In 1981, at a workshop by the same name, Houston discussed the term. She also related at the same time that the aging Teilhard de Chardin had befriended and encouraged her when she was a young child, and that they had taken long walks together in New York City.

6   The term *body-ego* was developed by transpersonal psychologist Michael Washburn, PhD, who contrasts it with what he calls the *Ego-I.* See Michael Washburn, *The Ego and the Dynamic Ground*, New York: SUNY Press, 1987.

7   Current research differentiates between recognition and recall. The infant may recognize his mother's face quite early but research pegs the age at which he can recall her image to memory when she is absent at or after 18 months. See Diane Pearson, MD, *Safe Sleep*, Chapter 4, "The Development of Memory in Infants," 21-22. Retrieved in 2005 at *http://www.safesleepforchildren.com*

8   Genesis 1:1-10. Abridged.

9   Michael Harner, PhD, anthropologist and founder of The Foundation for Shamanic Studies.

10 Mircea Eliade, *Shamanism: Archaic Techniques of Ecstasy*, Princeton: Princeton University Press, Bollingen Series LXXVI, 1964. *Author's note:* The shaman's Way is the Way of the 'wounded healer' and the traditional shaman was able to heal because he had known suffering. He accessed the root consciousness on his own journey inward, and it was that consciousness which wove dream, plant, and animal world together with his own. His creativity and his capacity to heal came

from a different kind of consciousness that included his suffering and the gifts from this deep foundation.

11 'Have traveled/*are traveling*' is a way of expressing two tenses that occur simultaneously in a different way of viewing reality. The same method will be used to express the simultaneity of opposite meanings.

12 There is a difference between *differentiation* and *dissociation*. I am laying the foundation in this chapter for an understanding of a Consciousness that is not a return to an infant or primal oceanic state. Rather it includes and transcends an intellect that has previously differentiated and transcended the emotional and instinctual being. Many of us grew up having repressed, for emotional purposes, the richness of these earlier aspects of ourselves, or else as we were developing our capacities for reason. We did not differentiate and then integrate these dimensions at these times. Instead, we dissociated from them. Chapters 7-10 describe, in part, the work of reclaiming this richness.

13 Jane Hirschfield in a lecture entitled, "The Artist and the Threshold Life," San Francisco, October 1996.

14 William Wordsworth, "Tinturn Abbey," *Complete Poetical Works,* London and New York: Macmillan and Co., 1888.

15 Poetry is the author's, unless otherwise indicated.

16 Source unknown. Van der Post grew up in Africa and has authored films and 23 non-fiction books as well as some novels. Most of his works are set in Africa.

17 The Rev. Ellen Grace O'Brian, Center for Spiritual Enlightenment, 'Daily Inspirations.' See *http://www.csecenter.org*

The Foundations of the Soul

5 Mind and Its Evolution— The Three Foundations of the Soul

If you have built castles in the air, your work
need not be lost; that is where they should be.
Now put the foundations under them.

Thoreau[1]

The song of the soul leads us unerringly toward a new way to live our lives. It guides us down through old foundations that lie within us, relics of an earlier time. These three foundations, personal and collective, teach us who we have been on the way to showing us who we are. Embraced, they become the scaffolding for a new consciousness that has been evolving in humanity for a very long time. This emergent consciousness embodies an understanding that is not of the mind alone, a capacity for relatedness, and a qualitatively different Love that has long been misunderstood. Such a Love is the vision inspiring every mystic's[2] quest, an Intelligence that embraces—*Fire for the second time*.

This is the awakening to which we are all heir and have been forever called.

o

When I was young, I longed to become an archeologist. In this first and very concrete response to my songline, I imagined digging in the rich soil at ancient locations in deserts and jungles around the world where the earliest layers of life had been lived. As I grew older, I followed my fascination with things underground. Seeking a deeper connection with the lives that had gone before me, I discovered I'd become, instead, an archeologist of the soul.

Not realizing I was looking for a footing for my own inner life, I remained drawn to foundations. They conveyed something I needed to understand—a sense of continuity, perhaps, but also something about who I was. The first was the underground church of my childhood.

Later, after I was widowed in my early thirties, I bought a small pasture on a dirt road in New Hampshire. Hidden in a tangle of bittersweet vines near the edge of the road, were the remains of an old granite foundation. It was constructed of huge, hand-hewn blocks, laid down by the land's first settlers, three hundred years before. I built a tiny home behind it so that the path to our front door wound between its lichen-covered walls. A few fallen blocks became stairs to the entry. The largest I saved for our hearthstone.

A decade older, I found some foundations that were far more ancient in the great stone mesas of Bandelier, New Mexico. The cliffs there are rough and jagged, pocked with ancient cave dwellings. In the afternoon sun, the sandstone turns pink, and shadows deepen the fault lines and dark hollows in the face of the cliff. To explore the many openings in the sheer canyon wall, you have to make your way up a rickety ladder of rough wooden poles lashed together. When I was there, I climbed the ladder past several cliff dwellings to the top, then clambered into the mouth of an ancestral cave and sat there as if it were my own. I looked out over the wide wilderness and imagined myself an Anasazi woman who lived there and listened to stories about her ancestors who'd come from Asia thousands of years before.[3]

Dug deep below another cave there, I found the first kind of sacred space known to man—a hole in the ground called a *kiva*. The Anasazi believed that by descending a kiva, one entered the earthly opening out of which the human family—*the people*—had come. When I went down inside it, a breeze brushed past my cheek and whispered, *"Home."*

I followed the whispered call of foundations for nearly fifty years before I came upon a scattering of broken white marble in an open field in Greece—all that was left of a temple to Athena. In a small roped-off area, an archeologist had carefully brushed away layers of accumulated clay and rock to reveal a single corner of the fallen temple's foundation. Peering down into the hole, I was awed. His work had exposed not one, but three separate foundations hidden beneath the temple floor, one on top of the other.

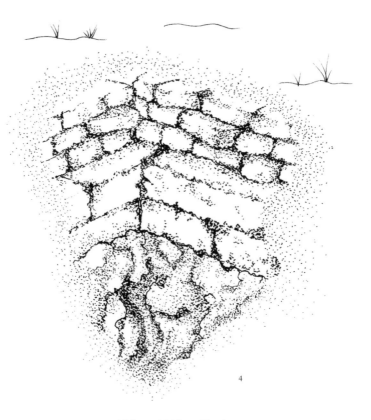

4

Ink drawing 2005 Denise Moynahan

The deepest one looked as if it had been chiseled out of the floor of a cave, like the kiva. The one above it was constructed of massive stone slabs. Those two layers supported a third, made of smaller blocks of carefully cut marble. All three had supported the temple. There was magic in this discovery, though I didn't yet know why—only that I sensed in these multiple foundations a revelation of something more than a history of sacred architecture, some kind of evolutionary template that spoke volumes.

I did some research and learned it had long been common practice for builders to use old foundations as a base for later construction on the same site. Ancient kivas dug out of rock became foundations for the grottos and temples of later, more evolved spiritualities. In many of them, whether in Greece, or Italy, Mexico, or the jungles of Cambodia, priests and priestesses had offered human scapegoats in sacrifice to the gods. Then, as religions continued to evolve, kiva, grotto, and temple became the foundations that buttressed later churches and cathedrals.

In Assisi, Italy, the Roman temple to Minerva went through many transformations and is now a columned church called *Santa Maria sopra Minerva*. The name is a wonderfully literal description, for the Italian declares it is the church of 'Saint Mary upstairs over Minerva'! When we were there, our guide pointed out two stone troughs in the floor, flanking the church's altar. Fifteen hundred years after the Romans, the troughs were still stained red with the blood of human sacrifices to their goddess Minerva.

I found my last clue to the call of the foundations in a dim grotto underneath the great cathedral in Florence. There, archeologists had just uncovered another triple foundation, and a sign revealed details that stunned me:

> Each of these three foundations was built of a different kind of stone; each represents a different form of construction; and each supports a structure built by a different civilization.

The archeologists' description immediately brought to mind what the eminent neuroscientist Paul MacLean had said of the human brain: that it contained three separate brains, each one constructed differently and each made of different kinds of cells:

> We are obliged to look at ourselves and the world through the eyes of three quite different mentalities.
>
> Two of these brains cannot speak. Each of the three brains has its own special intelligence, its own subjectivity, its own sense of time and space, its own memory . . . and other functions.[5]

No wonder I had been captivated by the triple foundations in Greece! MacLean's description of the amazing architecture of what he called the 'triune brain' was a mirror of life's long slow journey of awakening.

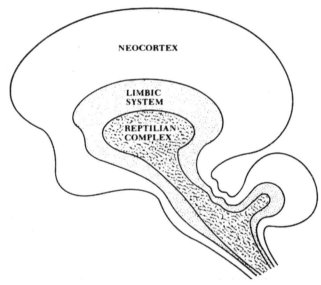

The Triune Brain[6]

We carry within ourselves three different brains, evolved over millions of years. Stacked one above the other like the stone foundations in Greece and Italy, they are a living inheritance from our long ancestry in the animal kingdom. Each one is a remnant of an earlier design: the brain of a snake, the brain of a mammal, and the brain of the earliest human being. It is as if the snake had been coiled in our minds since the Beginnings. So has the beast. So has the wild *Homo habilis*.

These three brains are our inheritance. They reflect the gifts and the inner discord that have made us so complex. They represent three entirely different worldviews which are forever in conflict. Not one of these brains gets along with the other two! Their quarrels with one another are a fundamental limitation of the consciousness with which we operate. All three shape our behavior. Most particularly, they shape the conflicts of our world. We don't usually pay much attention to their impact on our lives, but today's intense global conflict suggests that we examine them again; for each of these three minds is driven by life's passion to survive at any cost, without regard for the needs of others. If we hope to use a spiritual practice to help override our programming, it is essential that we understand the ways in which these conflicting brains control us. Once we do, they can become firm foundations for a new kind of Love—the very nature of which is to heal divisions.

o

While there are many sophisticated spiritual systems that parallel evolutionary development, the image of the three foundations provides a 'concrete' symbol for the way our three brains program how we act, how we feel, and how we think. Described here very broadly, these foundations provide a simple framework for our themes: 1) the gradual emergence of our species, 2) its repetition in our development as individuals, and 3) the way these developments are reflected in culture—particularly in *how we hear*. Briefly summarized below, they are further detailed in a footnote.[7]

The Foundations of the Soul

The Root Foundation: The Intelligence of the Body

The root foundation is the most primitive intelligence of the body. Called by MacLean the "reptilian function," this mind is similar to that of a snake. It is exceedingly intelligent and regulates our bodies and instincts, *but it has no feelings and no sense of relationship to others*. Its only concern is survival. Most powerful, yet least accessible to awareness, it fuels our passions, our desires, and our furies. Evolved over 500 million years, the reptilian brain does not separate sexual urgency and the instinct to kill. The silent ritual behavior of the snake still echoes in this part of our minds as a single embrace: creation and destruction. They are *one energy*. We tend to be unaware of how this energy drives our will to power, to territoriality, to social hierarchy and success: be it with a lover, on the road, or among nations. And we ignore this root inheritance at our peril.

The Heart's Foundation: The Intelligence of Feeling

The heart's foundation lies above the first and is the mind that controls feeling. MacLean named it the "limbic system" and this mind is also inaccessible to normal awareness. As mammals evolved over a period of more than 200 million years, this new brain added the kind of intelligence needed to nurture young and to maintain relationships with like creatures. This inheritance includes capacities for feelings, for memory, and for dreams, all of which are essential to our psychological, social, and spiritual development.

These first two foundations were the rock on which my *Homo habilis* grandmother stood. Like the kiva and temple, they were then covered over by a third.

The Mind's Foundation: The Intelligence of Thought

The mind's foundation, the neocortex, houses our intellect and is constructed over the first two. This uppermost foundation holds further capacities for memory, and adds the gifts of language, reason, planning, and conscious awareness. Our youngest and least experienced brain, it has far less power to shape our lives than the other two. But we tend to identify with this kind of intelligence almost exclusively.

What amazes me is this: The rudimentary swellings that ultimately became our three human brains were all present in the brains of fishlike creatures swimming in the primordial sea five-hundred million years ago![8] Our mental potential was already physically established in the fish and in the snake eons before mammals developed, and hundreds of millions of years before the first human ever set foot on earth. Only when it was Time, did the mystery of the human mind unfurl. Isn't that astonishing!

What Lies Beyond the Three Foundations?

What potential awaits us now? I am suggesting that the 'whisper' is an intimation of an emergent consciousness in us that we cannot understand; and that if we can learn to listen and are willing to risk the unknown, we might just serve that potential. Even if this were only a hint of the truth, *how we hear our call, and from which of our foundations,* become very important issues.

How we interpret the whisper—and then act on it—is influenced by the stories that inform our lives. Like the stone foundations of the kiva, temple, and cathedral, these stories have evolved over thousands of years. Joseph Campbell tells us that our most enduring stories hint at a far deeper pattern:

> Myths are stories that are transparent to something deeper, something universal. They are reflections of the ultimate design of the universe.[9]

If we hope to live lives aligned with the life of the greater Whole, the stories and myths passed on to us from previous generations may be able to help us. But it depends entirely on *how we hear them.*

Endnotes for Chapter 5

1   Henry David Thoreau, *Walden,* Introduction and Annotations by Bill McKibben, Boston: Beacon Press, 2004, 303. Reprinted from the first edition of *Life in the Woods,* 1854. The entire paragraph is lovely: "I learned this, at least, by my experiment: that if one advances confidently in the direction of his dreams, and endeavors to live the life which he has imagined, he will meet with a success unexpected in common hours. He will put some things behind, will pass an invisible boundary; new, universal, and more liberal laws will begin to establish themselves around and within him; or the old laws be expanded, and interpreted in his favor in a more liberal sense, and he will live with the license of a higher order of beings. In proportion as he simplifies his life, the laws of the universe will appear less complex, and solitude will not be solitude, nor poverty poverty, nor weakness weakness. If you have built castles in the air, your work need not be lost; that is where they should be. Now put the foundations under them."

2   The word, mystic, is often misunderstood. Put most simply by the historian of the mystics, Evelyn Underhill, it refers to 'a person who loves God.' It is defined more fully in Chapter 11.

3   *The Genographic Project* is an effort to map humanity's genetic journey through the ages and includes an Atlas of the Human Journey that maps the frequency of genetic markers in modern peoples and allows researchers to understand how ancient humans moved around the world. According to this research, the ancestors of the Anasazi tribe left Asia and crossed the Bering Straits to an unknown destination—what is now Alaska—then made their way down to what are now the western parts of North, Central and South America. See *http://www.nationalgeographic.com/genographic*

4   Denise Moynahan is an illustrator and author of children's books, the most recent of which is *The Great Cavern of the Winds: Tales from Backbone Mountain,* Johnson City, TN: Overmountain Press, 2005.

5   Paul MacLean, MD, Chief of the Laboratory of Brain Evolution and Behavior at the National Institute of Mental Health, quoted in Carl Sagan, *The Dragons of Eden,* New York: Ballantine Books, 1977, 57.

6   Sagan, *The Dragons of Eden,* 59. Others of Sagan's comparative drawings, 55 and 60, show similarities in brain structure of the human embryo to the brain structures of reptiles, birds, and other mammals.

7   The following summary is the author's, and is based on Sagan, 63-80:
    The first foundation of the brain: The human spine and cerebellum are structures borrowed from reptiles, birds, and fish, the earliest of which evolved 510 million years ago. MacLean called this archaic mind the "Reptilian Complex" because it controls the same processes in the human as it does in the snake. It governs the body's systems, among them: circulation, respiration, and metabolism, and also governs instinctual behaviors: eating, mating, sexual and aggressive rituals and self-defense. Its reactions are immediate, unmediated by thought.

    The second foundation of the brain: Above the cerebellum resides the limbic system or midbrain that appeared in mammals, which first emerged over 216 million years ago. It is also deeply involved in aggression and fear and monitors the coordination of inner and outer worlds, and the endocrine and sensory systems. What we used to call 'the unconscious' is now often called 'limbic memory.'

    The third foundation of the brain: The neocortex appeared within the human species 50,000-100,000 years ago and offered the capacities for language, logic, symbolic expression, complex perception, a temporal sense, conscious memory, and planning. It is the location of our conscious thought and our inventiveness. Probable dates are from Swimme and Berry, *The Universe Story*.

8   Sagan, *The Dragons of Eden*, 53-55. Sagan describes fossil endocasts of the brains of the earliest known vertebrates—ostracoderms and placoderms—and follows up with drawings showing the similarities between the brains of perch, toad, snake, pigeon, and cat.

9   Joseph Campbell, PhD, the great historian of myth, quoted in Carolyn North, *Seven Movements, One Song,* Berkeley: Regent Press, 1991, 14.

6 The Power of the Three Foundations— How We Hear

The world is made up of stories, not atoms.

Muriel Rukeyser[1]

From the foundations, from my bones, from the ashes of the fire, the root chants of my ancestors still sound in the myths and stories of my childhood. They were like a great song that brought to life countless people who'd lived out a destiny, taken a journey, fought a battle, or solved a problem posed by the gods. Their names echoed down the ages: Gilgamesh . . . Aeneas . . . Odysseus . . . Prometheus . . . Persephone . . . Joan of Arc . . . Deep with reality, their legends passed from one generation to another until they reached my own. Surely, the words that now give voice to our longings were energized by the yearnings of heroes and heroines like these! They may have made little sense to our intellect, but they *intended* our lives—propelled us and set us on our Way.

Intended! How I love the way language flowered in the minds of my ancestors! How the ancient Latin, *tendere*—to *stretch*, to *grow*, to *strive*—exploded into bloom! It brought us *intent* . . . *intention* . . . and *tendency* . . . And although we may discover that 'stretching' and 'growing' is not without *intensity* or *tension*—it is also not without *tenderness* and our yearning to *tend*—whether a fire or a child or another person. All the wisdom of human experience came down to me, first, through the gift of words in stories.

Encompassing those stories was a much larger epic: the immense story of the universe. I am awed by how its unfolding creativity is repeated in every infant in the womb: how the intricate form of each infant body was worked out in the bodies of countless earlier creatures—and before them, in the chemistry of stars. The depth and breadth of this great story of the lives of galaxies and planets and species and persons is, to me, the Great Composition.

In addition to these narratives, and grounding me from an early age, was the profound wisdom reflected in my own Judeo-Christian tradition. Beautiful and frustrating, paradoxical and so very human, I've sought in its stories infinite layers of understanding. By continuing to inquire into them—and by seeing how the wisdom stories of all the different traditions can light one another up—I have found in them living expressions of what I most needed for my own unfolding.

All these stories—of the universe, of the Greeks, of Moses' stuttering encounter with *Fire* and Mary's steadfast embrace of her baby; of Joan of Arc's trust in a whispered call and the compassion shown by Jesus—intended me. They set my direction and offered models for awakening to the energies of Love. I can no longer separate them from one another. I hear the whole Song as One—and I belong to them all.

As Ibn 'Arabi, the revered Arab Muslim poet and spiritual teacher of old, recited:

> My heart has become capable of every form: it is a
>   pasture for gazelles and a convent for Christian monks,
> And a temple for . . . the
>   tables of the Tora[h] and the book of the Koran.
> I follow the religion of Love: whatever way Love's
>   camels take, that is my religion and my faith.[2]

Stories are an example of how the three foundations of the soul actually work in our lives. They keep us mired in old forms—in *what we know*. Culture's stories not only intend us; they also help to tell us *who we are, now*. They have this kind of power because, like many human creations, they've been constructed in the same way as the three stone foundations—one right over the other. Thus the oldest stories provide many of the elements from which our later narratives were derived. Like the foundations, these oldest stories endure. Hidden 'underground,' they *strongly influence how we hear anything new*—just like our oldest brains.

In this chapter, we'll explore some creation stories like that of Adam and Eve in the Garden of Eden. Older tales like this are still alive in the earliest foundations of the human soul, but much of their power over us is unconscious. Hidden from awareness, they are like great stone buttresses bracing cathedrals. They literally reinforce our most deeply held beliefs and values—whether or not we know it—and whether or not we subscribe to them, intellectually.

But there is another side to stories, for they are not simply vestiges of the past. They also contain the seeds of the future. Just as the potential for the human mind was visible in the brain of a snake, our stories also provide the potential for *who we may become*. They are like grist for the mill—the grain to be ground for flour—and that grist intends the kind of bread we make with our lives.

The Evolution of a Creation Story

If we look at one of the earliest legends about creation, we can see how it has been evolving all along—and is still evolving. We can also see, in one of its most recent versions, how it hints at the emergent consciousness—who we are becoming. Actually, it reflects who we already are. We just haven't awakened to it!

Who am I? Who are you? What is God?

Whenever human beings have explored questions of identity, they've first asked, *Where did we come from?* After much pondering around the fire, they passed their understanding on, and the next generations learned what their forefathers learned— first in mime and chant, then in drama, song, and story.

The Anasazi Story

As we've already seen, the Anasazi told one of the oldest creation stories: of a group birth from a hole in the ground. They celebrated their story in a kiva like the one I found in the cave at Bandolier. In their story, 'the people' arrived—*the human family, as one.* This root human understanding was handed down to the Anasazi by their own hunter-gatherer forebears—clans that migrated from Africa to populate all the continents of the world.[3] This 'original story' defined every subsequent human generation on every single continent as *a people*—not individuals—who functioned within a group mind.

The clan's group mind—the *participation mystique*—still lies within all of us, buried deep in the triune brain. One of its present-day manifestations is the strong psychic bond between mothers and infants. In our Time, mothers may feel the bond, but most mothers haven't learned how to make use of it. To see it in operation, we need to turn to certain indigenous tribes: Women in the !Kung[4] tribe in Africa, for example, rely heavily on this deep bodily attunement to care for their young. A mother carries her naked infant on her back all day and when it needs to urinate, *she knows it*—in time to lift him down and hold him near the bushes. This kind of knowing still exists in mothers from so-called 'civilized' cultures—we may be unaware of it, but it is alive and well in the first foundations of our souls.

The Australian Aboriginal Story

Today's Aboriginal culture in Australia still rests on their 'song' about the first people emerging from a hole in the ground. A song! But this song had its roots in the far more ancient drama enacted by clans closer to the Beginnings—those who knew they were one, and one with the world around them.

The Hebrew Story

As human consciousness evolved, creation narratives evolved as well, and like nature, tended to incorporate the older stories and then add something new. Those who told them had to coin new words, an essential step in expressing a new kind of consciousness. In the Hebrew tribe, for example, Adam's creation *from* a handful of earth rested firmly on the kiva's story of humanity's birth *out of* the earth. The Hebrew word for 'tillable earth' (or soil) is *adamah;* and for 'man' is *adam.* Their language-making quite literally incorporated the essential ingredient of the kiva's older story: *Adam* (man) came from *adamah* (earth). The Hebrews' addition to the earlier story, however, reflected their own experience of a more complex human identity—the significance of a named individual. Adam was not enmeshed in a group mind. He was a separate person who lived in relationship—to others and to a divine creator.

The sense of self as an individual with the capacity for relationship required a mental and emotional separation from the shared group mind—the *participation mystique.* The stories of the long succession of peoples who accomplished this separation reflect a radical transformation of their behavior, emotion, and thought—and a complete change of identity. (An example of this radical change of identity in the people of India can be found in Appendix II.) This same transformation has now become innate in post-tribal cultures, and is repeated in every toddler's separation from his mother and his surroundings as he develops an ego.

The New Testament Story

The Eden story provided the Hebrews a means of answering the ancient human questions of identity. Later, Jesus followed the same pattern by building on earlier foundations and referring to himself as "the son of Adam."[5] The apostle, Paul, in his letters to the early communities of the first century, adapted those words and called Jesus the "new Adam." He described Jesus as an individual in whom *the boundaries between any one group and the rest of the human race had disappeared.*[6] Neither man was announcing a return to the identities of the past. They spoke, rather, of a new possibility for humanity: the emergence of the kind of person in whom ego's divisions had been reunited and transcended within a larger self. Their words describe a new potential: that which is inherent in the consciousness of Love. It is a possibility that lies within all of us.

Science's Story

Thus far, we've seen how each of these stories has included and then added something new to the story that came before it. In recent years, however, science has assumed responsibility for developing the creation narrative, and science is far less inclined to include earlier narratives within its own. Sometimes said to be our most recent religion, it tends to see the scientific story as the *only* creation story—and one that cancels out all of those that came before. *This is the way the foundation of the mind works: it chooses one perspective and tends to negate others.*

How that way of looking at the world can turn on a dime to blame and judgment! When we choose one perspective and stick with it—watch out! We end up smack in the middle of a conflict. Intellect's capacity for making judgments is a great gift, but when ego co-opts intellect to reinforce its own value, it can be profoundly damaging to relatedness.

The Emergent Story

The emergent story shows how these wounds might be healed, in Time. The potential we will explore in Parts 3 and 4, is that of an emergent consciousness, one that transcends intellect and at the same time, includes all three foundations of the soul—body, heart, and mind. This kind of consciousness has the capacity to heal the divisions created by our thinking minds: the wars within us, and our wars with others. It does not, as the intellect tends to do, make one story—or one position, one sex, race, or religion—right or wrong. Rather, as nature does, it gathers them up, takes them in, and then adds something new. I love Meister Eckhart's phrase in which he said that in such a Consciousness, *"all differences are one-d."* A mature spiritual path takes us in this direction.

In our long human history, those who have walked the more recent paths of Love and Compassion have told stories that include and transcend the stories of the first three foundations. The Buddha was one of them. So was Jesus. Paramahansa Yogananda[7] told stories like these in the twentieth century, as did Teilhard de Chardin and his student, Thomas Berry. It is Berry who calls us to reach "far back . . . to the shamanic dimension of the psyche," and in the same breath, tells a "Cosmic Story!"[8] His version of the unfolding story of the universe is rigorously scientific, but he also honors and enfolds all of the earlier narratives within it. As an historian of cultures, he is steeped in the old stories, and at the same time, adds a different perspective that is inclusive:

> We must find our primary source of guidance in the inherent tendencies of our genetic coding. These tendencies are derived from the larger community of the earth and eventually from the universe itself.[9]

Just as the Hebrews used *adam* and *adamah* to link the old and the new, Thomas Berry also coins words. As a linguist, he creates language that embraces polarities. Berry expresses transcendence by going deep. Listen for the whisper of the emergent consciousness in his language as he responds to the age-old questions of identity: *Who am I? Who are you? What is God?*

In response to the first question—*Who am I?*—he describes an identity that rests firmly on the creation stories of all three foundations, and exclaims, *"I am a geologian!"* If you listen to his language, you can hear how the earthy *'geo'* and the rational *'logos'* are no longer split but joined. But he doesn't choose a scientific term like *geologist*. No, he alludes to a deeper/*higher* Ground than earth and thought combined—and creates the word *geologian*. His word echoes *theologian*—one who studies divine things.

Berry invites us to "descend . . . to the shamanic dimension of the psyche," because he recognizes that *fundamental change takes place at depth*. His language reflects the same perspective.

By digging down for root words to create 'geologian,' he deepens us. At the same time, he also *intends* us. Such an intention calls us forward; for the word he coins to 'create the world' anew is inclusive, and within it, the schisms between stories from the kiva, Judaism, Christianity, and science are *'one-d.'*

Berry's answer to the second question—*Who are you?*—places all of us within the larger dynamics of life: *"We are geological formations!"* His language is concrete. It is earthy. His words set us thinking organically about our selves—as part of the earth's unfolding—and also leave us wondering about God.

When Berry creates new language to tell the Cosmic Story, he unifies the stories from all three foundations, and more, in a handful of words. He includes the literal, the heartfelt, the scientific, and the divine—and doesn't diminish any of them.

But it is in the *way their relationship to each other is held* that brings home the dynamic nature of the new consciousness. This kind of consciousness is revealed in his respect—indeed his reverence—for every point of view. Each story is more than simply included. It is wholeheartedly embraced. His embrace creates the container in which the enlivening energies of Love are sparked. Within it, as each creation story subtly interacts with the others, all are elevated and enlarged. *Together*, the stories are transformed and Berry's very human way of *one-ing* shows just how the consciousness of Love *acts*.

Thomas Berry would probably not have suggested the journey to humanity's shamanic roots, had he not made that inner descent himself. In every age, a courageous few temporarily set aside their intellectual point of view in order to enter the Unknown. When, well along the spiritual path, they approach the depths of the-shamanic-in-themselves, they consistently report their inability to express what they have found. Instead, their accounts state that all mental concepts fail and that differences—like those between dark and light, height and depth, knowing and unknowing—dissolve.

As St. John of the Cross told it, the more his journey into his own depths bore him in one direction, the more it also led him toward its opposite. Paradox was the only means he had to express an Intelligence that went beyond the language available to reason:

> I came into the unknown
> and stayed there unknowing,
> rising beyond all science.
>
> I did not know the door
> but when I found the way,
> unknowing where I was,
> I learned enormous things,
> but what I felt I cannot say,
> for I remained unknowing,
> Rising beyond all science . . .
>
> This knowledge is supreme,
> crossing a blazing height;
> though formal reason tries,
> it crumbles in the dark,
> but one who would control the night
> by knowledge of unknowing
> will rise above all science.[10]

John of the Cross pointed to an Intelligence that far transcended intellect's knowing. Jesus, the Buddha, and the many others who, over thousands of years, have excavated the same interior path say the same: Intellect is a stepping-stone in the human unfolding and not its final destination.[11]

John described the next stepping stone as the knowledge of unknowing. To observe his experience, however, he had to walk between the worlds. He also needed his intellect—but intellect was no longer in control. It was servant to a master: and that master was the power of Love.

John, Jesus, the Buddha, and others were attempting to express an uncommon realization of reality—one they knew would not be understood. By telling stories, they hoped to convey something of the nature of this radically different consciousness—for they had seen that it could heal the suffering of the human mind. Human experiences like theirs have become the stories that lie at the core of our religious and spiritual traditions, but the words in these stories could only hint at the larger truth.

Language must eventually betray reality. No text, sermon, or scripture, however sacred, could capture—then or now—what these and other masters were trying to convey. The subtle message beneath their words alluded to a lived experience far different from anything we are able to comprehend unless we, too, have lived it. Could an early human walking on a footpath in the jungle have imagined reining in a horse-drawn carriage, having never seen 'reins' or a 'horse' or a 'wheel'? Could a carriage driver on a dirt road have imagined using the 'steering wheel' of a 'car' on a high-speed 'highway' or a 'throttle' to raise an 'airplane' off the ground? Could we, only decades ago, have comprehended the infinities of instantaneous travel in 'cyberspace'?

How we hear our stories has a profound bearing on the religious conflicts and pain we face in our world today.

> *It is the great tragedy of our present civilization that religion is being _either_ promoted _or_ discarded on the basis of very limited interpretation.*

If we could only learn to hear differently! The best we can do, at first, is to try to become more objective about how we, ourselves, listen.

Gaining Greater Objectivity

How do we hear the stories that have informed our many different cultures? On which foundation do we stand? Do we know what foundations actually intend our lives, consciously or unconsciously? Are we aware of how they motivate us?

Where we stand on the foundations of the soul creates what the researchers at Emory named 'confirmation bias,' and any bias has a huge impact on the conflicts we have with others. When we stick to our own perspective, we are like the snake trapped in the garden shed that had single-mindedly followed its program and headed into every 'hole' it saw in the net. By taking a hard look at our own stance, however, we can each play a small part in a new and inclusive story.

As I explored the foundations of the soul, I came to appreciate the many ways in which the emergent stories call us to step past *where we stand* and *how we hear*. They invite us to a broader orientation—a new 'place' to stand in ourselves. What follows are five ways we might look at the nature of this call to a new orientation along with some common responses to it. As we explore these five ideas, we'll also examine how a mature spiritual practice can help us identify how our own ways of seeing and hearing keep us trapped in the net of our own convictions.

How We Hear An Emergent Story

The role of the spiritual throughout history can be viewed as a call to a transformation of consciousness. In this view, as each new spiritual awareness emerges, it serves to call forth the next immense leap of human consciousness over a very long period.

Natural selection operates on individuals, not species. Every person who sought a new unknown *that lay beyond his own understanding* was following his call. As more people followed, their changes gradually became incarnated in the species. More subtle feeling was a call. Language was a call. Ego-identity was a call. Ours is a call to Love.

In this sense, the original teachings of persons such as Jesus and the Buddha come from the future.

There were (and are) no words to express what these spiritual masters were trying to teach. The radical nature of their wisdom *was* communicated, however, and those who heard it, *heard, but not with their ears.* The fullness of what the great masters expressed did not come from the spoken word. It was transmitted differently, as we shall see in Chapter 11. As long as we remain at the threshold of conflict, the meaning they were actually communicating remains only a potential—whispered as if from the future.

People will hear a spiritual message from the perspective of the foundation on which they presently stand.

There are many ways to hear spiritual terms and texts, and underneath the inexpressible truth to which some of them point, many relative truths. From the inclusive perspective of the new consciousness, *truth is true at every level of its infinite dimension*.

This is a critically important point. The God of the body, the God of the heart, and the God/*no-God* of the intellect are among the truths that belong to the three foundations, and like those foundations, they endure. None of them is wrong. Some are meaningful to us; others are not. Those that have meaning for us make up our conscious worldview. *But the rest remain and intend us from underground.*

How We Hear Depends Upon Where We Stand

On the root foundation: People whose orientation to life may be more influenced by the root foundation—the intelligence of the body—are likely to be greatly inspired, and to hear a spiritual message more or less concretely.

On the heart's foundation: Those who ordinarily live more from the heart's foundation—the intelligence of feeling—may be deeply moved by the message and sometimes, also hear it more literally.

On the foundation of the intellect: The people who stand most comfortably on the intellectual foundation fall into three groups:

The first group is more likely to interpret the new message from an intellectual framework like history, theology, philosophy, biology, or psychology. However, the stepping-stone to this kind of interpretation is not commonly available. While some young people get help in high school to make the transition from concrete to abstract thinking in *academic* studies, few adolescents find adults to help them make the same transition in their *spiritual* understanding.

The second group on the foundation of intellect may not have had this kind of help. Those in this group tend to discard the new spiritual message because it is intellectually unacceptable to them. To let go—even temporarily—of the logical mind they've relied on is as great a challenge as early man faced when he let go the instinct to flee fire! But what is important is this: These intellectuals may think they don't care for the idea of God, yet not recognize that *how they hear the word* is still *literal*. For when any of us first heard the word 'God' as children, we understood it concretely. The Gods of the deepest foundations endure.

The third group consists of people who stand on intellect's foundation and continue to inquire *beyond* intellect. Seeking something they can*not* understand, they set it aside temporarily, then try to discern and follow what seems to be calling them.

Should they awaken to the energies of Love, however, they may find themselves in great danger; for as the stories of Prometheus, Jesus, and Martin Luther King remind us, if they try to bring the gift of *Fire* home, they may be exiled or punished by their communities.

> *The new threatens the existing mode of spiritual understanding in the populace and challenges the current power hierarchy and the social structures that keep it in place.*

People will war with each other when a new spiritual message seems to challenge the foundation(s) on which they, themselves, rely. They fear for their own survival but also, for the survival of their stories and their beliefs. As Ptolemy said:

Everything that is hard to attain is
easily assailable by the mob.

Jesus spoke to the same issue:

It is not peace I have come to bring but a sword.[12]

> *Without all of our foundations 'under us,' a spontaneous awakening to the energies of Love is like a house built on sand. It will not stand.*[13]

While awakening is ordinarily an infinitely gradual process, any one of us may awaken suddenly to the energies of Love—no matter which foundation we stand on. Though such a spontaneous awakening is an act of grace, it also carries with it the potential for inner danger, for the thinking mind is neither large nor strong enough to hold the energies of Love. Jesus made this very clear:

> Nobody pours young wine into old wineskins. Otherwise the young wine will burst the wineskins, it will gush out, and the wineskins will be destroyed. Instead, young wine must be put into new wineskins, and both are preserved.[14]

Homo erectus prepared a hearth to contain the fire he carried home. Since we, too, are gradually awakening, we also need to prepare a hearth for the energies of *Fire for the second time*. How do we create such a container? We can learn from the teachings of the great spiritual masters, past and present. Then we can use our practice to embody them.

These teachings are found in every tradition. Jesus actually used the image of foundations in the Sermon on the Mount,[15] and true to the way stories evolve, it was not original with him, but came from the Jewish tradition. He used the idea of foundations to illustrate a single point, one consistent with the practices associated with the emergent consciousness: He described two kinds of foundations for a house—rock or sand—and said that hearing his words without acting on them was like 'building a house on sand.' The common understanding of the examples he gave in the sermon has been that we need to change our *social* conduct—actions like "Love your enemies" and "turn the other cheek." But why, though we may try to follow these teachings, are they so hard for us to do? I suggest that it is because they require us to address ourselves at greater depth.

The things that intend us are not merely thoughts. In addition to the song of the soul that calls us 'forward,' the root imperatives of the three foundations—terror, desire, greed, aggression, pride, and control, among others—push us toward personal survival at any cost. In this sermon, which may contain some of his most authentic teachings,[16] Jesus is very specific about how *inner actions* are necessary to sustain *outer* change. These actions include a careful self-examination—of the attitudes, perceptions, thoughts, feelings, and behaviors that belong to all three foundations of the soul. These 'places to stand' are alive in us and exert enormous influence on our capacity to act as we would hope. Our ability to do so depends heavily on developing an inner orientation that is considerably larger than that of the three foundations. In our practice, we learn to have enough trust in this new orientation to dare enter the old foundations and *develop a relationship to what we find there*. This kind of mature spiritual practice can help us gain enough freedom from our programming to be able to make real choices about how we act in the outer world, even under duress.

Without conscious awareness of what lies in our depths, however, the three foundations of the soul remain dark, and when our body is dark to us, we're only able to see these root imperatives *in others*. Jesus called us, instead, to *see them in ourselves*.

> The eye is the lamp of the body. . . . If your eyes are unhealthy, your whole body will be full of darkness. If the light within you is darkness, how great is that darkness! . . . Why do you look at the speck of sawdust in someone else's eye and pay no attention to the plank in your own eye? How can you say, 'Let me take the speck out of your eye,' when all the time there is a plank in your own eye? You hypocrite, first take the plank out of your own eye.

He contrasted this darkness with an image of greater wholeness—with the unseen light that is transmitted by the emergent consciousness:

> A city on a hill cannot be hidden. Neither do people light a lamp and put it under a bowl. Instead they put it on its stand, and it gives light to everyone in the house.

This consciousness embraces *all* of our humanity.

How Our Stories Help Us to Inhabit All Three Foundations of the Soul

Every spiritual tradition tells us that if we hope to 'wake up,' we will have to use more than our thinking. Every tradition makes clear that none of intellect's frameworks can contain *Fire for the second time*—not biology, psychology, philosophy, or any of the religions, as we commonly know them. To create a hearth for *Fire,* both the traditions and authentic contemporary teachers offer stories and practices that demonstrate how to develop the inner strength that living deep in ourselves can provide.

Should we be graced by awakening to the energies of Love, our ability to bear these energies depends upon our capacity *to inhabit* all three foundations of the soul—our bodies, hearts, and minds—as consciously as we can. Self-examination is the stepping-stone that lets us get out of our heads and into our bodies. Then we *under-stand.*

The three foundations provide us with the crucial concept of *understanding.* Real foundations hold us up. Just as the kiva, grotto, and temple became the foundations of the more complex cathedral, the three foundations that make up the triune brain stand under something far more comprehensive—what I am calling *soul.*

If we hope to love, if we hope to make peace with one another and live as part of the community of life, we need to under-stand the heritage we bear. We come to stand under who we are by excavating the three foundations of the soul. If we don't inhabit them, the foundations will remain the warring and unconscious structures they are—"old wineskins" that cannot sustain the powerful energies—and demands—of Love.

Awakening to the energies of Love represents as extraordinary a birth as any before in the human journey. Should we come to embody this kind of Love—should it become incarnate in us and in our species—it will grace us with a capacity for a far deeper relatedness and a genuine communion with life.

What Time is it? Ours is a cosmic moment. Whether or not we attend the birth, we are all already pregnant—with *Fire.*

The whisper calls us to let go of who we think we are and enter the Unknown:

> Love is the willingness
> to give up a part of yourself
> you think you know,
> to discover a . . . self
> you never knew existed.
>
> John Squadra[17]

Endnotes for Chapter 6

1 Muriel Rukeyser (1913-1980), was an American poet. The source of this oft-quoted line is unknown.

2 Muhyi'ddin Ibn Al-'Arabi, Ode XI, *The Tarjuman Al-Ashwaq—A Collection of Mystical Odes*, trans. Reynold A. Nicholson, London: Theosophical Publishing House, Ltd., 1978, 67. Ibn 'Arabi, as he was known, was an Arab Muslim philosopher and a renowned teacher in the Sufi tradition (1165-1240).

3 See *The Genographic Project, http://www.nationalgeographic.com/genographic*

4 The exclamation point before !Kung indicates a clicking sound that members of the !Kung tribe (or Bushmen) make at the beginning of some of their words.

5 Matthew 8:20: "The son of Adam has no place to rest his head."

6 See Paul's letters to the Ephesians 2, to the Colossians 3:10f, and to the Galatians 3:27f.

7 Paramahansa Yogananda founded the Kriya Yoga tradition.

8 See Swimme and Berry, *The Universe Story*.

9 Thomas Berry, *The Great Work*, New York: Bell Tower, 1999, 160.

10 *The Poems of St. John of the Cross*, ed. Willis Barnestone, New York: New Directions Books, 1972.

11 See the writings of the saints, yogis, and spiritual masters from many traditions: the mystics of the church, the Jewish Kabbalah, and the Buddhist, Sufi (Muslim), and Hindu traditions. The disciplines they followed are based on specific training in repeatable experimental practices, which results have been tested and compared to standards validated by every major tradition for thousands of years. Now, neuroscientists are beginning to talk with spiritual leaders like the Dalai Lama who also asserts the importance of testing these conclusions empirically. See *http://www.npr.org/templates/story/story.php?storyId=5008565* retrieved September 2007, and related sites.

12 Matthew 10:34-35.

13 A reference to Matthew 7:26.

14 Matthew 9:16-17. "Jesus said, 'No one sews a patch of unshrunk cloth on an old garment, for the patch will pull away from the garment, making the tear worse. Neither do men pour new wine into old wineskins.'" The earliest version of this same teaching is found in *The Gospel According to Thomas*, ed. Raghavan Iyer, verse 47, London: Concord Grove Press, 1988, 29. Other versions are in Mark 2:22 and Luke 5:37.

15 The Sermon on the Mount is found in both Matthew 5-7 and Luke 6-12. The passage about the foundations is in Matthew 7:24-27 and Luke 6:47-49.

16 Robert Funk, et al, *The Five Gospels*, San Francisco: HarperSanFrancisco, 1993. Obviously, many sources address the issue of authenticity and have come to many different conclusions. This text expresses the consensus of 76 Biblical scholars from major universities worldwide and who come from many different traditions. They have evaluated and coded each statement in the gospels based on their criteria.

17 John Squadra, *This Ecstasy*, N. Ferrisburg, VT: Heron Dance Press, 1996, 84. First printing, Brooks, Maine: Hermes Press, 1996. Excerpt used with the permission of Heron Dance Press.

7 Retracing Our Journey— Excavating the Foundations of the Soul

> What can we gain by sailing to the moon if we are not able to cross the abyss that separates us from our selves? This is the most important of all voyages of discovery, and without it, all the rest are not only useless, but disastrous.
>
> Thomas Merton[1]

Thomas Merton reminds us that no matter how inventive we are, we need to live our lives on a more solid ground. The way to the ground winds through the three foundations of the soul. When they remain unexcavated, there is no one 'at home' and the conflicts between the three shape our attitudes and behaviors without our even knowing it.

A well-defined spiritual practice develops awareness. It leads us deep inside. This kind of preparation teaches us to quiet down in order to see who we are. We notice, first, what goes on in our minds, then listen to our hearts and bodies. Gradually we become more objective about ourselves. As we peel away the layers, we have to get more honest. And the more honest we are, the easier it is to hear the whispered song of the soul.

The light is dim in the interior world. It's like sitting 'at dusk' and waiting for our eyes to adjust to the dark. Then, just as our 16 month-old granddaughter Callista learned to name the objects in her outer world, we try to name what we see *inside*. By bringing the conscious light of awareness into the shadowy world of our foundations, we redeem them—quite literally buy them back. It is a costly purchase, paid for in significant personal change.

Many of us have made very important changes, but at this evolutionary juncture, life is offering the possibility of transformation. Transformation is not like changing lifestyle or location or a partnership. Transformation changes *us*.

In a longer poem, M. C. Richards, mused about how uncertain her path had been, and how the many changes in identity that had seemed so important to her journey—poet, potter, educator, author—were, at the same time, like clothes that obscured her real self. In this stanza, she *sees*:

> Clothes are the sheaths
> of my being—so many old dreams of
> changing dress, unable to decide . . .
> what to wear?[2]

For a long time, the only self I knew consisted of clothes like these. At midlife, in turmoil and poised at the threshold of the unknown, I'd spent a lifetime wearing clothes that consisted of roles, among them, musician . . . mother . . . consultant . . . neighbor . . . friend. A week before I had any idea I'd be taking the leap to face myself more honestly, my teenage daughter overheard me talking in my sleep. Afterwards, she told me I'd mumbled, *"I have to go to the duplex."*[3] She said she'd asked me while I slept, "Where is it? Who's living in the duplex?" and that I'd answered, still asleep, *"In Santa Cruz. In Santa Cruz, I have a separate identity."*

The dream told me that I had no idea who I really was. I didn't realize at the time how much I'd have to embrace before I found the makings of an authentic self. It would be a long and difficult passage to meet the mysterious personage in the other half of the duplex. From the start, I didn't want to go there. How could I have known that meeting her would set me free from *who I thought I ought to be* and give me back my *self*?

Though some people may seem to sail into the spiritual journey effortlessly, it is possible that one day—like me—you may hit a rough patch in your life that is bound to take you where you do not want to go. Few of us answer the call without a time of reckoning in our lives. It might be an illness—your own or another's—or the death of a loved one. It could be the loss of mobility, the loss of a job or the end of a marriage. Perhaps, life confronts you with some indignity—a truth that causes so much shame, you can't imagine it applying to you. Or someone whom you love dearly is furious at you and you cannot understand why. All of them signal the Way to the other side of the duplex.

However life throws you on your Way, you may wonder, at times, whether you'll ever be able to tolerate the challenge. You don't like what is happening to you. You may argue and use every tactic you know to sidestep it. You may deny it and in some cases, refuse it. Perhaps you decide to *think* your way through it. (Surely, I thought, I could figure it out!) You may become determined, use your will power, or get angry; or make jokes about what afflicts you. There are many ways of avoiding the gauntlet thrown down by Life.

None of them works. The challenge doesn't go away. Your body may have to convince you as only the body can: You may get sick or break a leg; you may fall into a depression or have a heart attack. Whatever the disruptive call, it is a powerful invitation to transformation—and the more usual kind of invitation for most of us.

Transformation Isn't Just a Change of Clothes

Transformation is something that wounds us and calls our very identity into question. This challenge asks us to step right into the 'refining fire' and let it burn away our old ideas about who we think we are. If we're lucky, it will have been one of many such fires in a lifetime, each an undressing that takes our old identity apart—and recreates us in an entirely new way.

A sage once said with a twinkle in his eye,

Awakening is an accident. It helps to be accident-prone![4]

We become accident-prone by increasing our receptivity to the primordial whisper, however it breathes through our lives. If we follow its call, it can lead us on an inner search for truth—particularly, truths about our selves. Each truth we meet is an encounter; each demands the courage to let go. As we begin to let go, we meet part after part of an unknown self we'd abandoned some place like the other side of the duplex. It may be an attitude we hadn't wanted to admit, a memory, or a yearning . . . It may be a longing for freedom, or a feeling we never expected to find. All along the way, we are surprised, however, for we also discover gifts we didn't know were within us. We may even stumble on the lifelong dream of our soul.

To become accident prone, we drop, first, from a selfhood identified with thought down into a breadth of feeling. Then, as we embrace the feelings we uncover, *they* take us down into the darkness of the body. The body cannot speak, but when we descend into its wordless wisdom, we find the way to an ease that was lost when we left the Beginnings. You know this kind of moment.

You are carried on an unseen current the way a seagull hangs in a strong wind over the ocean. It is effortless. You are lived by Life, itself.

The process that makes us accident-prone is not always a comfortable one, for as we drop deeper into the foundations of the soul, we clear away layer after layer of debris that reveals more of what it means to be simply human. As this uncovering process brings us ever closer to the Beginnings—closer to our core—it makes us increasingly vulnerable to awakening. We can feel quite naked, because without the buffer each layer of protection provided, we find we have become more and more sensitive. But we also feel very alive. Merton called this process a "true education":

[The true education brings us] to direct contact with "the beginning," the archetypal paradise world. . . . The fruit of [such an] education . . . [is] the activation of that inmost center . . . that "apex" or "spark" which is a freedom beyond freedom, an identity beyond essence, a self beyond all ego . . . and a consciousness that transcends all division, all separation.[5]

How do we put flesh on statements like these? We tell our stories—not only the great narratives of those who've walked the Way before us, but also honest stories about our lives. Though our stories may seem different from one another, they are, in many ways, the same, and to tell even a portion of them brings us into deeper connection with each other, deeper connection with the divine.

All of us hold within us the ultimate design of the universe, and your stories, like mine, reflect it perfectly.[6]

Perhaps our stories don't seem very 'fancy,' but shared, they become—like the world's creation stories lit up in Thomas Berry's embrace—elevated, enlarged, and transformed by one another.

Excavating the Mind's Foundation— The Intelligence of Thought

When I stood at the threshold of the unknown, I trembled at leaving my old ways. They were my only means of coping with life and I was very frightened. Did I want to take this leap? I did not. I wavered at the threshold for a long time, then took a first step toward freedom. That step gave me back my life. I began then to inquire into the only foundation available to me at the time—my thinking—and the lamp that lit my way was a desire to be honest. I explored layer after layer of my beliefs, attitudes, and judgments, and was stunned to see how many I'd held tightly out of habit—and never really assessed. Like the snake, I was trapped in a net of my own convictions.

One of the first convictions I faced concerned what it meant to be a good mother. While I was reflecting on it, a friend asked, "Why don't you do some of the things that *you* enjoy on the weekends?" What a question! I'd never even considered it. Being a working mom, I longed to spend more time with my son and daughter, and for ten years had devoted all my weekends to them. But I'd never questioned the self-judgment that also lay beneath my choice: that if I were to do something just for me, it would mean I was being selfish. My job, now, was to question that assumption. I struggled with it for days. Then one Friday evening after work, I said to the children, voice quivering, "I'm planning to do some things tomorrow morning, just for me." They answered in unison, "Go for it, mom!" I looked at them in disbelief—and cried.

The next morning, I sat on a lawn chair and asked myself, "Well, what do I want to do?" *I didn't have a clue*—not the slightest idea of what I wanted, much less, what I needed. My only option was to play 'eenie-meenie-minie-moe.' It was a long time before I realized that I couldn't know what I wanted until I knew what I felt. And I wasn't very familiar with feelings.

Excavating the Heart's Foundation— The Intelligence of Feeling

I learned what I felt in therapy. It was like opening my mind to a world I'd never known. As the work deepened, I was amazed at the rich variety of feelings that became available to me for the first time in my life. I had to be taught their names: *panicked . . . overwhelmed . . . terrified . . . patronized . . . depreciated . . . isolated . . .* and more. All of them had lived for a lifetime in the self I'd abandoned on the other side of the duplex. To claim them, I made a list and put it on my refrigerator door.

From this world of feeling came capacities that had also been in hiding on the far side of the duplex. For example, I'd already noticed—in the process of questioning my thinking— that insight into my self seemed to increase my insight into others. But now, as my capacity for feeling grew, it too, broadened outward. I not only understood other people better; I *felt with* others, too. I was so excited! This under-standing didn't divide *you* and *me* in judgment. It came from my heart. And so, I added more words to the list on the refrigerator: *sensitive . . . concerned . . . caring . . . gratitude . . . well-being . . .*

Excavating the Root Foundation— The Intelligence of the Body

After a long while, my heart led me down into the interior of a body that was completely unfamiliar to me. I began to feel sensations I hadn't noticed before, and learned to listen to what it had been trying to tell me. As I felt truths I'd never claimed— *enraged . . . grieving . . . dread*—the pain in my shoulders and neck and aching back went away.

I don't think we can excavate the deepest foundations of our souls without a growing tenderness toward the human condition, a growing concern for others. Compassion is the fruit of the spiritual journey and arises, quite naturally, right out of our bodies. I was being made aware of *who I already was* and hadn't known, and the list on the refrigerator grew longer: *compassionate . . . loving . . . more. . . .*

I've come to recognize that a spiritual path is only as good as the quality of truth-telling practiced by those who pursue it. To me, truthful living is not only what we say or do. It also includes a visceral self-knowledge that comes from knowing our physical selves *from the inside*. If you want, you can try an experiment. Just close your eyes and be still for a moment; and then direct your attention to your hands. You may need to take some time for this little trial, but in the meantime, you can ask yourself a question: *How do I know my hands are there if I can't see them and don't move them at all?*

When we reclaim our bodily homes from inside, we come to know their truths. Whatever form of intensive preparation we choose for a spiritual Way—whatever serious practice of attention we engage in—we will become sensitive to the interior of our bodies, organs and all; just as you became more aware of your hands in the experiment.

When we orient to life with our whole organism—body, heart, and mind—we become increasingly aware of more than what our five senses can detect. Then we realize that *we are instruments* and start to discover *what the body knows*.

First, we learn to register subtle interior sensations—slight movements that indicate an instantaneous *"Yes!"* or *"No!"* to what life is offering in any given moment. Whether these signals are an inner reply to headline news, or to invitations that we may (or may not) want to accept; whether they are reactions to another's behavior or to our own fleeting thoughts or feelings—they are a precise and honest bodily response to what we are encountering. When we are aware of this instinctual faculty, it also backs up the more subtle feelings we have uncovered and helps to support them.

But the mind and heart that have been socialized by our communities may argue with these messages and try to override them, saying, *"Not me!"* In some people, the mind may have long since repressed these sensations. Others of us may override them more consciously in order to comply with how we've been taught to behave. Often our feelings get in the way—especially in women! We don't want to rock the boat. We don't want to hurt others, or we care too much about what they think. But every time we ignore our body's intelligence, we are saying, *"No!"* to our selves. Each negation leaves us less able to hear its whispered messages—and less sensitive to ourselves and to others.

On the other hand, if we stay aware and attuned to our whole organism, we can use its authentic *yes* or *no* responses as guides. This kind of attunement is almost entirely absent in a culture centered on inventing new ways to entertain and distract us! How many hours a day does the average person sprawl on the couch and let TV images wash over his mind like waves? How often does he let the vibrations of the Blackberry on his hip interrupt the natural flow of events? Does he tell himself he's really alive when the restaurant is jammed and the music loud? These ways of so-called 'living' rob us of our attention and deaden our bodies.

In bodyminds that are *not* dulled, awareness is acute. You've known acute awareness in the last moments of a basketball game when the score is tied and the whole crowd holds its breath awaiting the final shot. You've felt it in a hospital delivery room, seconds before an infant's birth. It is heightened, focused, and alert. You can feel it now if you enter this scenario:

> There are no empty red velvet seats left in the glittering concert hall. It is filled with people, all chattering. You look at your watch and realize the concert is about to begin. The first violinist stands up and faces the orchestra. You stop talking and track his every move. He raises the violin to his chin. The hubbub fades; there is only a hushed murmur. You watch the musicians. Each comes to attention and waits. The concertmaster plays a single note. The orchestra tunes to the pitch and every instrument rings out one tone. The concertmaster sits. You wait. The conductor strides out of the wings and bows to thunderous applause. Your hands are burning and tired from clapping. He turns his back and in a single movement, steps onto the podium. A thousand people straighten up. Eyes on the stage, everyone watches. You breathe. There is absolute silence.
>
> The conductor lifts his arms. In that precise instant before the downbeat, his whole body is coiled. His energy is like that of a mountain lion, crouched and ready to leap. So is yours. There is one attention—yours and that of every single person in the hall: violinists . . . cellists . . . horn players . . . woodwinds . . . bass viols . . . timpani . . . chorus . . . audience. In this precise moment, there is no sound, no thought. No movement—only your breath; the breath of those present. Your hearts beat as one, awaiting a music that is *not yet*. An energy begins to gather; just as the fine oils of perfume concentrate thousands of subtle scented flower petals, this immense concentration of attention fills you, fills the hall. There is not a person here who cannot feel its presence. In some, it is palpable—an acute aliveness—an *awareness of energy*.

In the immediacy of this kind of attention to the energies of Presence, we stand at the *third Beginning*: the precise moment in which we are living. We will explore its nature in Chapter 15. In such a moment, we give wholehearted attention to the stillness in which everything occurs and listen with more than our ears.

Simone Weil said:

> Absolute unmixed attention is prayer.[7]

In the moment—in the acute aliveness of *not yet*—we become a prayer.

Tying the Foundations Together— The Attention of the Whole Self

But we are getting a little ahead of ourselves! In order to sustain this quality of attention, we need to tie the foundations together. Our attention will be mixed whenever the three are conflicted: caught in their inner and outer wars. Then we are stuck at the threshold. But as we clear out the debris on the inward journey, our attention will become increasingly refined, and over time we will develop an energetic awareness that comes not just from our heads but also from our hearts, bodies, and more— simultaneously. This quality of attention is a light.

Then we learn to use it. Just as a dancer first prepares by stretching her legs and torso, and then tunes her attention to the music, we do the same. We strengthen and span the body's feeling and instinctual foundations beneath our thoughts *in order to tune to Life.* To live from this quality of whole-bodied attention to the greater Life is *being.*

Softly present to the Silence, we begin to trust the sound-less sound of the whisper. Like a wind blowing through us, it knows and communicates in a different kind of way. When we are this open to its promptings, we can become Life's servants. It is the most essential practice of the spiritual journey—and a far cry from the ego's fearful *"Not me!"*

There will be times, as we develop this quality of atten-tion, when a feeling arises that is very close to the bone—raw, instinctual, and unmediated. It is a primal feeling, one that has no name. We run from it every way we know how. As we prac-tice, we watch ourselves run away, return, and run away—over and over again. One day, we learn to join our experience and— whatever the feeling—*stay*. Staying requires a kind of strength that contains within it vulnerability. Reader Pat Sullivan offers an analogy:

In the building trades, they speak of structural integrity. Structural integrity means that the form of a structure meets the purpose for which it is intended, and that it is strong enough—and flexible enough—to handle the stresses and strains it is likely to encounter.

Our own "structural integrity" comes from unlocking the door to the other side of the duplex and saying, *"Yes!"* to the self we find there. By learning to inhabit all three foundations in this way, our choices are more likely to be informed by the wisdom of our bodies, hearts, and minds. Then, we're more able to stay.

Like a toddler who learns how to put on her shoes by first taking them off, I had to learn to *be* in stages. I gradually learned to say, *"Yes!"* to much of my body's truth. But it took a long time before I could hang in with it enough to stay.

The Party

When I decided I wasn't willing to live on the fast track any longer, I knew I didn't want to define myself by the title on my business card. I wanted an identity that didn't depend on 'what I do' or 'what I've accomplished,' but didn't yet know what it was. Occasionally, I'd laugh and repeat, half facetiously, "I know who I am on the East Coast and I know who I am on the West Coast, but who am I on the airplane in between?!" Still, I kept at it. I was being pressed by a whispered, *Clear out!* And the whisper was emphatic.

I began to clear my outer world first, and shrank my work life—hour by single hour—until it faded to black. It took several years before I cut my business card in half and dropped it into the wastebasket. Then I cleared out my home. I emptied closets and drawers and gave away half of my possessions. Only then, was I ready to tackle my life.

The first props to fall were my jam-packed days. For some time, I'd been hearing another inner whisper: *Just how little structure can you tolerate, anyway?* I moved very slowly into the uncertainty of not knowing what I'd be doing, and experimented by inserting longer and longer empty spaces in the calendar. It was a year before the emptiness began to shout. When it did, an old question flew up in my face like a startled quail. *Who am I now?* And while I knew I was more than a role, or my work, or where I lived, or what I thought—it frightened me.

That same month, George and I received a gracious invitation to a party from some people we hardly knew. I'd always been uncomfortable at stand-up events but I also wanted to go to this party. What a conflict! I was afraid. I couldn't imagine being at the party without labels to hide behind. What could I possibly say about myself and still stay true to the whisper's call? *Clear out! Don't define yourself in the old ways!* I asked George if he'd be willing to go in two cars, so in case I got scared, I could leave early. Ever the gallant partner, he replied, "If you need to leave, I'll leave with you."

It was an elegant affair: beautiful home, lovely flowers, and a crowd of people. Our hosts were gourmet cooks and the buffet table was laden with exotic dishes. I stood for a while at the edge of a small group, listening to strangers talk to one another. An academic crowd, they cited their latest books, described the committees they chaired, and the famous people they knew. I felt safely on the fringe of the conversation until someone turned to me and asked solicitously, "And what do *you* do?" It was the question I'd dreaded. I stammered something utterly inane and ran for cover.

As I made my way through the crowd looking for George, the dream of the primitive woman flashed into my mind, but I wasn't having any of *her* pioneering ways! I wasn't ready yet. I found George and whispered, "Let's get out of here! I don't know how to do this!" He hugged me, "Let's go get some of that great food first!" We heaped our paper plates, ate out of sight, and fled. It seemed another failure to me then. In fact, it was a small step toward the greater aliveness of being simply who I am. I just hadn't learned how to stay!

A few days later, I sat on a garden bench with a friend. When I told her about my dilemma at the party, I was amazed at her reply. "Why, when they ask what you do, all you have to say is, *'I'm living my life!'*" What a statement! Every time I've used it since, I've seen a wistful look in people's eyes: the lure of just living their lives . . .

The experience of the party exposed a new vulnerability in me. I liked my growing softness but now, it was beginning to cause trouble at home. I was afraid to admit what my mind saw as weakness to George; I knew he'd courted the apparently confident outer self I'd presented to the world. He'd admired the consultant who made presentations in paneled boardrooms to clients far more powerful than she. Now, this same person was tender and uncertain, and exploring inner worlds he didn't understand—even writing poetry! Sometimes, it seemed as if he wanted me to change back into my old self. But inside, I knew that if we were to have the kind of truthfulness real intimacy required, I had to drop my façade. It was a difficult period of transition for both of us.

In fact, we were both afraid. It took us a long time and some skilled help to navigate those waters. And it was a revelation that the more we were able to stay—to be still and remain present to our own exceedingly tender feelings—the more we felt inwardly strong; the more we were able to love.

To sustain the bonds of deeper relationship, we need more than everyday thinking and feeling can provide. For us to mend our conflicts with others—personal or communal—we have to *see* where we're in conflict with ourselves. If we are to address the issues of our Time, we need to search out what is hidden from awareness in the three foundations of the soul. The whisper invites us to look beyond our current mode of functioning and undertake a 'true education,' one that has long been called for by the wise: *"Know thyself!"* cried Socrates. *"Cross the abyss!"* echoed Merton. *"Harness the energies of Love!"* wrote Teilhard de Chardin. All their voices ring encouragement.

When we are more consciously aware of *how* we think, *how* we feel, and *how* we are reacting viscerally, we can come Home to our selves. 'At Home,' we can be present to the moment, whatever that moment brings. To maintain this kind of presence requires a considerable amount of spiritual 'muscle'—an ability to stay in the most uncomfortable of situations and not react.

It is the beginning of the end of conflict.

The whisper sounds:

> When you know yourselves, you will be known.
> Then you shall know you are sons and
> daughters of the Living One . . .
> The Gospel According to Thomas[8]

Endnotes for Chapter 7

1. Thomas Merton, *The Wisdom of the Desert,* New York: New Directions Publishing Co., 11.

2. Mary Caroline Richards, excerpt from "Poet," *Imagine Inventing Yellow: New and Selected Poems,* Barrytown, NY: Station Hill Press, 1990, 3. A more complete version of the poem can be found in the last chapter entitled "Presence."

3. In New England, a duplex is a 2-family house split in half vertically, with two entrances, side by side.

4. One of the many variations of this statement is attributed in somewhat different form to Zen teacher, Richard Baker, known as Baker Roshi, in an article by Ken Wilber in *What is Enlightenment? Journal.* See *http://www.wie.org/j18/wilber.asp*

5. *Thomas Merton: Spiritual Master—The Essential Writings,* ed. Lawrence S. Cunningham, New York: Paulist Press, 1992, 361-363. This is from a late essay on education written for Columbia University, 1967.

6. Carolyn North, *Seven Movements, One Song,* p. 17.

7. Simone Weil, *Gravity and Grace,* New York: G. P. Putnam & Sons, 1952. Weil was a twentieth century mystic. See also Evelyn Underhill's description of the mystics in Chapter 11.

8. Iyer, ed., *The Gospel According to Thomas,* 17. I hear 'the Living One' to mean the divine energies of Love.

8 Awakening the Heart and Body—The Power of Emotional Truth

For the Garden is the only place there is,
   but you will not find it
Until you have looked for it everywhere and
   found nowhere that is not a desert.

W. H. Auden[1]

To descend into truth, to let it break us open—that is how love and healing happen. A 'true education' is the search for the Garden-at-depth—for the vibrant place inside where we are fully our selves. In this Garden, we belong. To find it, we face what we have refused in our minds and hearts and bodies—our dark qualities *and* our promise.

Every time we have said, *"No!"* to a thought or feeling or sensation, we've diminished the wholeness of who we really are. This deeply ingrained pattern of Self-avoidance is the desert of Auden's poem, but we can inhabit our selves again. If we make a fierce commitment to the truth; if we don't override these thoughts and feelings, but dare to venture beneath our protective *"Not me!"* we can face our inner wars—the conflicts between our foundations. If we persist in this self-honesty, we may not only uncover the gifts that hide behind *"Not me!"* but also come closer to the mystery of *I AM*.

When we inquire beneath each *"No!"* we are doing more than feeling our feelings. We are opening to the power of emotional truth. In the process, we may find ourselves leaning into a time well before words, down into the felt and sensed identity of an infant body. Preverbal memories that set the template for a life are difficult to find. Sometimes, the work seems to take place at almost a cellular level. There is no other way to describe the heart's search for its own memories. We descend into what feels like darkness where only the nuance of dream, myth, and the most subtle, visceral hints point the direction.

As I continued to follow the whispered song of the soul, my sense of 'I' gradually dropped down into my body's primal world.[2] It soon became clear that I had surrendered only conditionally, for I was heading in a direction that the 'me' who lived on the far side of the duplex *did not want* to go. I didn't know this 'me' whose existence I'd learned about in a midlife dream, but clearly, she had a lot of power. Her *"No!"* to the ensuing work was enormous: I got pneumonia. I dreamt of falling off cliffs, then into a cavernous abyss, and finally, of plunging into a gaping hole in the ice. I had come to the edge of an internal precipice beyond which was only a void. At least, to my thinking mind, there was nothing there.

If you follow a spiritual path, it is likely you may also encounter an abyss like one of these. Maria wrote a description of what she called a 'hole':

> I feel as if I can sense the outline of a hole inside of me. I get near the edge and then I'm compelled to step away. It's as if I can feel heat radiating from the hole—the heat of sadness, shock, disappointment, disbelief—and anger that *this is what is*. I'm afraid of it, afraid of what's in the hole, afraid of how big it is. Recently, I was right down in it, right inside the edge and the pain and sadness were overwhelming. Yet, somehow, getting inside the hole was what allowed me to see it, feel it, try to define it. It was cleansing to feel and to cry. It's like I am safely walking deeper and deeper into the truth.

As I approached my own abyss, I felt like a Jacob warring with an unknown angel in the Old Testament story.[3] It was as if the two occupants of the duplex in my dream had entered a pitched, subterranean battle. At this threshold, I was locked in combat. I wanted/*didn't want* to do the work: I wanted/*didn't want* to feel in my own adult body, the same sensations I'd felt so deeply in the past/*still carried in my flesh*. At the same time, one of my teacher Richard Moss'[4] statements resonated in my mind like a mantra:

> Nothing gets healed in the past. The only place healing happens is in the present.

But I was not prepared to feel *now*, my infant body's own sheer fury for survival, its desperate need, its craving for tenderness, or the torment of its helplessness. I was stuck—right at the threshold of an abyss with both sides of me in conflict: I wanted Love badly/*I fought it fiercely*. I was refusing suffering.

Suffering Begins With a "No!"

If we follow the whispered call of transformation, the *"No's!"* of our past—personal and collective—will confront us repeatedly. However, when we look more closely at the many times we said *"No!"* so vehemently as toddlers, we can see that it was a blessing. *"No!"* helped us to draw a line in the sand between who we were and who others were; it also lifted us out of the chaos of two brains that had no words. Neither our reptilian nor limbic brain could help us discriminate between 'me' and 'you,' 'inside' and 'outside'; nor could they tell the difference between who we were and our surroundings. But when we started to use language and said, *"No!"* we began to define a separate self.

This gift of separateness heralded an immense interior transformation: the emergence of the subject/object consciousness that my granddaughter Callista used to name her world. Seen from a larger perspective, this consciousness that divides one thing from another is *both* a blessing *and* a curse: It may help us draw a line in the sand with others, but it also serves to divide us from our selves. This intellect cannot ordinarily reach the feelings, sensations, attributes, and memories housed in our two wordless brains. They remain hidden in an unconscious location within us like far side of the duplex of my dream. Locked away in a place like 'Santa Cruz,' they create a conflicted mind. It bears repeating that this inner conflict is the source of many of our conflicts with others.

How Dreams Can Contribute to the Healing of Conflict

If this transformation at an early age left us in conflict, is there a way we can heal it? Fortunately, we can learn to hear how the two wordless[5] foundations of the soul *do* communicate. Dreams can help by showing us how to listen to something other than thoughts. It can be like playing detective: Sometimes, we follow a single strand of feeling to its roots and find, hidden in the depths of our own foundations, a very old human story. When we hear that story in a different way from how we once understood it, it will often tie both of our Beginnings together: our childhood and the childhood of the race. To let ourselves see and feel the truths that dreams and stories like these can expose, is one way we can bind together what has been torn apart by intellect. In this case, dream, feeling, and ancient story reflect more than our own little lives. They show us a broader *human* identity and sometimes, a glimpse of a self that is vast.

There are dreams that spin slender filaments of an ongoing conversation between portions of mind, two of which cannot speak. The many facets of such a dream tend to reflect our wholeness and can reveal aspects of an identity that extends far into the past, whether or not we are aware of it. We carry more in ourselves than we realize: untamed characteristics that came from our long animal-human heritage, from the childhood of the race, and from all our ancestors—parents, grandparents, and great . . . great . . . great . . . grandparents.

I've also discovered that the inner storyteller who creates dreams is not only mine. She's also offered her images and adventures to the creatures of the earth for millions of years. "All animals dream," says dream scholar, Jeremy Taylor.[6] His statement suggests that our dreams can bind us at depth to other species, to other times, to our heritage from the past, and to our covenant with the future. In dreams like these, she weaves a slow integration of *life's* under-standing—an accumulation of *being* from all three foundations.

My own dreams have fairly hummed with overtones from the primordial world—dark-skinned peoples, menacing tigers, and jungles filled with danger. They've presented dramas of passionate love in medieval castles and shown me vast cathedrals drenched in light. Dreams can disclose a different kind of order than thought, and reveal life's whole story in us, *mis-under-stood* by intellect.

The dream that follows provides a foundation for the remaining chapters. If we hope to heal the conflicts in our hearts, this dream may help us to under-stand why a *"No!"* to ourselves from the Beginnings still has such an impact on every one of us:

> *I'm with two people, trying to talk without being heard about something I'm not supposed to say. The dream is like a series of photographs: frozen stills of groups of babies. They are different ages—toddlers able to sit up and infants who are younger. All of them are naked, putting themselves and each other in ice water at the edge of a lake. They are freezing. You can see their agony yet they're trying to smile, pretending to have fun even while they suffer.*
>
> *There is a balance to be achieved! I want to find a way to thaw them out, but only enough that they can talk about it—no more—and the words are available only at a certain temperature. My shout wakes me: "Thaw the babies just enough to get the words out, but <u>no more</u>!"*

When I wake, I am still terrified, for the dreamer has taken me into the visceral world of infancy, far from the safety of thought. Even with my eyes wide open, I can feel the physical echo of my body's *"No!"* I'm shaking and my heart is pounding. Immersed in the lingering sensations and feelings of the dream,

I can feel every hair of my body standing on end. My waking mind may know that I've struck pay dirt, but *I* sure don't want to dig around in it! *I don't want to thaw those babies out and feel what's frozen in my body. I don't want to know what the words stand for! Abstractions are OK—but no more! I don't want to feel the feelings I had before there were any words! I don't want to feel my body's story either—the sensations the ice water has deadened.*

In the daylight world, I may have believed I wanted to visit the other half of the duplex—but in the dim light of the sleeping world, my heart and body were telling a different story. It was as if I was poised on a precipice at the edge of the world. Trapped in conflict and unable to move—I was just like the snake in the garden shed.

The Dreamer Can Give Us a Larger Perspective

Just as little Callista 'stepped back' from her usual way of seeing in order to name her world, we can 'step back' from our ordinary perspective and let a dream give us a more objective view of ourselves. When I stepped back from this dream, I saw that the dreamer had painted a Technicolor war in which the two sides of me were shouting opposing messages simultaneously: One screamed, *"Leave those babies frozen in the ice!"* and the other, *"Let Love thaw them out!"* The dreamer's broader view exposed the conflict raging inside me between my thinking mind and the minds of the deeper foundations.

Dreams Can Lay Bare the Structures of Consciousness

In this dream, the larger dream awareness showed me the three structures of consciousness in which I was imprisoned—those mediated by the triune brain. She gave me a vivid experience of all three mental structures that governed my body, heart, and mind. She employed the freezing *bodies* of babies to enact the agony of physical contraction. And although they'd apparently been socialized to hide their suffering under a smile, she transmitted genuine *feelings* of terror, then offered an abstract *thought* that attempted to avoid them: *"There is some balance to be achieved!"* From the dreamer's timeless perspective, she had dramatized—in the present—the minds of all three foundations of the soul, frozen in a terrified *"No!"*

How Contractions Close Us to the Energies of Love

The early childhood world is not forgotten. It is remembered *by the body*. Uncovered in adulthood, the body's sensations can be nearly intolerable; in infancy, they are unbearable. No wonder the dreamer cast her characters into icy waters! Their 'freezing cure' is a vivid enactment of contraction, an innate process that robs us of our aliveness. There are three kinds of contraction: physical, emotional, and mental.

The "No!" of the Infant is a Physical Contraction

Contraction begins in infancy.[7] How tender we were as babies! How terrible our need; how desperate our love! When I combine visceral memory and imagination with what is known about the infant world, it appears to be like a drama in which we engaged huge characters against a backdrop painted in the colors of life and death. On this stage, we lived our lives utterly. There was no buffer against the all-consuming pain of unmet need. No feeling was tempered, no desire small. Born vulnerable, we were susceptible to hurt—and hurt was often bestowed *in relationship*: When we cried out in hunger, loneliness, or fear, anything that denied our experience was a wound.[8] And innocent as any inaccurate response may have been—a misunderstanding by a caretaker or an unwitting expression on a parent's face—we registered it as a *"No!"* to *who we were*. With each *"No!"* we recoiled and closed a little.

Unable to speak, we cried and protested our hunger, our loneliness, and our terror: *Would we die?* We fought against that visceral dread with the only means we had: our bodies. Most of us learned very young to 'freeze ourselves.' Starting with the muscles over which we had some control, we held on—first, with those in our scalp and face, then in our neck and shoulders. We clenched our fists. As we grew older, we set our jaws and swallowed hard to press back our tears. We locked our diaphragms, held our breath, and contracted our organs. Later, we locked our knees or curled our toes.[9]

The "No!" of the Heart is an Emotional Contraction

With each bodily contraction, our hearts closed too, and because the heart's foundation cannot speak either, we remained unconscious of the feelings that lay within it. Contracting, we numbed our own tenderness and became increasingly closed to others, increasingly closed to the divine—to Love.

The state of contraction eventually comes to feel quite normal. Unaware that we are contracted, we don't notice, don't sense, and don't feel.

The "No!" of the Mind Leaves Us Trapped in the Contractions of Our Beliefs

Over the foundations of the body and the heart, we construct a third set of contractions that leave us trapped in the net of our own convictions. A toddler, for example, fervently believes that when something bad happens, it is her fault. Such a belief does not come from outside her. It is the construction of a very young intellect. By blaming herself, the world makes sense, for *surely* her parents are good parents and love her; and *surely* they wouldn't cause bad things to happen to her. *She* must be to blame. *She* must deserve the punishment.[10] Living her life based on such unripe convictions, her mind eventually closes, too.

Poet Colin Oliver writes in response:

> Self-contempt was my curse . . . [my] dark secret. How do we assuage our own suffering? How do we transform the hounding and pitiless . . . 'bad ones' [inside us] into the 'good'? We say, at last, "I hear you." We weep and weep until it seems like bleeding.

Two Examples of Contraction—Guilt and Shame

When my first husband Milton died tragically, I knew enough about the terrible burden of responsibility a child assumes after a trauma, that I worked very hard to reach my own small children's hearts. I repeatedly assured them that the plane crash that had taken their father's life was not their fault. What I didn't know at the time was that I, too, carried a child inside me who believed her responsibility, still. And I didn't reassure *her*.

No wonder the human need for forgiveness! We crave it not only for past deeds. We also *crave it unconsciously* for perceptions and feelings tangled with the body's memories: our passionate infant desires and our helplessness to meet them; our desperate feelings of need and their frustration in childhood; the strange sense of responsibility for what is happening to us—and the shame that accompanies all of them.

Unearthed in adulthood, the sensations of shame are nearly intolerable because they are felt *as they were originally felt: by an un-contracted (undefended) animal body*. We tend to forget our animal nature; but ours is the same bodily shame that Frankie Brogan saw in her dog—when it knew it had misbehaved:

> Oh! the abject crawl of my poodle, her tail between her legs, and her eyes pleading for forgiveness when I returned after having left her home alone too long. She had torn up my arrangement on the coffee table and stripped the fake bird of all its feathers!

The Deeper Contraction of Shame in the Child

A great gift, early in my spiritual journey, was to learn that the shame I unearthed as I excavated these deeper foundations was not mine, alone. Much of it had passed to me 'underground' in my earliest interactions. What was resonating in my body *now* was a deeply intoned chord of feeling that had begun far back in the animal world.

Those Who Went Before Us Felt the Shame First

It was not 'my' shame that I was feeling, but The Shame. How, then, did it come to feel like my own? This is what I found out: If a child expresses a need or a feeling for which a parent once felt shame in his own childhood, the parent's unconscious shame is transmitted wholesale to the child. We are heirs to the shame of our parents. They were heirs to the shame passed on to them from their parents . . . and their parents . . . and the long line of parents before them.

The young child soon learns to 'freeze' any expression of pain or need that reminds *her parents* of their childhood shame. The adults may be completely unaware that their own pain has been triggered, but a warning has flashed inside them—a bodily *"No!"* that has shielded them from the debilitating feeling of shame since infancy.

As we shall see next, this very subtle contraction—the parents' inner *"No!"* to their own suffering—is innate, long since inherited from the childhood of the race. Its unconscious communication to the child is also innate, a vestige of communication that once took place within the group mind, the *participation mystique*. Although no word has been spoken and no visible body language expressed, the child gets the message. 'Freezing herself,' she completes the transaction by saying *"No!"* to her need or feeling—whatever she'd expressed that triggered her parents' shame—and then, takes their shame on *as her own*. It is all automatic, all repressed. Every time she appropriates a painful feeling that her parents deny, the child joins them in their Self-avoidance and carries the human process of contraction forward: *She grits her teeth and pretends to be nice to her little brother when she's really feeling jealous. He hides his hurt under a forced smile when someone teases him. She doesn't show how scared she is when her parents are away for a week. When they return, she acts nonchalant, and never lets them see how angry she is.* Now the meaning of the opening line in the dream of the freezing infants becomes clear:

> *I'm with two people, trying to talk without being heard about something I'm not supposed to say.*

But it is far too late: The shame—conferred on my own child-inside by the procession of parents, grandparents and great . . . great . . . grandparents who preceded her—had long since been engraved in the deepest foundations of her soul, "along with the burden of the ways that the parents either tried to hide it or expiate it," writes Marvin Hiles, from his own experience.

When we let ourselves fall beneath the intellect in a dream or feeling or bodily memory, we drop deeper into the reality of *who we are*. The greater the depth, the more our perspective is enlarged, and the more our compassion grows. To feel, consciously, so profound a feeling as shame is to know ourselves to be part of the larger human experience—all the way back to the Beginnings.

The Contraction of Shame in the Child of the Race

The *"No!"* of our past is both personal and collective. The same suffering occurred in both our Beginnings: our childhood and the childhood of the race. In prehistoric times, however, shame was first a blessing.

The Jungian psychiatrist Esther Harding explored the nature of the arduous awakening that occurred in a Time when our prehistoric ancestors' survival demanded they band together in tribes.[11] She described archaic human creatures that had once been solitary, foraging alone or in very small families, and eating—even gorging—on whatever food they happened to find. Her studies led her to believe that *when they joined the group,* these old ways no longer worked: When one individual continued to satisfy his own hunger, thirst, or sexual desire without concern for the rest, it raised havoc in the tribe. To enforce a new conformity, the angry group probably killed outright those who were too greedy or too aggressive. Otherwise, it is likely that they were exiled—a sure death sentence.

As I see it, the call from the future for these creatures had been a call to community—and shame became the community's tool. Some tribes made scapegoats of nonconformists. Others offered them up in ritual sacrifice. It did not take long for the terror of that sure death—whether from rejection, abandonment, exile, or sacrifice—to be deeply carved in every human heart.

To move beyond the threshold of conflict, these early humans had to leap a gap that threatened their very survival, for what lay on the other side of the gap was unknown. How would they survive if they gave away *what their bodies knew* they needed? Those who lived to pass on their genes, temporarily set aside the guidance their bodies offered. By ignoring the instinctual wisdom on which they'd always relied, they learned to share the available food, water, and females with others. This new Way of self-control broke open the seed of potential in the human mind—a consciousness beyond a purely animal instinct. Served by shame—and by the physical and mental processes of contraction—their Way was passed from generation to generation until it became innate. It was an awesome evolutionary accomplishment.

The tribe's conserving role—that of ensuring the community's survival—also became innate, part of the ongoing evolution of culture. In our Time, we still offer scapegoats for sacrifice. We need only remember the Puritan's practice of 'shunning' to recognize that although this kind of exile is brimming with shame, it is still rampant on today's playgrounds, in high school hallways, in our penal systems—and in our families.

The "No!" That Almost Extinguishes the Fire

Since the Time of the first tribal injunction, parents have trained their young to survive in the group. That training is both a blessing and a wound. The blessing includes learning to share with others; but the wound is a loss of the self one has heretofore known. A child learns to cross the divide between each of the foundations by discarding vast dimensions of who he is; and whether the *"No!"* to self comes from an outer voice or his own inner one, it is often accompanied by shame. The child then contracts against the pain of shame *along with* the offending behavior. It is another layer of freezing himself.

In the process of contracting, he gradually loses access to the tender connection with Life at the core of his being. It is a devastating loss of the freedom *to be* that only an innocent knows. In order to enter the amazing ego-consciousness we now enjoy, each child sacrifices his original and created self on the altar of his parents' love for him—a love essential for his survival. It is a huge inner conflict.

No wonder the 'terrible twos!' Every toddler 'puts himself naked in ice water.' The original conflict—between his own "*Yes!*" and "*No!*" to himself—will remain 'frozen' unless, as an adult, he makes the choice to leave the threshold of conflict and shine a conscious light into the foundations of his own soul. Then he may thaw out *more than the words*.

How Can We Contribute to a Change of Mind?

Those who *see* or *hear* differently begin the awakening process. (Three examples of major transformations of human consciousness are given in Appendix II. Each involves a radical change in perception.)

Today, as yesterday, most people tend to see the collisions of old and new *outside* themselves, and then try to resolve those conflicts 'out there'—between countries, religious persuasions, political parties, race or sexual orientation, 'haves' and 'have-nots.' But when we trust enough to begin to look more deeply into the roots of these issues *inside*, we discover the same collisions in our own hearts. They may be conflicts between how we want to be with those we love and how we actually behave. Or our deeply held values of peace and non-violence may conflict with a desperate need to protect our families from terrorists, at any cost. Our stated principles of religious freedom may conflict with our criticism of beliefs that others hold. Or our trust in democracy may coincide with hatred for a politician who represents a value we decry. We may pride ourselves on being open-minded, and then discover we're terrified by others' sexual behavior. It is easy to understand why most of us would rather not look in this mirror.

We have seen that transformation can carry with it both blessing and curse, but as fairy tales and myths remind us, no curse can be transformed until it is faced head-on. The frog must be kissed; the dangerous task completed; the buried feeling felt.

Then suffering becomes Love.

We Can Risk Dangers, Physical, Emotional, and Social

To leave the threshold of conflict and face the *"No's!"* of our personal past may challenge every one of our fears—but we can learn to *stay* in order to *see*. Dream work, bodywork, the martial arts, or other spiritual and psychological paths can help us release layer after layer of contraction in our bodies, hearts, and minds. As we proceed, we may also stumble upon the *"No's!"* of humanity's collective past. To see the truths of these Beginnings may leave us dismayed, yet, taken together, they are gifts from the child and the children of the race. Their gifts offer us a more conscious glimpse of who we are, and from that larger perspective, we come to recognize that we are far more than the little separate selves we defined at the age of two. We belong to an entire species and stand on very solid ground: the profound unity of Life.

How Myths Can Contribute to the Healing of Conflict

How we lost that felt sense of unity is dramatized in many ancient myths and, as Joseph Campbell observed, myth is more than just a story. Myth speaks to our depths and if we really listen, it can take us by the scruff of the neck and shake us to our core. When we allow both myth and dream to shine a light into our foundations, they work together to help unfasten the grip of a long-contracted identity and thus, can bring us to a more authentic self.

The dream of the freezing infants reflects a theme from the myth of the Garden of Eden, and together, they illuminate the *"No!"* from both our Beginnings. In that primordial Time, as the story goes, Yahweh spoke directly with humans:

> God called to the man and said . . . "Have you eaten of the tree of which I commanded you not to eat? . . . Behold, the man has become like one of us, knowing good and evil."

How do we hear the words *God* or *Yahweh*? And how do we hear that this God spoke with humans? The community's version of the story is clear and provides a necessary moral lesson. Adam and Eve, like Prometheus, had made the mistake of stealing something that had always 'belonged to the realm of the divine.' Prometheus was therefore punished by the god for taking fire; Adam and Eve, for eating the fruit of the tree that gave knowledge of good and evil.

Hearing the myth from the larger perspective of the awakening process casts a different light on their story: Like those early humans who tamed fire, Adam and Eve had broken the Law that had always guided their bodies. In this view, it is understood that the body doesn't care about choices, but rather, follows its own Way. 'Right' and 'wrong' are meaningless to a body that takes what it wants—food or female—and is not concerned with consequences. In the context of the awakening process, 'eating the apple'[12] broke the Law of the body and precipitated the gift of human consciousness—a new intelligence that incorporated and transcended the older wisdom. The empowerment that came with making choices was a blessing but from the intellect's new point of view there were consequences. This new way of knowing made a judgment—and proclaimed a curse from outside itself:

> Yahweh expelled them from the Garden of Eden . . . . He banished the man . . . and in front of the Garden he posted . . . the flame of a flashing sword to guard the way.[13]

Before Adam and Eve tasted the fruit, they had only to follow the whispered sound of their songline to be intimately connected to the greater Life that enfolded them. They belonged to the Garden and their bodies knew it—they ate, slept, played, and made love, attuned to a subtle song that permeated their bodies, the earth, and the galaxies. In those Beginnings deep in the first foundations of the soul, they never had to make a choice of their own. Then they took a bite of the fruit—and lost the whisper's silent harmonies. When they knew they'd 'tampered with the powers of the gods,' they were ashamed and hid themselves—their wild and animal beauty—from the Wholeness out of which they had come. The apple's gift of discernment had given them the power of knowing all kinds of differences—but it had also cost them their safe and unconscious Home.

Masaccio, *Expulsion from the Garden of Eden*[14]

In a fresco painted on the wall of a Florentine chapel, the artist Masaccio reveals the depth of the Eden story. He shows the suffering inherent in Adam and Eve's expulsion from the Garden and lets their bodies express it.

Much of the conventional understanding about this story was constructed, not from bodily experience, but from an abstraction—the idea of 'original sin.' What an unfortunate interpretation! Like the child who believes she's at fault when she loses someone or when something 'bad' happens, this way of hearing the myth was the product of a very young intellect.

A mind when it is young judges. It is concerned—as were Adam and Eve in humanity's childhood—with distinguishing right from wrong. A judgmental mind projects a judgmental God. And such a God leaves us exiled.

The transformation of consciousness in our Time requires that we leave this threshold of judgment and learn to see and hear in a different way. To move forward, we can't rest on intellect's laurels, for even defining the Eden myth as a naïve story makes it far too easy and lets us off the hook. If we hope to awaken, we, too, have to make the leap into an unknown.

No great myth is carried forward just because it is a crude moral whip or a pretty tale of creation. The story of Adam and Eve is a step forward in human under-standing—the result of thousands of years of pondering under the stars. Constructed over the foundations of earlier stories, it represents the wisdom of untold generations: the testing of their intuitions, their extensive witness of human experience, and the outcome of their deepest reflections. Now, as we incorporate their experience and thereby claim more of our humanity, we can add to what our ancestors compiled.

To the bodymind of *Homo habilis*, thought was supernatural. To the mind of *Homo sapiens*, 'the one who knows,' God is supernatural. To listen to the Eden story with thought alone, however, is to listen with only one of our minds. Even if intellect professes to understand the story's accumulated meanings, *it does not stand under them. The words have not been thawed out!* A maturing intellect is willing to let go of its old ideas in order to deepen what it knows. Thought deepens when we move from our heads down into our bodies and under-stand a story *there*. We thaw out 'more than the words' when we feel our way down beneath the mind's safe abstractions—and learn *what the body knows.*

To hear the Eden story in this way reveals the body's truth: that our deepest connection with life was broken early in human experience. The route to this kind of truth often taps the depths of need and loss—the grief, loneliness, and terror that belong to our humanity—and the shame that attends all of them.

In our Time, these feeling-sensations are not consciously available to most people. Many of us still struggle just to let ourselves know they are there. But when we consent to the presence of these primal realities and make them conscious, we belong to a larger Life. We know in our bodies that we are geological formations like Adam, creatures emerged from the unfolding of *adamah*, itself. We also know that we are not only independent: We need. We depend on others, on the earth, and on much that we can only call the Unknown. We may be surprised to discover that the closer we come to our primal identity as earth/*adamah*, the closer we are to the divine. *As adamah,* we are humbled—and therefore vulnerable to the energies of Love. And *that* Consciousness holds our betrayal in the Garden with compassion. It is a far different perspective than judgment.

> *From the emergent spiritual perspective, we recognize in the Eden story an intimation of our earliest pain—the profound human separation from Life.*[15]

The Garden is more than nature. The myth of the exile from Eden dramatizes our separation from Wholeness, what Thomas Hand, SJ, called our Ground Consciousness.[16] (Beware the mind! It will want to equate all these words—it can be helpful to remember that they are only abstractions!)

As best I can express my own inner experience, the deep relatedness to this Ground was the communion I'd lost when I began to name my world in childhood. I felt it again in the beauty of stained glass, the pageantry, and flickering candlelight of my underground church—and in the breath of the chant that brushed past my cheek when I stood down inside a kiva. Torn from union with this profound inner source and sustenance, I knew in my bones I was exiled. It mattered not, as I grew older, that my mind could rationalize this original separation. *My body remembered it.* It was the root of a great chord of grief in my cells.

Every one of us relives the original human loss of our profound connectedness when, as children, we navigate the abyss between the combined foundations of body and heart—and learn to live from the foundation of the mind. In the moment when we begin to name our world, we gain a great gift: our subject/object consciousness—and lose our ability to hear the voice in the Garden: that which our subject/object mind has called God.

God is not an object! To give so seamless a Mystery a name is to be severed immediately from the Ground of who we are!

To name is to wield a knife. No wonder the Hebrews refused to speak the name of Yahweh. To name it 'God' is to be exiled from whatever that mystery may be!

What have we done as a civilization by giving mystery countless names, then judging those who've chosen different ones? No wonder we feel separated! The rupture of our prior relationship to this Ground is the root of human loneliness and human isolation. Tangled with it is the shame of the unspoken Sorrow we carry in our souls.

It is not the sins of the fathers we need to heal. It is their sorrow.

Says the Rev. Mark Goodman Morris, in response:

I think the unnamed/unhealed sorrow is the result of the separation— what the church has called 'sin.' Maybe the naming and healing of the sorrow is our work . . . maybe the healing of the separation is the impossible work we leave to God.

The mind of ego cannot repair the tear that separates us from Wholeness. We can, however, become 'accident-prone'— in the hope the impossible work may be done.

The Way is a deeper and deeper acceptance of the fullness of being human.

The soul's slow undressing is a letting go and an embrace— as if a hard shell around our core had cracked open and the garments that had covered it fallen away. In that exposure of our naked humanity, our *"No!"* is transformed. We no longer carry the long human process of contraction forward because we no longer deny who we are. Instead, we have strengthened the foundations under a self that is no longer in bondage to ego.

Though it uses ancient language, the Gospel of Thomas carries a present truth:

> When you shed your shame, and take your clothes, place them on the ground, and trample them underfoot like children, then you will see the Son of the Living One and will not be afraid.[17]

I hear "the Son of the Living One" as a way of expressing the lived experience of the divine—the Presence of Love.

Letting Go is Grief

Underneath our lives flows a river of grief seldom brought to awareness. The poet and the mystic[18] drink from it. When Polish poet Aleksander Wat wrote of the grief that had accompanied his lifelong journey, he also tapped my own:

> But my life, oh my life, had been a constant search for an enormous dream in which my fellow creatures and animals, plants, chimeras, stars, and minerals were in a pre-established harmony, a dream that is forgotten because it must be forgotten, and is sought desperately. . . . I loved that harmony with a passion.[19]

Long hidden within the human heart, grief is a great gift. It is real. It is beautiful. It is irreversible. We grieve the past that was and the past that was not; the loss of our youth, the shortness of life, the dead. We weep for the suffering everywhere and for the way the world actually *is*. We mourn the loss of our dreams and the ashes of how things were supposed to be. Out of grief, rise new responses to life. Maria describes her own:

> I am on a rapidly moving river. . . . All my familiar emotions are along for the ride—anger, abandonment, disappointment, sadness, fear. Some new ones are along as well. Something that feels like joy . . . so fragile and tiny I want to cup my hands around it to protect it so the flame won't go out. A peace that feels deep, knowing, restful; a trust in God and a sense of place that is new to me. And an acknowledgment that I am loved and don't have to do *all* of the paddling on this ride—indeed, that I'm not *supposed* to. What a relief!

The Blessings and Wounds of Increased Awareness Are Intertwined

"The pure in heart[20] are self-aware at the core of their being," said Father Hand. I hear the words, "pure in heart" differently than the exact translation in the footnote. 'Pure' suggests, to me, a heart that is wide open to the energies of Love, right down to our primal Beginnings in the first foundation of the soul. From these dark recesses of the Elemental comes a multitude of gifts: among them, the joy, peace, and sense of belonging that become part of our daylight world. These energies also inhabit our dreams. There have been times when the joy in my dreams has been so intense, it's catapulted me out of a deep sleep. Joy woke me from sleep as explosively as nightmares had wakened me in the past. Joy is not a feeling. It is pure energy, and the *condition* of an awakening body.

The gifts of the Elemental offer balance: there is movement; there is repose.[21] Consciousness brings amazing experiences, some of them new and fragile, like Maria's new kind of joy. We're so alive! We are energized! We are blessed! There is light in us—but we pay a price for it.

Consciousness Entails Suffering

When we open to a past still alive in our bodies, we will hurt, physically. The more awake we are, the more we will feel the pain of whatever contractions still hold our bodies captive. To release the pain of each bodily *"No!"* we need to feel the emotion we were trying to avoid.

Richard Moss said:

> That which does not yet know how to love hurts dreadfully on its way back to Love.[22]

His statement also reminds us that the angelic and the demonic live side by side in humanity's duplex. When we come to acknowledge that truth, we also recognize that it is accompanied by another—one that ego doesn't like at all.

The More Light, the Longer the Shadow

We need to remain alert to the signs of our shadow within/ *without*. It presses back, even as we are aware of our joy. In the aftermath of September 11, 2001 (which coincided with a dark night in my own journey), I despaired for almost a year. Despair is not depression. In the daylight, my life went on quite as usual—but underneath in the darkness, hope and despair kneaded one another. I learned that despair is a doorway. Allowed, it becomes despair/*hope*. The two are not separate.

Whenever we embrace our shadows, hope, compassion, and forgiveness arise, too. They are not things we do. They are Elemental: our very grain.

Irene Claremont de Castillejo wrote about the "colossal task of holding together, without being split asunder . . . [the] conflicting opposites . . ."[23] I had to learn how to bear this growing reality inside me—all the opposites joined. It was far too much to encompass with my mind.

"Who can hold all this?" I asked. "I can't contain it!" I had to call on something larger to embrace its many dimensions. I named it 'God,' not knowing what God was, or whether this God was 'out there' or 'in here.'

Why Does Awakening Matter?

You may ask, "Why work so hard? Why not just take a pill and dull the pain?" It has to do with Love. We know, intuitively, that the spiritual journey has never been about our singular short lives or about our own particular future. When we bear pain—physical or emotional—we bear it with and for the human race. The grace of claiming our own suffering joins us to the world. We recognize *as our own* the suffering of others—of children, some grown, some dead, some yet unborn; of our parents; of people living under all kinds of conditions in different times and different places; and of other species. We know this Suffering intimately. We know it because we are not an isolated 'I.' We are also a 'We' rooted in a Ground Consciousness that binds us to the community of life.

I believe that a people which under-stands the profundity of loss and pain is compassionate, not aggressive, and that it empathizes with the pain of every species and every culture. We need this kind of under-standing to meet the pressing require-ment of our Time: that of becoming a community larger than tribe, race, religion, or country.

Ego's conviction of a sole and separate identity stands at the core of the conflicts that divide our world. That perception is a mis-understanding. As our stories show us, *who we are* includes and transcends all that we have been. These stories also dem-onstrate that once upon a time—at our Beginnings—each of us knew ourselves to be the whole human family—*the people*—born from the kiva, as one.

Since that Time of the tribe, we in the West have traveled far from the unconscious wholeness of the kiva—the hole in the earth from which we emerged as a group. Focused—as ego necessarily must be—on our individuality, our independence, and our entitlements, we've become increasingly divided by dif-ferences: the abstract divisions our minds create. As a result, certain groups and entire cultures carry the debilitating shame of being either *dependent* or *different*—people who are needy, people of a different color, people whose sexuality may not be like our own; people who represent diversity in body, feeling, physical or mental capacity, or age—people who are thereby outcast.

Cultural anthropologist Angeles Arrien asserts that *the overarching subject of communication in all groups is about inclusion or exclusion*. That 'metacommunication,' as she calls it, is grounded in the terrible fear of exile. Arrien suggests that people deal with the fear of being excluded by excluding other people; that we project our own unconscious tendencies out-ward, and then scapegoat those who are different—judge them, wage war on them, leave them out.

When we ask, *Who am I? Who are you? What is God?* there lives, hidden in our bodies, a yet more terrifying question: *Will I be excluded?* The question is interwoven with feelings of fear and shame that go all the way back to both our Beginnings.

The saber rattling of our world is not caused by the peculiarities of a particular tyrant or group or nation. It is rooted in the heart and horror of humiliation, the dread of isolation, and of exile. The heart of terror*ism* is the terror of being excluded from Life. Then a person is likely to reach for the nearest stone.

Thirty years have passed since I dreamed of the duplex in Santa Cruz at midlife when my daughter told me I'd been talking in my sleep. *"In Santa Cruz,"* she'd said I'd mumbled aloud, *"I have a separate identity."* As the dream comes to mind these many years later, I reflect on its wisdom and exclaim to myself, *Santa Cruz? Cruz comes from Crux!* I run to the dictionary:

> Crux. [L. Cross.] Anything that vexes or tries in the highest degree. Crucial. The essential, most important point.[24]

The root meaning of the word 'Cruz' explained why—as any human being afraid of exile might have done—I'd sealed away much of who I was on the other side of the duplex. At the same time, the dreamer's choice of 'Santa Cruz' confirmed in advance that the thirty-year journey ahead was a sacred one.

If we hide our truth and cannot find a way to accept all of ourselves, we will scapegoat and exile others, unconsciously. With a *"No!"* at our core, we will only add to the world's suffering. It is the crucial, essential, most important point.

> *We are unable to see with the eyes of the mind what is deeply known by the soul.*

The soul knows that separation exists in minds that fragment the world—but that it does not exist in Wholeness. Much of the suffering we have known ends when we turn to that greater reality and trust it. Thich Nhat Han from an Eastern tradition writes:

> We are loved by the whole cosmos . . .

Paul extols the same truth from an ancient Western perspective:

Neither death nor life . . . nor principalities . . . nor powers, nor height, nor depth, nor anything else in all creation, can separate us from the Love of God . . .[25]

Who am I? Who are you? What is God?

If I have learned one thing on my journey, it is this: We are both separate and joined. The Consciousness of Love embraces all separation, and in the immensity of that Mystery, everything belongs and we belong to each other.

And the whisper echoes:

"Yes!"

Endnotes for Chapter 8

1   W. H. Auden, excerpt from "For the Time Being," *The Collected Poetry of W. H. Auden,* N. Y: Random House, 1945, 412.

2   The experience of embodiment is described in greater depth in Hillman, *The Dancing Animal Woman.*

3   Genesis 32:22-31. The story of Jacob and the angel is described in the Interlude.

4   Richard Moss, MD, is a modern-day teacher of consciousness studies and has been my spiritual mentor for many years. He left medicine as a young man, and staked his life and work on his own profound awakening. His lineage is eclectic. He is the author of several books, the most recent of which is *The Mandala of Being,* 2007. Other works include *The Black Butterfly, The Second Miracle, How Shall We Live?* and *The I That Is We.* He made this statement in one of his many mentor groups.

5   See the reference to Paul MacLean's description of the human brain in Chapter 4.

6   Dream scholar Jeremy Taylor, DMin, said in a 1988 lecture that every species of animal except one bird dreams(!) He is the author of three books that have become the gold standard for learning to work with dreams: *Dreamwork, Where People Fly and Water Runs Uphill,* and *The Living Labyrinth.*

7   I am focusing on only a few of the contractions from infancy, here, but it is important to understand that contractions are also necessary to survival. There is too much information for an infant to deal with in his environment unless some of his energy is spent organizing it in some way. In the process of organization, some of it falls through the cracks of the organizing structure—the ego—and is lost.

8   In the West, parenting skills, like the *mirroring* needed to soften these effects, were *not even named* for the general culture until the 1980s.

9   *The Dancing Animal Woman* describes a way of learning from the body's contractions. Each contraction, in my experience, represented a specific feeling or set of feelings. Other resources are the seminal work of Alexander Lowen, MD, or a serious practice of systematic bodywork. Options include oriental systems such as yoga or the martial arts, and also Rolfing or deep tissue massage. See also the recently developed *somatic therapy,* described in the academic catalog of the California Institute for Integral Studies, San Francisco.

10 Esther Harding, PhD, *Psychic Energy—Its Source and Its Transformation,* Princeton: Princeton University Press, Bollingen Series X, 1973, 3-116, is the psychological and anthropological resource for this chapter.

11 *Ibid.*

12 In no version of Genesis is the fruit of the tree called an apple. However, we tend to learn as children from images rather than words. And most of us saw pictures of an apple!

13 Genesis 3:9, 11, 22 (abridged), and 3:23-24.

14 Masaccio, *Expulsion from the Garden of Eden* (c. 1424-28), a fresco at the Brancacci Chapel, Florence.

15 When excavated by theologians of all traditions, 'sin' is understood, not in moral terms but as the human state of separation from God, Life, the Essential Self, Brahman, Unity, or the One, etc.

16 The late Thomas G. Hand, SJ, of the Mercy Center, Burlingame, CA. used this term in a conversation. It can be so tempting to try to equate words like Life and Love, Ground Consciousness and Self with what we haltingly name 'God!' God is, indeed, not an object! This is one reason why the Hebrews, calling it idolatry, gave the Mystery no name—only the initials for Jehovah.

17 Iyer, ed., *The Gospel According to Thomas*, 27.

18 Evelyn Underhill's description of the mystic will be found in Chapter 11.

19 Aleksander Wat, Polish poet, quoted in Edward Hirsch, *How to Read a Poem—and Fall in Love with Poetry*, New York: Harcourt Brace and Co., 1999, 177. This and Jane Hirschfield's *Nine Gates*, are two of the finest books of any type that I know.

20 A reference to the Sermon on the Mount, Matthew 5:8. "Blessed are the pure in heart . . ." 'Pure' is translated from the Greek, *katharos,* and as used by Homer and Plato, means (in ascending order), *physically, ritually,* and *morally,* clean. I am taking the phrase to another level: to that of *awareness.* The 'heart's clear light' is the kind of awareness that is *clear of mental debris*—an important addition to these other forms of cleanliness.

21 A reference to *The Gospel According to Thomas,* ed. Iyer, verse 51, p. 30.

22 Richard Moss made this statement in conversation.

23 Irene Claremont de Castillejo, *Knowing Woman: A Feminine Psychology,* London, Hodder & Stoughton Ltd., 1973.

24 Daniel Webster, *Webster's Second Unabridged Dictionary*, ed. Jean L. McKechnie, New York: 1979, 439. Abbreviated.

25 Romans 8:38-39. Condensed.

9 "Yes!"— The Gateway to Freedom

> If your everyday practice is to open to all your
> emotions, to all the people you meet, to all
> the situations you encounter, without closing
> down—then that will take you as far as you can
> go. And then you'll understand all the teachings
> that anyone has ever taught.
>
> Pema Chödrön[1]

From the time the littlest child floats warm and wet in the
womb until well after her birth, she is wide open to life. Swept
into the world on an unbroken lineage from origins deep in the
universe, nothing has ruptured her primal trust. Hers is a state
of *"Yes!"*—albeit, an unconscious one—and all of the energies
of the universe flow through her. Her antennae for relationship
are raised high, but as we have seen, life outside the womb is
not perfect. Little by little, she contracts her body, her heart,
and her mind to protect herself from pain. By saying, *"No!"* in
these ways, she closes herself down and loses what is deepest
within her. Jesus' puzzling statement then makes sense to me:

> If salt loses its saltiness, how can it be made salty again? It is no
> longer good for anything, except to be thrown out and trampled by
> men.[2]

From a psychological point of view (a spiritual perspective appears in Chapter 15), to have 'lost one's saltiness' can be heard to describe the human condition of self-avoidance. Every time we contract our bodies, hearts, or minds, we are choosing not to be salty—not to be who we are. And each time we obstruct the energies of Love with a contraction, we turn the key to our prison door.

If we want to know true freedom, we need to reverse the process. As participants in the great human transformation of our Time, we don't just stop saying, *"No!"* We actively say, *"Yes!"* instead. We ask, *Who am I, really?* and excavate the foundations of the soul. Our minds might view the descent as an orderly, stepwise process, but without a protective shell to pull into, it can feel like we are falling. Like the stone falling into the water, we drop deeper and deeper, and as we do, we gain more of our selves. As difficult as Pema Chödrön's challenge may be, we "open to all our emotions, all the people we meet, and all the situations we encounter, without closing down." As we fall, we keep saying *"Yes!"* to the intelligence of our feelings, to the wisdom of our bodies, and to the greater Unknown. This lifelong process of becoming more authentic often begins at midlife, as the next stories portray.

Saying "Yes!" to Our Selves

Bruce,[3] 54, was the president of a very successful company and found himself experiencing serious heart palpitations. They didn't go away. When his doctor diagnosed the contractions as atrial fibrillation, Bruce began to question how he was living his life. He studied meditation with a Buddhist teacher and after his mind began to quiet down, saw a film that moved him to tears. The movie *Rivers and Tides* is about Scottish artist Andrew Goldsworthy who often fashions ephemeral art in nature—from beach sand that disappears in a rising tide, fallen leaves that blow in the wind, or icicles that melt in the sun.

Newly aware of the fragility of his own life, Bruce began to examine his thinking. In a *Mining Your Life for Meaning* group, he first questioned his beliefs about work:

No one can really be over 50, at least not someone my age. Snuck up on me like a bad cold. Maybe the real disease is denial—that I will die, or that what happens this minute really counts.

Andy Goldsworthy speaks in a language I can feel but I can't *know*. What speaks to me is his *work*. He is of the earth. I am of the mind. He is like a child, marveling, or a lover playing with his love. Without his work he says he loses *who he is*. Without my work I lose who *I* am. So what of this thing we both call *work*?

Next, he reflected on his father's work and what happened when he'd lost his job:

My Dad was an inventor, an engineer who helped to put a man on the moon. Then he got fired. Without his work he was lost. *He didn't know who he was.* I'd see him feeling alone, sitting in the backyard
. . . .

Soon he had a heart attack. It made him completely change his life. He stopped drinking and learned to live in peace. Ten years later, he showed me some photos he'd taken and developed. He had no work any more but *he was whole that day.* I could feel it in my bones. Three days later, he was dead at 67. But he'd had 10 extra years.

Loss brought Bruce face to face with the crux of his inquiry:

My work is meaningful, with concrete measures. My dad's work was meaningful, with concrete measures. Andy Goldsworthy's work has *no* measures, is *not* concrete, and can collapse in a moment. But tell me: whose heart swells with wonder, aches with the beauty, or who has tears in their eyes when they look at *my* work? And tell me if you believe Andy's work will kill *him*?

Bruce was asking deeply human questions. Although trained as a scientist, he realized that the kind of truth he sought now was of an entirely different order from that which concerned his intellect. Intellect is disembodied. It has not yet been tempered by *Fire*: It lacks the kind of flexibility and strength we access at depth. The truth Bruce wanted now was not the kind that solved problems or analyzed information. It transformed hearts.

Saying "Yes!" to the Intelligence of the Heart

Bruce took his questions seriously enough to begin to address his feelings. He had understood his heart's challenge and made a commitment to some long-term therapy. As his inquiry deepened, he began to see that his focus had always been on what others wanted. He had no idea what he needed, or what he felt, or what was important to *him*. He hadn't thought about these things because he didn't want to be 'selfish.'

Though this kind of fear is usually rooted in family dynamics, it is reinforced by the mis-under-standing many of us have absorbed about the commandment to "love others as ourselves."[4] Bruce needed to understand it in reverse: To love others as ourselves implies that we must first be able to love ourselves.

After great personal struggle, he left a marriage to a talented woman he loved, but who was caught in the vise of alcoholism. Later, he let go of a job that left him no time for himself. After three years of inquiry, Bruce learned how to say, *"Yes!"* to what he found inside. In the greatly abridged selection that follows, he recognized a much larger identity than the one defined by his work:

> Rich and growing
> Alive
> Anxious
> Split
> Soulful
> Curious and creative
> Divorcing
> Transforming my relationships
> Redefining my self from the inside out
> Wondering about the future
> Capable of serenity and compassion
> Open to new ideas
> Confident and not
> In awe of each day . . .

Bruce continued to question and to let go of his old ways. As time went by, his writing showed how he was seeing, not just problems or characteristics, but the rich complexity of his personhood—one that included the capacity to stay with deep feelings. He also reached an understanding of what was meaningful to him that went far beyond his work, thoughts, roles, or activities, and began to live the fullness of his own life:

> I've opened to creating my life from full consciousness, to listening to my 'still small voice.' I've found feelings of sadness and disappointment and have practiced sitting with them. I've discovered my body-mind doesn't know past or future. It's just opened or closed. I sit now with the grief of having lived with a closed and protected heart—a limited life; I relive what I didn't see, what I didn't feel and I *see what I couldn't see . . . and why I couldn't see.*
>
> I know now how much I love to play and I'm playing more. I know how deeply I value community and I've created a cupful. I still struggle to accept being cared for and occasionally see where I squirm to escape it. I struggle to stand openly in the brilliant suit that is me, all visible, all present. I can finally stay for long periods of time in my own dark fears, and not move from them. I can move forward and create, even then. I turn to the task of loving my whole self and then, perhaps, open a door to loving others. My small voice tells me that this love matters, though sometimes another voice says I should get a real job and bury all of this. I cry more often now and I know that all this matters; and when I get lost, that matters too—it's all just a part of it.

Learning the Ways of Love

We investigate our minds and our hearts, not as a self-centered activity, but to learn the ways of love. Bruce had begun by examining his thoughts about his outer life—his work and his marriage—but it was not long before he turned inward. The feelings he found there led him into the larger question of love. Love is not what we think, not what we'd like it to be. It is not all goodness and gentleness and peace. Love holds all of our humanity. We have not believed it was enough to be human— to be ordinary, to make mistakes, to embrace, then push away. Therefore, we contract.

The contractions that have defended us against further heartbreak are deadening to aliveness, destructive to society and devastating to love. Though they were meant to protect us from painful feelings and memories, they've kept us locked in self-made prisons—unable to let ourselves *out* or another person *in*. Judgmental of our thoughts, our feelings, and our gut reactions, we've dared not show who we are to ourselves or to others. In this closed state, how could anyone conceivably love?

Maria learned how true this was for her when she started to release her own contractions. When she saw how her driven-ness kept her from feeling, she stopped *doing,* slowed down, and began to write. The first time she read aloud to her group, her sentences were flung across the page like hot coals. Maria was saying, *"Yes!"* to feelings she'd not allowed since childhood.

I Am Angry

I just want to die, to avoid this pain and unsafety.
There is nothing good.
It is all unsafe.
Hell comes when you are not looking.
If I don't pay attention
    and think through everything
I will get caught . . .
I can't breathe for fear I will be found and hurt.
I can't stand the pain.

And I am very angry to be this unsafe.

Anger is *precious*. But anger locked away is a barrier to relationship with ourselves and with others—a refusal to risk authenticity. To open the inner lock, we thaw out more than the words. It takes patience to drop deeper than thought within ourselves and to listen for what the wordless foundations might be communicating. The answers don't arrive quickly. We redeem the ways we've said, *"No!"* to our selves one at a time: feeling by feeling, characteristic by characteristic, and failure by failure. We learn that it is human to dance, to fall, to fail! Letting go, our hearts slowly open.

The gift of a heart that has opened is compassion. If we have not allowed our own feelings, will we be able to feel genuine empathy with the feelings of others? If we have walled off certain needs, will we not be disdainful of them in others? If we haven't under-stood their pain, will we be able to feel *with* them? We may feel pity; we may feel contempt. We may put ourselves in a helping role. But helping is a very far cry from loving. We may feel safer in that powerful position, but *it is not love*.

We tend to mis-understand the nature of love. I surely did. Since childhood, I had thought I was supposed to be good. I had goodness all tangled up with perfection, but Love was not asking for perfection. *Love was asking me to be whole.* To be whole, I needed to say, *"Yes!"* to who I was.

As I fell more deeply into the truth of myself, it felt like an undoing. Trying to "open to all my emotions, the people and situations I encountered, without closing down" was a challenge to everything I knew—my thinking, my beliefs, attitudes, behaviors—all my ways of coping with life. It was a gradual surrender until the old structures from which I'd always viewed the world lay at my feet. Still, I had an uncanny sense that all these aspects of me were being raised up, offered, and in this strange ritual, made holy: pride and willpower . . . weakness and self-doubt . . . control, determination, and incompetence . . . anger . . . shame. Flaws, failures, and points of view, *Something* had need of them all—the good, the bad, the sacrifices and sins, the beauty and the despair.

Saying "Yes!" to the Body's Wisdom

Who am I now? I asked as I was doing this work, and a dream brought forth two figures from the Beginnings. They hushed the *"No!"* of the conserving community (which expected me to be 'nice'), and offered, instead, a wordless ritual that my body under-stood:

> *There is an old Native American grandmother who sings very beautifully. I want to join in and harmonize with her. The community starts to shush me as I sing, but she says, "No!" to them and together we sing the Song.*

Afterwards, she turns me around and cuts a lock of my hair. A Native American man makes a beaded headband for me, and when I put it on, I raise my arms straight up over my head to the sky and stand there naked—and it doesn't matter that I am naked, for I am whole, and I am One, and I am beautiful.

The dream showed me how to let others see me as I was: both vulnerable and strong. By harmonizing with the primordial grandmother-in-me, I was consenting to the treasures of my body's foundation. Joined with this older, more primal self in song, I stood naked to my need, my tenderness, but also to my animal-body's ways of survival—the depths of its violence and its passions. I was a human creature, openly acknowledging the very vulnerability of being alive—along with the instinctual powers meant to ensure it.

In *being*, the youngest one in us meets the Elder—the most ancient and universal in us. It is as if an old and wordless self speaks to the one hiding on the far side of the duplex: *"It's all right, there's room for you in here!"* Hearing it, the younger leaves her dark hiding place and enters the Elder's embrace. It is almost like holding a little baby.

In this sacred dialog, the little girl who had been captivated by the Virgin Mary in a picture book *became her*—gave birth to and embraced the Christmas child *in herself*. It is painful growing up as a human person, but I believe we are called to cradle humanity's Child. She is innocence. She feels much, and in feeling, she enlivens us. She is creative, spontaneous, and real. She is wounded/*a healer*, born repeatedly in all of us. May we continue to give birth to our infant child of the Spirit, whether within a tradition or not.

If we can honestly embrace the oppositions inside us, our compassion will grow for the same qualities in others. Friend or stranger, each shares with us the same loneliness and the same terror; each needs the same love. I believe that as we make this kind of peace within ourselves, it contributes to peace in the world. In the midst of all its conflicts, it is something we *can* do. Every time we embrace both sides of an issue within ourselves instead of trying to change the point of view of others, we cooperate with life's painstaking work of testing and integrating new forms of life. In this case, the form is the gradual shaping of the human mind.

Each inner embrace adds more light to life's deep need for it at this Time. Each contributes to the realization of second *Fire* in the same way that the first fire passed from hearth to hearth across the face of the earth.

Sometimes, as we work, we are surprised by 'more than the words.' Once, when I asked myself, *What shall I do with my "No!" to this hatred I'm feeling?* my body became inventive: Quite spontaneously, one arm stretched wide as if to offer hatred an embrace. I thought, *It's trying to show me how to put my arm around it!* At first, I was afraid it might look kind of silly; but then, nobody was looking, and so, after a few minutes, I extended the other arm too. Colin Oliver's response to the story astonished me:

> I believe our inner intelligence is amazingly conversant with the ancient art of mime. It can be so telling.

Only then did I realize that the primordial mime-in-me— the *Homo habilis* woman who'd danced and dramatized before she could speak—had helped me create an inner spaciousness I didn't yet have. Her ritual embrace was a Way of *one-ing*. It let me know that if I could make a big enough space inside, there'd be room for more—even the most difficult parts of me. This was not to be a space in my thoughts, but the spaciousness of *being*—the liminal space where I could be at-one with myself.

We will never be whole without our body's exuberant joys, its tender vulnerabilities and the demonic torments hidden in its dark recesses. It holds our root terrors, our archaic gluttony and feral sexuality, our fierce furies and jealousies. Their presence created the terrible beliefs we consequently held about ourselves, said, *"No!"* to—and then dragged with us every day. But when we carry our heart's conscious light into our body's depths, we are like the little girl in Picasso's drawing who climbed down a ladder into the cavern of the half animal/half human Minotaur. Like her, we raise a candle to his face—

—and see in it a mirror.

When we light up our own interior wilderness, we *see*: We are far more than who we think we are. The makings of humiliation lie buried here, but we're no longer split in two: the side that lives in the half of the duplex hidden from the community, and the side that shows itself. Instead, by consciously reclaiming the primal self we have lost, a measure of humility emerges—enough to begin to hold who we are in our hearts.

How we hold anything in our bodies, hearts, and minds determines how we ourselves are held.

When we embrace the visceral inheritance we've received from the animal kingdom, compassion arises—and at this unspeakable depth, the shame of the child and the child of the race is transformed. It is then we under-stand what has always been true: that all three foundations of the soul rest on yet deeper Ground.

Endnotes for Chapter 9

1 Pema Chödrön is a contemporary Buddhist nun. Source unknown.

2 Matthew 5:13 (NIV). *Author's note*: Matthew added a context at the beginning of Jesus' original saying that commended Christians as the 'salt of the earth.' But this is contrary to Jesus' teachings. Jesus was inclusive and rejected 'outsider-insider' discriminations of every kind. See Robert Funk, et al, *The Five Gospels*, San Francisco: HarperSanFrancisco, 1993, 139.

3 Bruce is a pseudonym. His unpublished writings are used with permission.

4 Leviticus 19:18 is the root of this commandment, variants of which are found in 21 of the world's religions. The phrase will be discussed further in later chapters.

5 Pablo Picasso, *Minotauromachia*, Brooklyn Museum. *Author's note:* The Minotaur as half animal/half man, was an ancient intuition of the bodymind. The title of *The Dancing Animal Woman* was inspired by a dream in which I was a female centaur: with a woman's torso and the slender legs of a hoofed animal, like those of a deer.

10 The Three Foundations Transformed— The Embodied Soul

Thus far, our preparation for the spiritual journey has been a way of trying to reach a deeper Ground—and some means of deepening our connection with it. In addition to examples of several spiritual practices, we have explored a few aspects of what is already known: what disciplines like archeology, anthropology, biology, and psychology have discovered about our origins. Their discoveries have mapped the amazing evolutionary journey inscribed in the three foundations of the soul: the long story of awakening from cell to reptile to mammal to humankind that is reflected in the human mind. Our inquiry then led us in the reverse direction—a descent of these same foundations beginning with the most recent. We dropped from reason as a means of engaging life, into successively deeper layers of awareness, on down to those more ancient.

We saw how Bruce developed greater awareness when he turned to a more interior path, and how the practices of meditation and therapy led him to a significant change in the way he saw his world. As a result, he created a larger context for his life, made new kinds of relationships, and extended his concept of who he thought he should be. Bruce found more of himself.

His writing helped him to express the new sense of identity that had emerged, along with new thoughts, new feelings, and new purpose. To uncover his authenticity, he learned to pay attention to feelings he could not reach with his thinking mind: his need, his loneliness, his hurt, and his longing for deeper meaning. When he began to listen to what his heart had been trying to tell him, he made the painful decision to change his life. He took the leap, and left both his work and his marriage for the unknown. His atrial fibrillations ceased. And even though he feared the loss of his beloved daughter's love, he learned to remain trusting. As time went by, he created a new kind of relationship with her—one that was far more real.

Likewise, when Maria began her inner journey, she let go of what she called "do-do-doing" in order to find her feelings. Though her mind disagreed with her heart—it *knew* anger wasn't allowed—she took the leap and wrote about what she felt inside. Her honest expression of anger empowered her. It was the first fruit of saying, *"Yes!"* to herself.

Along with these stories, we tapped sensations, dreams, and myths to see if they might lead to greater understanding. At first, we may have doubted their value but if we worked with them even tentatively, we found ourselves led down into the far more subtle unknowns in our bodies. The dream of the freezing infants and the myths of Prometheus, Eden, and the Minotaur's cave offered new means of under-standing our contractions—the tight places that keep our hearts closed to Love. Another dream—the song of the primordial grandmother—dramatized the way our bodies and their wordless rituals can also teach us about ourselves. 'Listening' to sensations, dreams, and myths is very different from accessing thoughts or feelings; but it can help us create a more conscious connection to our own nature—and to a humanity that evolved and developed in the natural world. If we practice these ways, and if we can embrace what we find beneath the surface and *stay*, we will embody our selves. Then, like our ancestors who tamed the first embers in the wild, we will have made a hearth for *Fire*.

The journey down through the foundations is one of the many ways we can begin to recover the realities of the past—

those of the child within and the children of the race. In each, we will uncover the same self-centered fear: *Is there enough?*

Will I *have* enough . . . money . . . food . . . safety . . .
    love . . . control?

Do I *do* enough . . . in my work . . . for others . . . or
    for the world?

Am *I* enough?

The response from the greater Love—is *"Yes!"* When we trust that whispered *"Yes!"* enough, we can dare to leave the threshold of conflict and set out for the Unknown. This begins the spiritual journey.

To confuse what is spiritual with what is psychological is a mis-understanding. The disciplines that helped us create a hearth for *Fire* were investigations of the known. What is known cannot take us further than the three foundations of the soul. No intellectual endeavor, feeling, or belief—not archeology, anthropology, psychology, philosophy, or religion as it is ordinarily understood—can awaken us to *Fire for the second time*. The spiritual journey requires that we develop a new kind of relationship to an Unknown *that has no name*. It is this turning away from our inner *"No!"* to the abyss of not knowing and toward Love's *"Yes!"* that opens us to the possibility of transformation. It bears repeating here that transformation is different from the kinds of changes we make ourselves—changes in attitude, location, friends, jobs, partners, and the like. Transformation is not an extension of what has gone before. It implies a *change in form*—and *that* is out of our hands. Transformation brings into being the *not yet*. When that happens, it is a complete break in continuity with the past. Between the known and the *not yet* is a gap, and what lies on the other side of the gap is brand new:

There was a gap between the foundation of the
    body and that of the heart.
There was a gap between the foundation of the
    heart and that of the intellect.
There is a gap between the foundation of the
    intellect and the life of the soul.

We are more than we think. We are body, a sea of untamed energies and wisdom. We are heart with its profound capacity for empathy and relatedness. We are intellect that repeatedly stuns us with its capacities for invention and understanding. *And we are something more.*

The Turning Point in Our Journey

We stand at the brink of an Unknown that is a radically different kind of consciousness—what Merton called the "abyss that separates us from ourselves." Shall we leave the threshold? William Sloan Coffin suggests there is only one thing to do:

> When you find yourself at a precipice—*leap!*

How Shall We Learn To Fly?

I am relying on the ancient word *soul*[1] to express a different way of being, but the deepest mysteries of soul transcend human language. Soul is not an object—not an identity—because it is not something we 'have.' Perhaps we could say it is more like a process—one we're just becoming aware of.

> *Learning to orient our attention to the soul process instead of to our thoughts is the change of mind to which we have been called. This radical reorientation is at the heart of transformation.*

To engage in a living relationship with the power of Love is a revolution in the very concept or substance of 'mind' or 'awareness.' Attention comes not only from the mind, as we know it. It comes from our body, heart, and mind, *and more*—what I am calling 'soul.' Soul inquires into and relies on a far deeper and more ephemeral Intelligence—one that can't be accessed by intellect.

> *Soul registers the Presence of Love differently from the ways we register signals from our bodies, hearts, and intellects.*

We have seen that in the transitions between each of the first three foundations, as human creatures moved from a reliance on sensation to feeling, and then to the greater nuance of thought, they developed the capacity to 'tune in' to increasingly subtle signals. Reacting automatically to an adrenaline rush was very different from recognizing feelings of anxiety; noticing anxiety was, in turn, entirely different from listening to thoughts about choices of what to do.

The transition to the soul process follows the same pattern. It involves an even more subtle means of perception than thought: We 'listen' through the soul process—and register Presence.

Jesus repeatedly admonished, *"Ye who have ears to hear!"* and called our contractions "hardening." He asked his disciples:

> Do you still not see or understand? Are your hearts hardened? Do you have eyes but fail to see, and ears but fail to hear?[2]

1600 years later, the mystic Angelus Silesius elaborated on the same statement:

> See where you do not see
> Hear where no sound comes through
> Go where you cannot go
> And God will speak to you.[3]

As I hear their words, Jesus and Silesius were speaking of listening *with* and *as* soul. *As soul*, we *are* relationship. To listen *as relationship*, requires the acute and open attention of people who are functioning in a different way. When we "see what we do not see," and "go where we cannot go," we have become instruments—of a Love, a peace, and a kind of perception that our current view of the world finds utterly incomprehensible.

Leaving the Old Way for the New

For each of the heart's and mind's foundations to gain ascendancy, the essence of the prior foundation(s) had to be negated.

During these first two transformations, the 'virtues' of a prior foundation became undesirable in the next.[4] And so, at each of these gaps, the child and the child of the race said *"No!"* to themselves. When *Homo erectus* saw that his greediness and aggression excluded him from tribal life, he leapt the first gap by setting aside a total reliance on his body's proven wisdom in order to gain some sensitivity to others' needs. In entering the subsequent transformation to a thinking mind, archaic *Homo sapiens* negated his feelings. Both practices eventually became innate. *Children learn to share. Men don't cry.*

Our ancestors transcended their bodies' and hearts' foundations by burying them. So, to 'grow up,' have we. Then as now, what the community saw as undesirable often remains far from conscious awareness. It is probable that in order to gain control over our own instincts and emotions, all of us have had to oppose or deny much of *who we are*. We began the practice in childhood, and as the dream of the freezing infants so vividly dramatized, we most likely found a way to 'freeze' the raw instincts and feelings of our young bodies 'in ice.' As adults, even though we may think we want to thaw them out, our contractions may be telling us, *"No! Maybe it's all right to give them a name—but no more!"*

We are still reaping the wind of these solutions! The *"No!"* we said to our bodies, as children, has left us living from an intellect largely cut off from instinct and feeling. We have lost the connection to our root selves—and with it, our fundamental relatedness to others and to all of existence. But deep inside, we still yearn for that communion. D. H. Lawrence describes it as a longing shared with all living things:

> In every living thing there is a desire for love, for the relationship of unison with the rest of things . . . Oh what a catastrophe for man when he cut himself off from the rhythm of the year, from his unison with the sun and the earth. Oh what a catastrophe, what a maiming of love when it was made a personal, merely personal feeling, taken away from the rising and setting of the sun, and cut off from the magical connection of the solstice and equinox. That is what is wrong with us. We are bleeding at the roots . . .[5]

We live in a universe that is alive with energies and powers beyond our wildest imaginations. In this unbroken communion, there are no boundaries, no edges; we belong to a Whole. Without a deeply felt experience of this Communion, however, we tend to view reality in parts. That ordinary way of *seeing* leaves us with the conflicts that plague our world: conflicts between cultures, between nations, and between religions that have culminated in the horrors of genocide in Cambodia and Rwanda, and the disastrous war in Iraq. The chaos that results from the divisions inherent in this form of consciousness will be greatly increased by global warming—and made worse by conflicts over resources: oil, water, soil, and food. What are we to do?

In a speech at Harvard, the Dalai Lama clarified what is most needed in our Time:

> In this century, human knowledge is extremely expanded and developed. But this is mainly knowledge of the *external* world. In the field of what we may call "inner science" . . . there are many things, I think, that you *do not know*. You spend a large amount of the best human brain-power looking outside—too much—and it seems you do not spend adequate effort to look within. . . .
>
> Perhaps now that the Western sciences have reached down into the atom and out into the cosmos finally to realize the extreme vulnerability of all life and value, it is becoming credible, even obvious, that the inner science is of supreme importance. Certainly physics designed the bombs, biology, the germ warfare, chemistry, the nerve gas and so on, but it will be the unhealthy emotions of individuals that will trigger these horrors. *These emotions can only be controlled, reshaped, and re-channeled by technologies developed from successful inner science.*[6]

The rent in our communion with the Whole is a wound the ego cannot heal. Intellect and ego cannot see Wholeness; they function by tearing apart. We need now to find a way to cooperate with something the mind can neither see nor understand.

The New Way

Only the Whole can repair the Whole, but we can begin to cooperate with that process by repairing our relationships with others. An important preparation for making those honest amends is to become aware of our own inner conflicts—and to find the hidden characteristics in ourselves that we've only been able to see in the people around us. This work illustrates the essential difference between the *"No!"* we used to leap the gaps between the foundations and the Way we follow to enter the soul process.

> *To cooperate with the emergent consciousness of Love, we do not negate the traits inherited from the three foundations. We embrace them.*

We will always need the wisdom of the triune brain—that of instinct, feeling, and intellect. For this work, however, we need to quiet their demands differently than did the child and the children of the race. At the gap between a life driven by the three foundations and the new life lived from the soul, it may feel like we are negating our old ways altogether—perhaps even losing ourselves! But that is only ego's perception. From the larger perspective, they become incorporated, for that is true of all transformations. Both the old and the new are preserved—like the old and new wine in the parable.

We stand at the gap between the foundation of intellect and the life of the soul. At this gap, we say, *"Yes!"* and embody ourselves as deeply as we can. We say, *"Yes!"* to our pain, *"Yes!* to our anger, and *"Yes!"* to the feelings that lie beneath it. In the same way that Thomas Berry embraced the older stories within the cosmic story, we learn to embrace What Is. We assert our *"Yes!"* to the greater Wholeness with all our hearts and minds and strength: a *"Yes!"* to the past, to the present moment, and to what lies ahead. When the worst happens, we don't shut down; we let go.

It is the beginning of Love.

It is a melting, not a journey,
an enlargement, not a path;
a relinquishing—
nothing held
nothing saved
nothing safe—

Then a great moon
swells inside and rises
    silent
        luminous
            without edges

Letting go is our leap to freedom. This kind of *"Yes!"* to Life runs counter to every protective device the ego has perfected—counter to our plans, our expectations, and our hopes—especially our hopes. It leaves us open to hurt and to disappointment, and unprotected against unexpected wounds from others.

So does love.

o

The Interlude that follows offers an opportunity to experience our *fundamental relatedness*—not only to other persons but also to the whole of the natural world. If we can feel our joy in its colors and textures, how deeply bonded we are to its creatures—and if we can sense in our bodies their active efforts to engage us—perhaps it will help us to realize that we are neither as alone nor as isolated as we think.

The Way of fundamental relatedness rides on the breath of a whisper:

> For all that has been—Thanks! To all that shall be—Yes! [7]
>
> Dag Hammarskjöld

Endnotes for Chapter 10

1   The ancient Hebrew word for soul, *nephesh*, is closest to the usage I intend. Most simply, it meant the essence of a person in his or her wholeness. Much later, Plato and his followers defined a split between matter and spirit, often called the *separable soul*. This became the more conventional understanding, but it is not an accurate or a relevant interpretation of *soul* within either Judaism or Christianity. One cannot, in truth, objectify the experience of *being soul*. Nor is it accurate to say that *soul* represents a new kind of identity. *It is the lack of the usual kind of identity* that allows the life of the soul to flourish. Even using 'the' before the word *soul,* objectifies it, and though I occasionally find I have to use it, nothing that objectifies soul/*the soul process* is really appropriate.

2   Mark 8:17-18 (TNIV).

3   Angelus Silesius (1624-1677), in H. A. Reinhold, *The Soul Afire*, New York: Pantheon Books, 1944.

4   Adapted from Harding, *Psychic Energy*, 75-76.

5   D. H. Lawrence, *Lady Chatterley's Lover and A Propos of 'Lady Chatterley's Lover,'* ed. Michael Squires, Cambridge: Cambridge University Press, 1993, 323.

6   The Dalai Lama, from a speech at Harvard University, 1984. Italics mine.

7   Dag Hammarskjöld, *Markings*, Ballantine Books, 1985, 89.

Interlude

From Loneliness to Communion

To be awakened is to be intimate with all things.

Dogen[1]

An Interlude is like a bridge that links two parts of a piece of music. This Interlude links the two parts of the song of the soul: preparation and awakening. Our preparation showed us how to listen to what lies inside us: to the whisper, to dreams, to myths, and to the messages from our bodies. It taught us to say, "Yes!" as we went down through the three foundations of the soul. The Interlude takes us steadily in a new direction: toward the experience of awakening to the energies of Love.

o

I want to trace the long path between loneliness and Love, to give it form and flesh. Who does not know the loneliness of the human heart, the deep yearning for connection that is drowned out by background music, noisy restaurants, and chatter on cell phones and computers? This loneliness rises and falls in our lives like the slow swell of an ocean wave. It's not a matter of being alone; we sometimes feel it when we're surrounded by the people who love us. Loneliness steals into our hearts when we lie awake at two in the morning or when we're washing the dishes or shaving—and thought has fallen away. We're aware of it most when we pull away from our selves. We feel it then: a hollow in the gut . . . a slight constriction in the throat . . . an emptiness . . .

Loneliness has its own rhythm. It simply comes and goes. We know the moment it arrives, though, for it falls over us like a blanket and deadens our energy. What haunts us is a nameless feeling that lies at our very core, and we do everything we can to avoid it. Strangely, it is both our deepest wound and our blessing—and often propels us on our spiritual journey.

The spiritual journey is a slow opening, a path from separation to Wholeness, and from judgment to Love.

The word *communion* describes the Love of which I speak, the mystery of belonging we think we have lost and seek on the spiritual path. If we have learned to listen to our bodies, however, we've become familiar with the many obstacles we've put in our way: all the *"No's"* to thoughts and feelings and urgencies disapproved by the community. We've seen how these contractions can block our authenticity, a genuine engagement with others, and the capacity to be fully alive. But if we have persevered, stayed with our practice, and let go, we have laid the groundwork for Love's emergence. The rest is out of our hands.

Surely, we are all already awakening. But in such a subtle and gradual process, it is difficult for us to imagine how radically different the soul's communion with the greater Life actually *is* from its foundations in thinking, feeling, and instinct. And although we may have had glimpses of it all our lives, the voltage of an abrupt or spontaneous awakening tears the scales from our eyes. Immersed in this "transforming Fire of love and union,"[2] we *see/feel/under-stand* that this Life is entirely different than we had realized.

There is a vast difference between the textures of stone and the temperatures of Fire.

The second Fire that comes spontaneously is a flash of illumination that changes our lives forever. Discontinuous with everything we have ever experienced, it *will not fit* within our established frameworks of thought, feeling, sensation or any other familiar way of knowing—yet it includes them.

When we awaken, we are ferocious with life. 'Waking' implies everything new: a new being, a new orientation, a new kind of awareness, and a new body. This fundamental realization is a genuine birth, as if we had opened from a tight bud and were just as tender. Afterwards, we adapt, but slowly, for we have entered an entirely new environment. Life's horizon has expanded and with its increase, everything has new significance. Still, the old remains: that is the nature of wholeness.

To wake up is to be disoriented. We may think we have lost ourselves, at least the selves we knew. On the first half of the journey, the path through the foundations was fairly easily mapped. On the second, there is no map. It is a different world.

The Way of the Soul

To connect the worlds, this Interlude improvises. Improvisation is not orderly; it modulates, and in this case, not just to a different key or from a major to a minor mode, but *to an altogether different kind of music*.

It is not unlike the slow metamorphosis of a Beethoven symphony. Beethoven often begins with a few musical themes, mere fragments of melody. Then, as anyone might who loves what he is doing, he starts to *play*. As we listen, he plays with his themes in a series of transformations that leave us utterly lost. Where is he going? What happened to the melody he started with, the familiar rhythm, the harmony?

As Beethoven plays, he transports us into far-reaching harmonies and embellishes his themes. Then in a flash, we step into a clearing and find ourselves—where we started. The symphony's destination is the same place it began. We hear the original theme played in the original key. We are Home, but see it in an entirely new light—just as T. S. Eliot's poem had whispered:

> And the end of all our exploring
> Will be to arrive where we started
> And know the place for the first time . . .[3]

This Interlude starts in a similar way, with themes of *uncertainty, wandering,* and *paradox.* As it begins to digress, the themes change shape. They are transformed into *yearning* and *vulnerability* and *love,* and resolved in stories told by a new voice—not the familiar one of the mind. Rumi announces the first theme:

> Straying maps the path.

The soul's journey into the unknown is fraught with uncertainty, filled with confusion. The direct, goal-oriented ways we've tended to follow in the past are not the Way of the soul. We're used to making plans and traveling on a road that has a beginning and an end. Soul moves in an unfamiliar terrain, in a more organic unfolding.

After I spoke at a conference 'down under' in Sydney, an Australian actress Clare Dunne told me about her long friendship with an aboriginal woman.

> When we take a walk, Miriam *belongs* in the walk: she loves the movement, the feel of her feet touching the ground. My head is already at my destination. The walk is only a means of getting there.

The Way is formed quite by accident. The spiritual path is shaped by serendipity. It is a meandering, not a highway. Yet as we grow older, we often look back at our lives and sense that somehow, every step seems to have led in a single direction, and every failure has been a necessity.

Soul speaks the language of paradox. Language creates reality through opposing definitions, but outside its world of opposites lies a reality that is vast. Intellect calls the larger reality 'paradox.' Soul calls it *Wholeness.* To express this reality, you will notice in the stories that follow, some experiments with words that show up unannounced. You may be surprised by textures or senses blended without explanation, like this:

> There is a shade of green, a shade of wrinkled, barely unfolded leaves that I heard whisper long ago . . .

You will find coined words with more complex meanings like *joignance.* The making of *joignance* helped me to express the razor's edge of human love: joy and poignancy reunited. In this book, you've already seen opposites tied back into wholeness with a slash, like loneliness/*communion.* I've joined them this way because, ordinarily, when we're immersed in one of these opposites, the other seems nonexistent. It is like the dark side of the moon—present but unseen. But the communion we seek on the spiritual journey obliges us to live its true paradoxical nature: loneliness/*communion* as One.

Until we are lonely, we shall be lonely. We may have initiated our quest to be relieved of a painful isolation—for that is the legacy of the ego. Eventually, however, the journey into communion requires that we enter the inescapable depths of our own loneliness. Those who let themselves *have* their loneliness, who feel it in all its ramifications and allow its presence in their bodies—are more likely to enter a genuine intimacy with Life.

The Paradox of Blessing

By receiving our loneliness—allowing it and taking it in—we continue to deepen, and sometimes, encounter a wound that is deeper yet. For many people, there is a relationship between a wound and the spiritual journey, and on my journey, I found it to be paradoxical: a wound/*blessing.* One day, I was looking for a model, and turned to the old tale of Jacob's battle with the 'angel,' also called 'a man.'[4] After the two had struggled, so the ancient story went, the angel wounded Jacob, and even then, Jacob asked him for a blessing. Jacob carried the wound of the angel's blessing for the rest of his life. He also carried the blessing of the wound. *Together,* they transformed him.

His story gave me even more confidence when I looked once more at the roots of its language, for those ancient words under-girded my own. I discovered that the French, and Old English roots of *bless* meant *to wound* or *to open,* and the German meant *the sacrificial blood* sprinkled on archaic altars. In Hebrew *to bless* meant *to kneel.*[5]

We have so domesticated language! The ancient founda-tions of the word *to bless* are wild and have their origins in the rituals of kiva, grotto, and temple. But with the increasingly refined abstractions of intellect, the wholeness of its original meaning has been split off and lost.

With this realization, I understood: I had known blessing all my life. It had flowed from the most painful of events; it had laid bare my wounds. It had opened my heart and made me vul-nerable. And as kneeling does, it had begun to humble me.

Poet Jennifer Welwood voices the wholeness of this wound/*blessing* from her own life experience, and at the same time, paints a Way that is common to our human journey:

> Willing to experience aloneness,
> I discover connection everywhere;
> Turning to face my fear,
> I meet the warrior who lives within;
> Opening to my loss,
> I gain the embrace of the universe;
> Surrendering into emptiness
> I find fullness without end.
>
> Each condition I flee from pursues me,
> Each condition I welcome transforms me
> And becomes itself, transformed . . .
> I bow to the one who has made it so . . .[6]

Poet and mystic weave the language of paradox and vulnera-bility. So does the one who tells stories. This ancient voice-in-us presses up from the ashes of the fire, from the bone and tis-sue of our ancestors. When this Storyteller begins to chant, she sings of her love affair with life—and of the tenderness that makes it possible.

She reminds us of the little child-inside who still lives in her own body—the one who knows the living landscape, and is intimate with the animals and the trees. As we listen to her cadence, she lets language loose. Then, sense and color and liturgy tumble together and unfold in her first story—a reverie meant to be read aloud.

Green

There is a shade of green, a shade of wrinkled, barely unfolded leaves that I heard whisper long ago. It is a green that has light shining through it, green that is somehow light itself

> light of light,
> light reflecting itself

and, being light, is more than green; it is gold—the color of early morning sunlight slanting past the soft new tips of oak leaves, setting them afire beyond the stand of yellow lilies that float above their long leaves; fashioning the radiance of daffodils trumpeting light in the meadow.

It is a green of young pasture grass so tender my mouth waters and I want to graze and nuzzle its moistness; the same green of soft velvet slung across fallen logs in a dark forest or draped, new-mown and fragrant over the many faces of my beloved lying under white stones, chiseled with names and dates in the hope of permanence.

This green-gold of new life is a color I first knew in the fields of my childhood; fields of long, sweet-smelling grass and pink clover, a green over which yellow and white butterflies, fresh from the cocoon, skimmed over tender milkweed, and overhead, darting swallows I tried to draw with crayons in a big soft 'V'; but my drawings could not speak the beauty of feathered grace, the glory of flight, the early morning sounds of nesting, or the sticky stems of dandelions.

It was the gold of dandelions that we'd brush underneath each other's chins, *"Do you like butter?"* we'd ask ritually and bend to look at the underside of each other's chins to see whether there was a reflection of the flower's gold light. *"Do you like butter?"* We asked the same proof from buttercups later in the season, believing fervently that light illuminating soft down was proof of butterlove.

We knew it wasn't love of butter we were measuring, but love of something else our bodies knew and arched as if to embrace, something we yearned for that was always just beyond our grasp. We knew, somehow, that it signified more than a game—that we, too, were part of the glory, reflecting the dappled green-gold light.

I tried to write my first book about it when I was nine, about brown shoots of grass, like little people who'd waited underground all winter, until it was time to pull on their new green clothes and poke up through the wet earth. I don't know what happened to those carefully colored pages smudged with wax, but I realize now that I have spent a lifetime trying to tell about the green, perhaps in the hope of keeping it forever.

In my twenties, shortly after I was married, I saw a photograph in a magazine, a picture of a small screened porch with white wicker chairs, green ferns and a fabric of delicate green and yellow leavery against a white background. It whispered the sounds of dandelions and meadow grass, new leaves and daffodils. I tore it out and put it away, for it was too late to use; we'd let the furniture-sale prices decide our first color scheme of orange and brown and olive. But over the years, though I lost the clipping and forgot the shapes of chairs and patterns in the picture, I never forgot its message. And in every house and every apartment, in every state I've lived, I've had one small green and yellow room; tried to recreate with fabric and paint and plants what I had heard and felt and smelled in the meadows each spring; tried to find a way to reflect the light of green leaves and fragrant grasses that spoke so deeply after the harsh New England winters of my childhood.

The same promise drew me forward like a magnet through the long years of tears and loneliness, and it still draws me today at dawn when sun, slanting across the spring garden, models with shadow the undulating meadows in the distance, shapes the curve of each rolling pasture and each tree trunk in the early light. I say to my husband, "Look!" and he says, "Yes, the flowers in the garden are beautiful!" but I say, "It is *more* than the flowers! It's the *green,* the new yellow-green of the leaves, the hills, the tips of oak leaves; the light shining through them . . ."

And my voice trails off, for I cannot put into words that which I've always seen and never been able to capture, loved and never been able to paint or write or have inside my home, even as it lies forever inside me and all around me in the green-gold light. I tell him about the picture in the magazine, the way it has helped me try to express a longing I have carried in my heart for a lifetime. "Do you have a picture like that, too?"

"Oh, yes!" he replies. "When I was a boy, there was a Harley Davidson ad, a drawing really, not a photo, of a motorcycle entering a bend on an open country road that winds up a long hill and disappears"—he draws a serpentine road midair—"and the caption underneath was '*Sing the song of the open road!*' Every day when I drive up that hill"—he points in the direction of a nearby road—"I think of the picture in that ad."

What pictures, I wonder, do other people carry of something seen with reverence before that word was ever understood; an image taken in and embraced, a companion that speaks to the hidden layers of their souls, not of lofty goals, but of the ordinary; a picture they carry for a lifetime and try to make real until they too pass underneath the carved white stones to lie in hollows and join with the soft green gold forever . . . ?

o

Life tugs at our hearts like a magnet. It allures us—draws us into relationship with all that is. It was this *allurement*[7]—this power of attraction calling everything into communion—that seduced and sang to my whole being. I was attracted to life the way the earth is attracted to the sun, the tides to the moon, and flowers to light. From some place deep down in my body, I knew from this yearning in my bones that everything in existence was utterly woven together.

I say that it touches a man that his blood is sea water and his tears are salt, that the seed of his loins is scarcely different from the same cells in a seaweed, and that of stuff like his bones are coral made. I say that physical and biologic law lies down with him, and wakes when a child stirs in the womb, and that the sap in a tree, uprushing in the spring, and the smell of the loam, where the bacteria bestir themselves in darkness, and the path of the sun in the heaven, these are facts of first importance to his mental conclusions, and that a man who goes in no consciousness of them is a drifter and a dreamer, without a home or any contact with reality.[8]

The Storyteller calls us home to this reality. She reminds us that we are creatures too, part of the animal world, and that other animals, like us, express their allurement in curiosity and in play.

Play

A week ago, we made a new swing and hung it from a high branch in a Monterey pine. I love to swing out over the field! The first time I sat on its maple seat and pushed off into the air, a movement near a split-rail fence to the north caught my eye. I had startled two young fawns grazing at the edge of the meadow, and they had scattered fast. But their curiosity got the better of them. They seemed enchanted by what they saw—a human being swinging in the air! They started to come closer, got part way, and stopped. Not quite daring to come further, they stood stock-still and watched.

The day before, one of the fawns had tried to get a jack-rabbit to play. She sneaked up on the baby rabbit as it nibbled the spring grass and jumped in place as if to scare it. The rabbit turned and ran a little way and the fawn gave chase, then stopped and waited for the rabbit to return. Sure enough, the rabbit came back, sidled as close as it dared and waited for the fawn to take up the pursuit again. They kept it up for several minutes until the doe got tired of the ruckus and chased her fawn into submission.

Another day, we watched a similar game between a puppy and a calf. When they encountered one another unexpectedly, they sniffed around a bit, tested each other with the same star-tle behavior, then pretended to menace one another, jostling and chasing about for half an hour. It seemed strange to see the comparatively huge calf romping with a puppy, but they were allured to relationship . . .[9]

We arise out of relationship. It is the ground of who we are.

The Storyteller sings more about the theme of allurement and the wild ones who yearn to engage us. The first is about another creature that wanted to play—a whale.[10]

The Gray Whale

The grey whales appeared as if out of nowhere and surfaced next to our tiny raft. It is extraordinary to be afloat in a small rubber boat amidst these huge 35-ton mothers and their enormous infants. They are expressive. Beautiful. While most of the pod remained hidden or stayed in the distance blowing and breaching, these few clearly wanted contact with our small group. They were seeking relationship.[11]

So powerful they could capsize the rubber raft with the movement of a single flipper, they were utterly careful. One mother whale pulled straight up out of the water as if standing on her tail—the better to look at us. But her calf came closer and lay in the water right next to the raft. When I knelt and leaned toward her, she stared into my eyes with her one eye only a foot away. I felt bonded to her very heart.

Later, she rolled over on her back and slid under the raft, offering her belly to be stroked. To touch the warm flesh of this gentle giant in the wild and to feel the soft springiness of her satin skin was holy.

It wasn't that she expected food; we couldn't have provided her kind of food anyway! No, she was magnetized. She wanted to see us and to be seen, to touch us and to be touched. She knew what she needed.

There is a Deep Need in Everything for Everything

We are not different from the whale. The Dalai Lama says:

> The need for love lies at the very foundation of human existence. It results from the profound interdependence we all share with one another.[12]

Allurement expresses the deep need of life for life.

We are more than woven together; we are utterly dependent for our existence on the life around us; dependent, as well, on all of existence that has gone before—animal, vegetable, mineral, and more . . . How difficult it is to admit need in our super-independent culture! Can we correct this blind spot? Other mammals recognize need; and they cross the gap between species to respond. We're familiar with the comfort a dog or another pet can offer when we are sad or lonely. They just know it, lean hard into our bodies and lick our hands or face. Now, the Storyteller tells of an empathic creature in the wild.

The Sea Lion

Our little craft bobbed in the vast crater of a submerged volcano in the Pacific, and the group we were with had decided

to snorkel. I knew I was out of their league! Still, I was *here*—
and would probably never again have such an opportunity. With
some trepidation, I had borrowed a mask and flippers from the
ship's supply, but now, looking down into the dark sea, I had
second thoughts: Though I had confidence snorkeling with my
own gear close to a beach or to rocks where I could 'touch base,'
here, we were suspended over the bottomless crater of a volcano! Was I mad? I gripped the side of the raft, anyway, slipped
the ill-fitting mask over my face, positioned the snorkel, and
slid down into the salt water. Facedown, I started to paddle
toward a nearby 'island'—part of the rim of the huge and hidden volcano.

The mask began to leak. Out of practice, I momentarily forgot how to clear it, and before I knew it, had a nose-full of water.
I looked out of habit for a footing so I could stand to adjust it,
but I was groping for a bottom that wasn't there! There was no
place to rest, and fathoms of water below me. I panicked, and
the mask took in more salt water as I thrashed about. Flailing, I
tore it off and threw it aside.

Out of the corner of my eye, a full-grown sea lion plowed
toward me from the shore where she'd been sunning. In seconds, she was swimming circles around me until she knew she
had my attention. Then, she rolled over on her back and showed
me how to float on the tide.

Many of us have experiences like this; then, push them
aside because they make no *sense* (and besides, no one would
believe us, if we told them!) However, if we pay attention to our
feelings of connection with other creatures and listen in a different way—what they have to teach us can be profound. In
her tales of the two fawns, the gray whale, and the sea lion, the
Storyteller dramatizes how empathy and need are woven into
the fact of relationship, and are often expressed through play.
Telling stories about animals, she shows us aspects of relationship that reflect a deeper kind of knowing. This knowing is not
thought, not theory. It is very subtly felt. And like the longing
for relationship, it is communicated not in words, but from *body*
to *body*.

She also reminds us that true relatedness requires risk, and that some creatures make themselves vulnerable to other species because they are in tune with something deep inside them—their own allurement.

The Dolphin

Once upon a time, I was allured to a dolphin, and responded from my heart. I heard a whispered suggestion that seemed impossible—and decided to follow it anyway. It was partly a matter of yearning, partly a matter of trust, but first, I had to quiet my intellect's argument. When it laughed at my idea, I told it firmly that it was behaving just like my *Homo erectus* grandfather—the one who thought his brother foolish when he tried to carry fire—then set my thinking self aside, temporarily.

o

The small Hawaiian lagoon sparkled in the morning sun. There was not a scrap of shade but I didn't mind. I was awaiting the dolphins. It was a local exhibit for some forty tourists standing along a narrow lagoon, and I felt like one of the kids there, as excited as if the circus were coming to town. We'd arrived early to watch the great sea turtles feed. Monsters, they measured three or four feet from end to end and moved deliberately about their habitat. Knowing food was coming, they were trying unsuccessfully to clamber up some slippery rocks, perhaps in the hope of getting the first bite. The park ranger, a young woman with an advanced degree in marine biology, gathered the little children around her and gave them fresh lettuce for the feeding. These children were serious. They wanted to learn. They listened carefully as the ranger lovingly explained how to feed the creatures, some of them hundreds of years old.

The feeding was like a ritual between an ancient species and a more recent one: between great age—wrinkled, cold, and slow moving—and warm and wide-eyed human young.

In an instant, the sounds of the small crowd changed abruptly—"*o-o-ohhhhhh!*"—as out of a gate at the far end of the lagoon, light flashed on silver. The group turned as one. Two gleaming young dolphins sailed through the air toward the tanned young trainer who called them by name. As I watched, I felt a kinship with these mammals, so close to my own species, yet at home in salt water. I was enchanted by their intelligence and the quality of joyful movement they displayed. They went through their paces, and after a while, one female had everyone's attention. She literally danced on water, then rode a surfboard and raced after a ball, tossing it back and forth to her teacher. They were playing 'catch.'

Lost in delight, I found myself remembering fragments of a friend's long-ago musings: *Do you suppose that dolphins and whales might have the same kind of unbroken consciousness we experience when we meditate? . . . They live and move in three dimensional space . . . they communicate across oceans . . . and they don't have hands to manipulate objects, so maybe they don't objectify things? . . . Maybe they don't perceive anything as separate from them? . . . Maybe their awareness is more inclusive than ours?*

The questions dissolved and in their place was a feeling of tenderness toward this lovely creature gliding across the lagoon. Then came the whispered inner suggestion. Ignoring my intellect, I said, "*Yes!*" and decided to make the experiment: I imagined my body hinged at the spine . . . pictured it opening along that seam like a warm peach, exposing the softest parts of me—heart, flesh, belly. And out of my core poured something I can only describe as *bodily love.*

It was an embrace-without-touching.

Quite given over to the moment, I didn't see the ball come at me from the far end of the lagoon, only felt a sudden, sharp *smash!* against my face and cried out in pain. The metal rims of my sunglasses dug deep into the bridge of my nose and it throbbed so intensely, I was sure it was broken. My eyes stung with tears, but it was as much from humiliation as from the impact.

It wasn't until much later that I realized that the young dolphin had *grokked* me,[13] and had responded as any friendly dolphin would have done with a companion. She wanted to play, and tossed me the ball, nose to nose, in the hope of having a game.

o

The dance with the dolphin was my first experience of its kind, one in which I reached out from within my body to express a felt relatedness to a creature from another species—and seemed to receive a response.

I suspect that you, too, have had moments with other creatures that seemed unparalleled—occasions when the connectedness between you was unmistakable. Perhaps, at that time, you heard or felt or sensed something that had been there all along. Perhaps, it had been out of awareness because it was out of sight.

Sometimes, what has been out of sight or hearing is suddenly perceived—I shall never forget the sound of a blue whale singing.

The Song of the Blue Whale

We stood on the deck of the expedition ship, spellbound. Below us, in the clear water swam an enormous blue whale. We could see the whole length of him, his flukes, his flippers, and his massive head. Then he dove out of sight. When he had completely disappeared, the ship's captain lowered a microphone into the ocean.

We heard the whale sing.

His song was like an ancient Gregorian chant—pure melody, with a free-flowing rhythm that lingered first on one note and then on another. The sound rose and then dipped, rose higher and fell again. It was the chant of an ever-constant, ever resonant *yearning*.

The captain told us that what we were hearing was this whale's own particular song, and that the song would continue to radiate throughout the waters of the world's oceans. The whale would begin to sing it again each year at the exact place in the music he'd left off the season before. He would continue to compose it for the rest of his life.

Several of us wept. We had heard his songline—the sound of allurement broadcast to all his companions in the deep.[14]

How did he know where to begin his song again? I wondered . . . *Where in his body had it waited for him? Do all animals have a howling or bleating or whistling songline somewhere inside them? If I listened, could I find my ancestors' chants alive and sounding in me?*

Why, you may ask, when human beings have so many problems with relationships, personal and collective, does the Storyteller focus on those between species? Why animals? And why stories about that early human animal, *Homo habilis,* who thrived on earth before she had words?

Relationship is Fundamental to Existence

Everything is in loving relationship. Animal, plant, human, we fell into being together."[15]

The spiritual journey takes us from the loneliness of life as an ego to a Way of relating that ego cannot understand. In all of these stories, there was a felt connection, a subtle bonding between two kinds of creatures. It is clear to me that the sea lion was responding to my distress, and that in the bay with the gray whales, human and sea animals sought to touch and look at one another. It also feels true that the dolphin had asked me to play. We were all participating in the greater allurement, the larger Love. And though we'll never be able to define this kind of love, these stories demonstrate that it is not rooted in human thought. Unmistakably, each experience of relatedness took place *between the bodies* of creatures from different species.

The Body Loves

The whale's sonorous chant is an energy that resonates throughout the planet's oceans, a vocal embrace-without-touching that creates a living communion with whales the world over. Sound waves never end. Neither do the energies of Love. These energies are something we, as a species, haven't yet understood. They also radiate—but in a different mode.

Love Is Radiated, Not Spoken

With these stories, I've hoped to illuminate what is omitted by thought; to shine a light into places we don't often look—places not of the mind. In these scenes of intimacy between creatures, something else begins to come through, something prior to/*beyond* our thinking, a depth and dimension of reality that has been *entos*: in/*around*/*between* us from the Beginning.

Someday We Shall Harness for God the Energies of Love

The energies of Love in Teilhard's magnificent koan belong to the greater Life: to nature, to the universe, to the divine. They are not supernatural. They are subtle—sent and received *at depth*. These energies are registered beneath thinking; beneath feeling, seeing, hearing, and touching. I am suggesting that many of us cannot access this dimension of existence because we are immersed in thought—nay, run by it. But when we learn to let go of the loop that goes round and round in our minds and does not stop—we can.

The energies of Love are registered in an interior stillness. In our culture, it will take a leap of faith to quiet down. Something about our restlessness tells us that. The irritable highs—the intensity of work, the highway's speed, and a media that serves up thrills and special effects—trick us into thinking that we are more alive. In fact, they obliterate our innate aliveness: They keep us from feeling our joy and our pain—and from engaging the energies of Love. Inured to chaos, trapped in contractions, and imprisoned by thought, we have lost our connection—this radical, whole-bodied intimacy with life, seen *and unseen*, that *is* Consciousness.

The New Consciousness Is Relationship

In the universe, among the stars and planets, it is silent. The grass does not speak. Within the heart of a tree or a plant, it is quiet. The water of the lake is still. The deer in the field, the hawk on a branch, the tiny lizard, poised, throat pulsing, tend to silence. But their minds are not empty. They are filled, not with the staccato of self-talk, but with the Life they inhabit.

When we rest in that Stillness, we find ourselves in the mysterious place of the gap. In the gap, we don't know *about* what surrounds us in our usual objective way. *We are continuous with it.* We *are* it. Here, we are connected to all that is. We live life as a continuum-without-edges because we *are* life, not separate from it.

This is the quality of being I call 'soul,' and Parker Palmer points the way to it:

> The soul is like a wild animal. . . . It seeks safety in the dense underbrush. . . . If we want to see a wild animal, the last thing we should do is go crashing through the woods yelling for it to come out. But if we will walk quietly into the woods, sit patiently at the base of a tree, breathe with the earth, and fade into our surroundings, the wild creature we seek might put in an appearance. . . . [It] is not about solving a visible problem: it is about honoring an invisible thing called the soul. . . . [Only then can] we learn to trust the invisible powers within us . . .[16]

Palmer and the Storyteller are suggesting that we are *intended*—that we have an innate tendency—to communion, but that in our thinking mode, we are asleep to it. It is not the fact of thought that is at issue; it is our *inability to withdraw our attention from thought*. When we are imprisoned by an allegiance to thought, that gift—that blessing/*wound*—increasingly obliterates Presence, the dynamic energies of Love.

The wild, two-million-year old creature inside you knows this; and she will show up if you walk quietly, wait, and listen. But the key to your prison door is your preparation. It will show you how to *be*.

Our preparation softens our contractions and relaxes our judgments. It helps us let go of our need to know. It also teaches us how to live in relationship to the mystery of our own bodies.

It is the body that awakens—the entire bodymind with its innate sensitivity to the sea of energies in which we live. 'Out of our minds,' embodied, we participate in the oneness of being. We cannot live in this communion and have the answer. We cannot be in such intimate relationship and be in control. We cannot exist in unbroken wholeness and leave anyone out. It is the end of loneliness, as we know it.

To enter this communion, we turn, and like the ship's microphone dropped into the ocean, drop our attention into the Love that bathes us. We listen with *ears to hear* for the soundless sound of the ineffable whisper—the eternal song that calls us Home.

Let the music begin.

Endnotes for Interlude

1   Dogen (1200-1253), was the founder of Soto-Zen or Dogen-Zen. Source unknown.

2   Ursula King, *Spirit of Fire*, 58.

3   T. S. Eliot, "Little Gidding," *Collected Poems 1909-1962*, 208-9.

4   Genesis 32:22-31.

5   The verb *to bless* comes from the French, *blesser*, which means *to wound*. Related to blood (*blod* in Old English, *blut* in German) it describes sprinkling an altar with blood sacrifices and other means of marking with blood.

6   Jennifer Paine Welwood, excerpt from "Unconditional," *Poems for the Path*, 1998, 21.

7   Brian Swimme, PhD, whose first calling as a mathematical astrophysicist was to gravitational attraction, calls attraction on any scale 'allurement.'

8   Donald Culross Peattie, *An Almanac for Moderns*, quoted in Heron Dance Journal, March 2004.

9   David Quammen, *Natural Acts,* as quoted in *Heron Dance Journal*, April 2004 (abridged): "Animal play is common, at least among certain mammals, especially in the young. Play—by definition—serves no immediate biological function for survival and reproduction. Ravens play toss with themselves in the air, dropping and catching again a small twig. They lie on their backs and juggle objects (in one recorded case, a rubber ball) between beak and feet. Crows perform for other crows: tip backward dizzily from a wire perch, holding a loose grip so as to hang upside down, spreading out both wings, then daringly letting go with one foot; finally, switching feet to let go with the other, all. "

10 Every fall, hundreds of female gray whales migrate from the Bering Sea to the safety of San Ignacio Lagoon in Baja California where they give birth to their 2000-pound infants. Here, safe from the killer whales and other predators in the wider ocean, they remain to nurse and train their calves before the spring return migration, a 10,000 mile round trip.

11 When whales were still being hunted, they had a reputation for being vicious. "The first whale in modern times known to scientists and the native Mexican populace to approach humans was in 1977. Charles Scammon, a nineteenth century whaler . . . related that some whalers harpooned calves in order to lure the mothers within killing range. . . . 'The mother, in her frenzy, will chase the boats, overturn them with her head or dash them in pieces with a stroke of her ponderous flukes.' . . . Such attacks endured long after the species received belated partial protection from commercial whaling in 1937. . . .
"In 1977, researchers Steven Swartz and Mary Lou Jones wrote that '(a whale dubbed) Amazing Grace, doubtless moved by . . . curiosity, first indicated we would be welcome if we came in peace. . . . From our very first encounter with her, she readily adopted us along with our 14-foot inflatable boat as her personal toys. She would roll under our boat, turn belly up . . . then lift us clear off the surface of the lagoon perched on her chest between her massive flippers. . . . Grace would often lie quietly alongside the boat to be rubbed. . . . She was the exception rather than the rule . . . friendly whales find you, you don't find them.'" *National Geographic*, June 1987.

12 The Dalai Lama. An undated selection from 'Thought for the Day' from *http://www.wisdomatwork.com*

13 The word *grok* was 'Martian language' first used by Robert Heinlein in his 1961 science-fiction novel, *Stranger in a Strange Land*. It literally meant "to drink," but metaphorically, it meant "to take it all in," or to "be at one with." In Heinlein's view of quantum theory, *grokking* was the intermingling of intelligence that necessarily affected both the observer and the observed. As a character in the novel said: "'*Grok*' means to understand so thoroughly that the observer becomes a part of the observed—to merge, blend . . . lose identity in group experience. It means almost everything that we mean by religion, philosophy, and science. . . [But we don't yet get it] because of our Earthly assumptions." Retrieved online 2007 at *http://en.wikipedia.org/wiki/Grok*

14 Brian Swimme's response to this chapter was eloquent: "You've shown how the whole ocean is filled with song; the whole ocean, filled with compassion."

15 *http://www.RichardMoss.com*

16 Parker Palmer, *A Hidden Wholeness*, San Francisco: Jossey-Bass, 2004, 58-9, 66.

The Unknown

Artist unknown, Kyoto, Japan, 19th Century

Home—The Soul's Ground

God is at home. It is we who have gone out
for a walk.

Meister Eckhart[1]

Shortly after 1868, an artist in Kyoto, Japan spread before him
a small two-panel folding paper screen. On it, he painted a pair
of Japanese yellow buntings, vivid green and yellow birds with
sharp, black and white details. They perch in a maple tree, itself
unseen except for a rough, somewhat blurred branch that he
inked in darkly along one edge and a few small branches with
deep, orange leaves. The birds look so real they might fly away
in the next breath.

Before he painted the screen, the artist applied thin squares
of silver leaf to the paper and painted them over with a very subtle gold. The sometimes-gold/sometimes-silver leaf reflects the
movement of natural light by day and the flickering of candlelight by night. Its effect is a soft shimmering: a quality of living
light that shifts and changes as one moves across the room in
front of the painting.

There is no horizon in this golden/silver space. Instead, the
artist has created a luminous ground with a life of its own—a
field of energy and movement that expresses more than backdrop, more than air, more than sky. When I look at his work,

I make a slight but unmistakable shift of attention from the figures of the birds to luminous gold ground—and my entire perspective changes. I see, in a sense, with different 'eyes'—with a larger self that interacts with the moving background and its contents. The effect on my body is unmistakable. The painting's luminosity is *felt*.

This is how I'm learning to interact with life. I don't find it easy, but when I shift my attention from figure to ground—from a tree, for example, to the space that flows between and beyond its leaves—something inside me softens. What lies before me is no longer an object, for I fall into place in the scene. With my attention on this quality of spaciousness, everything changes. I am no longer separate; I have come Home.

The presence of Home is everywhere. If I could paint it, it would be like the gold that grounds and surrounds the birds in the painting. But like words, a work of art can only hint at it, for Home is not merely external. It is inside, outside, and throughout—*everything*.[2] Philip Newell speaks of it as 'light,' but this is not the light we think we know: neither visible light, nor the opposite of darkness. *It is the heart of life*:

> The whole fabric of creation is woven through with the thread of God's light. It is like a material shot through with silk. If somehow this thread were removed the whole of creation would unravel.[3]

We long for solid ground. We want the assurance of something we can see and feel, something tangible on which to rest. But this Home is neither tangible nor visible. It is *alive*. Like the light in the painting, Home is a vibrant, ever-changing matrix—a boundless energetic presence. It has substance as a thundercloud boiling overhead has substance, and its energies are felt—known, not by the mind but by one's entire being.

Home has neither beginning nor end, is neither here nor there. It is not a place; not a thing. It is power. Something substantive among/*beyond*/*within* us, it is holy. This inexpressible and inexhaustible Presence is the field in which we live, the Song that sings us alive.

Endnotes for Home—The Soul's Ground

1 Meister Eckhart. Source unknown.

2 All of us have had moments of grace when this invisible reality has penetrated our lives, yet we are dependent on language tied to space and time to articulate a paradox that is subject to neither. In *The Dancing Animal Woman*, Home was symbolized by the universe and more immediately, by the earth. It seemed the best way to express the sacredness of the tangible world and at the same time, point beyond nature to the spaciousness within which it turned. Images for the sacred—whether the gold in the painting, or the earth, the universe, or other symbols—call us to *return* and at the same time, to *go beyond*. The use of return/*go beyond* reaffirms the tension between two different views of union: One view sees it as identification with an underlying ground or a return; the other stresses a union with a higher, transcendent center or one that is yet to come. Theologian, Paul Tillich, embraces both dimensions by calling this origin/*destination* the 'Ground of all Being.' This Ground is the depth and vastness of our own being/*the depth and vastness of Being*.

3 J. Philip Newell, *The Book of Creation, An Introduction to Celtic Spirituality*, New York: Paulist Press, 1999. *Author's note:* Newell is a Scottish mystic of the Anglican tradition and has been warden of Iona Abbey.

So late in coming, Love?
So quiet a step
through the open gate

So gentle a trespass
I didn't feel you enter

Or even know
You had arrived
and filled me
like a river at flood

Until you spilled over,
took me with you
banks and all

Into your vast
and infinite

Ocean

11 Awakening the Energies of Love

> Light up a fire of love in thy soul,
> Burn all thought and expression away!
> Moses, they that know the conventions are of
>   one sort;
> They whose souls burn are of another.
>
> Rumi[1]

Rumi points to the difference between a conventional understanding of religious meaning and the Fire of Moses' awakening. The ultimate value of awakening is a new awareness of the living Presence of Love—and the souls of the awakened burn with it. They radiate Love like the heat from a fire or the sound of a blue whale singing. They radiate *light*.

Love Is Not Consolation—It Is Light[2]

Those who have awakened to the mystery of Love are lights. Persons such as Jesus, the Buddha, and Mohammed are luminous—exceptional Carriers of the *Fire*. Treasured vehicles of the Unknown, they are conduits of its power.

Others who have awakened are also lights, part of an infinite continuum of illumination. Mystics like Rumi and

Meister Eckhart are lights, as are Lao Tse, Blaise Pascal, and Pierre Teilhard de Chardin. More recent are Thomas Merton, Krishnamurti, Paramahansa Yogananda, and Franklin Merrell-Wolff. In our time, Richard Moss, Eckhart Tolle, Adyashanti, Ellen Grace O'Brian, and many others, known and unknown, follow in this long lineage. Among those represented on the ongoing trajectory are humanity's greatest poets, scientists, artists, composers, and philosophers—along with countless ordinary people. Living and dead, they are all Carriers of the energies of Love.

Shining with something we cannot see,[3] their light magnetizes the soul. You recognize them, not through what you hear them say or see them do, but *through their conductivity*. The more time you spend in the Presence of these men and women—however you attend that Presence, be it in person, in meditation, or another means of inquiry—the more sensitive you become to what they emanate. As you learn to *listen with ears to hear*, something within your bodymind becomes capable of detecting increasingly subtle signals. When it registers the energy of Presence, it knows Who they are.

Transpersonal psychologist, Michael Washburn calls this energy "the power of the Ground":

> The power of the Ground is a force that, under certain conditions is discernable not only subjectively but also physically. This . . . movement of the power of the Ground within the body begins once primal repression is lifted . . . and is [physically discernable] only by those in whom the power of the Ground has become active as spirit.[4]

The power of the Ground is like a magnetic field, and this power radiates through those who have awakened. When their attention to the divine is whole and undivided, all thought of self has fallen away. In such moments, these persons are as transparent to the energies of Love as a clear pane of glass to sunlight.

In a statement central to his teaching, Richard Moss describes this availability to Life as a gift:

> The greatest gift you can give to another person is the quality of your attention.

What he refers to is far more than giving one's full attention to another. The gift these persons give is the *quality of their attention to the Ground*, which allows its power to flow through them. It is a physical transmission—a current—a palpable bodily communion that affects you profoundly over time, whether or not you are initially able to feel it. In this presence of Presence, *you are transformed*. You do not change yourself; you are a receiver.

An old proverb declares:

> The iron is put in a magnetic field until it becomes a magnet.

Life's gift of awakening to the communion of Love is a 'non-action' like the *wu-wei* of Taoist teaching, and carries a transformative energy that changes lives, heals, serves. Isak Dinesen eloquently describes its outcome as an eternal bond:

> There are many things in life which a human being . . . may attain by personal endeavor. But there exists a true humanity, which will ever remain a gift, and which is to be accepted by one human being as it is given to him by a fellow human. The one who gives has himself been a receiver. In this way, link by link, a chain is made from land to land and from generation to generation. Rank, wealth and nationality in this matter all go for nothing. The poor and downtrodden can hand over the gift to kings, and kings will pass it on to their favorites at Court or to an itinerant dancer in their city. . . . Strange and wonderful is it to consider how in such community we are bound to foreigners whom we have never seen and to dead men and women whose names we have never heard and shall never hear, more closely even than if we were all holding hands.[5]

It is the original laying on of hands.

o

Thus far, in our exploration, we've focused on the more gradual kind of awakening in which we are all participants; one that operates in accordance with nature's conserving wisdom. In the midst of such a slow unfolding, however, it is difficult to illustrate the *fundamental difference* between our ordinary subject/object consciousness and the fullness of the consciousness of

Love. This Consciousness is not simply an extension of thought. It lies across the gap from thought—even though it is already present in us. We are far more than our minds and hearts and bodies. If only we might realize it!

The Mystic

There are mystics, past and present, however, who have awakened to the Presence of Love and it is vividly reflected in their lives. Wide-awake to its energies, they are our mirrors, and in their words, we catch a glimpse of *who we really are*.

This chapter allows us to hear some of the voices of those mystics who've suddenly awakened to Love and who, therefore, can be our guides. Though some of them describe their experiences in similar terms, it will still be hard for us to imagine what they mean. But should we, too, suddenly awaken to this Mystery, their words will have helped to prepare us for what we *see*: For in the wonder of that moment, *everything* we know will have changed—our perception of reality, our sense of identity, our motivation, and our lives.

Matthew Fox[6] has said many times, "We all have a scientist and a mystic inside." The scientist in us breaks things down in order to understand them. The mystic in us helps to bind them together again.

"Mysticism," writes Evelyn Underhill, using the religious language of the church ". . . is the direct intuition or experience of God."[7] Underhill, the renowned historian of the mystics, includes all of us in her definition of a mystic: "Every human soul has a certain latent capacity for God," she continues, "and . . . in some, this capacity is realized with an astonishing richness. . . . Such a realization may be of many kinds and degrees—personal or impersonal, abrupt and ecstatic, or peaceful and continuous. . . . If we take all of these experiences together . . . we find that they are, as a matter of fact, the actual foundation on which all the great faiths are built."[8]

Underhill sees the mystics throughout history as the world's spiritual pioneers. She emphasizes that the mystical experience of waking up to reality is, indeed, one of communion, and adds,

"This communion, in all its varying forms and degrees, is always a communion of love . . . . Mystics never keep their discoveries to themselves," she writes. "They have a social meaning, and always try to tell others what they have known."[9]

In this chapter, we turn to some of their 'tellings,' mindful that any attempt to express discoveries like theirs is like trying to lasso water. Our own experiences and our choice of words to express them may differ from theirs, but we share the same dilemma:

> *How to articulate the experience of awakening to the Presence that the mystics called God?*

I Am

As I sat in the garden one morning before dawn, the image of Moses' encounter with a burning bush in the wilderness arose in my mind:

> Now Moses led his flock to the far side of the desert and came to a mountain where he saw a bush on fire, yet it didn't burn up. God called to him from within the bush, *"Moses! Moses! Take off your sandals, for the place where you are standing is holy ground."* Moses hid his face, because he was afraid. God said, "I am sending you to Pharaoh to bring my people out of Egypt." But Moses said to God, "Who am I, that I should go? Suppose I go and say, 'The God of your fathers has sent me to you,' and they ask me, 'What is his name?' Then what shall I tell them?" God said to Moses, *"Say to the Israelites: 'I AM has sent me to you.'"*[10]

In the darkness that morning under the stars, I heard Moses' story from a new perspective. I had always seen in my mind's eye the vivid picture of a burning bush painted for me in Sunday School. This time, I recognized with a shock that Moses might have been trying to express something quite different from what I'd understood as a child. I began to ask for the first time whether Moses' *Fire* might not have been an inward one—and if the blaze that had confounded him might have been like that of St. Teresa of Avila who, in her love for God blurted, *"my head is on fire!"*

Her words evoke the passionate awakening that those mystics describe who have experienced an abrupt realization of *I AM*. More than an insight or feeling, more than imagined 'bliss,' they have been struck like a gong in the midst of the ordinary by a profound revelation, a sudden entrance into what might be called a direct perception of truth—a spontaneous awakening to the larger Life that lies *behind* the life we see.

As I sat there in the silence, I mused: If Moses' burning bush was, indeed, an awakening, what did *he* think it was? Perhaps, in his dumbfounded condition, he perceived its explosive aliveness as something outside of himself—a projection.[11] We cannot know, of course, but however he understood the phenomenon that had seized him, he communicated its intensity with an image—*Fire*.

I have since learned that the images we see as young children tend to construct our worldview.[12] No image, however, can convey the fullness of what someone like Moses may have been trying to express—something behind/beneath/*beyond* what he could conceive. The point, however, is this: *How did his listeners hear him?* Since they had no comparable personal experience to draw on, they had no choice but to see the scene as concretely as I'd imagined it in childhood. They listened to the phenomenon he described, saw a bush that raged with fire yet 'didn't burn up'—and passed the story on.

The people of that long-ago desert tribe heard Moses' tale, not *with ears to hear,* as Jesus later admonished his listeners, but *with their thoughts.* They could not know that the *Fire* of Moses' story was a metaphor for the overwhelming energies of Love. No ordinary Love, this: Moses recognized it as the Divine, a power that called itself, *"I AM."* No wonder he took off his shoes—for where he stood, indeed, was holy ground.

A similar Old Testament story is that of Elijah's awakening in the book of Kings:

> And as Elijah and Elisha went on walking and talking together, behold a fiery chariot and fiery horses parted them both asunder; and [all] of a sudden Elijah was caught up by a whirlwind into heaven. . . .[13]

The stories of Moses and Elijah contain images of immense power—a fire, a whirlwind, and a fiery chariot—to express an unspeakable moment of communion. Each image conveys that this communion is hardly the static circle of devout and angelic beings some people might imagine. *It is dynamic and alive.*

A third mystic, Pierre Teilhard de Chardin, was a scientist, a paleontologist, and a Jesuit priest whose excavations of life— inner and outer—has stirred the creativity of countless others. He included in his autobiography two stories of the inward *Fire,* his own mystical experiences of union.[14] Because he is more our contemporary, he used modern language: He described, not a fire or a whirlwind, but an intense *energy* that seemed to be outside him yet also poured into his body—and he felt it intensely:

> First I noticed the vibrant atmosphere which formed a halo . . . [that] radiated into Infinity. . . . [and] in which could be seen a continuous pulsing surge.
> *The whole Universe was vibrating.* And yet when I tried to look at the details one by one, I found them still as sharply drawn, their individual character still intact.
> This scintillation of beauties was so total, so all-embracing . . . so swift, that it reached down into the very powerhouse of my being, flooding through it in one surge, so that my whole self vibrated to the very core of me, with a full note of explosive bliss that was completely and utterly unique.[15]

Teilhard's abrupt awakening to the powerful energies of Love is what Underhill called a "direct intuition or experience of God . . . the foundation on which all the great faiths are built. . . . a communion of love." He felt radically alive—alive from his root *(L. radix),* his core. He was Home.

Teilhard ended his story by saying it was about a "man whose soul was in instinctive communication with the unique Life of all things."[16] This conscious awakening to the soul's "instinctive communication with the unique Life of all things" is described in the traditions of both East and West. Morihei Ueshiba was history's greatest martial artist. His was the Way of Aikido, "The Art of Peace." One day in 1942, after a match in which he had defeated a formidable swordsman, he went down into his garden. As he entered it, he was stunned by something so powerful, it seemed almost to be a vision:

> Suddenly the earth trembled. Golden vapor welled up from the ground and engulfed me. I felt transformed into a golden image, and my body seemed as light as a feather. All at once, I understood the nature of creation: the Way of a Warrior is to manifest Divine Love, a spirit that embraces and nurtures all things. Tears of gratitude and joy streamed down my cheeks. I saw the entire earth as my home, and the sun, moon, and stars as my intimate friends. All attachment to material things vanished.[17]

His communion with existence was not a vision, but a radical awakening to Love.

However Moses, Elijah, Teilhard, or Ueshiba described their encounters—fire or whirlwind, energy or golden vapor— something utterly unfamiliar poured into the place where each one stood. They'd had a life-changing experience with an overwhelming Thou that both lived outside who they knew themselves to be—yet filled them.

Such a mystical awakening, says Franciscan, Richard Rohr:

> is precisely not like the layers of an onion. It's one great truth that you know in a moment. . . . You don't work up to it. It's not cumulative. It's an epiphany.[18]

Envisioning a Mystical Awakening

This is a moment when language fails. We've come to the edge of a precipice and are about to leave the familiar behind.

I invite you to join me in an experiment—a 'walk between the worlds' with a present-day mystic. To do so, you'll need to abandon the sharp focus of your intellect, and instead, proceed with soft eyes, a soft heart, and an open mind. The following story is told as if it were your own. If you can enter the experience with me, perhaps the mystics' stories, combined with your own moments of wonder, will add to your sense of the matchless power of an awakening—and of that mysterious energetic

Field so like the gold in the Japanese painting—the nameless, timeless, formless Presence.

o

Quite unexpectedly one day, like a jewel sparkling in the sunlight, Love stands at your doorstep. You don't recognize it, at first, for in this moment, you have no expectations at all. In fact, you've been thinking to yourself as you sit in the familiar conference room, *Why did I come here? I had plans to be with friends this evening, yet at home this noon, when I was standing in my kitchen, it was as if something had suddenly picked me up and turned me around—then put me back down in the opposite direction. I still don't really know why I'm waiting with this handful of people to hear a speaker I've never even heard of! How strange* . . . But you settle down anyway and wait, because the speaker is the respected teacher of a friend who'd asked you to come to hear her.

Now a woman enters the room. She is perhaps in her early sixties and wears a plain white blouse and a long dark skirt. She talks for a short time, tells a little about her childhood and her own awakening, then sits quietly before the small group in a straight chair, her hands folded. She is utterly ordinary. After a moment's quiet, she suggests that you simply sit with your eyes open. You sit . . . and the small room becomes very, very still as she begins to meditate. . . . That's all she does.

You watch. You are very alert. The silence deepens . . .

Suddenly, something in you—not sense nor sight nor sound nor smell but *some other faculty*—beholds a vast and boiling ocean that pours itself into the room/*into you* and leaves you streaming with energy. You are stunned. You occupy the same space and time as usual, yet in this moment, they seem infinite. You feel as if you have been blown open, your boundaries exploded, and stretched wide. *Who you are* is no longer bounded by the limits of your body, your life experience, or your mind; they have been forever shattered.

It is ecstatic.
The edges of me
are gone—

Where space was
is filled to overflowing

with
Substance
Presence

—Thou—

The room is filled with a radiance that *moves*. It seems at
once to compress itself, to squeeze down toward the woman so
still before you, and then to expand. It squeezes down and then
expands . . . again . . . and again. The light has substance.

The very air afire—
alive, incandescent,
thick with itself like soup . . .

Is someone dimming the lights? your mind asks, and you turn
out of habit to look, but the light isn't dimming. It has *weight*. It
is like a power so vast, so much greater than yourself, yet somehow, it is *in you*, flooding you. The intensity of it is palpable. It
pervades every atom of your body. An unmistakable Presence, it
is immediate and intimate and fills your whole being—and you
know it to be Holy.

The weight of You! Your density,
The room, my heart, the universe
—filled—
and I, for the first time,
perceive

Immensity.

The moment is compelling and unparalleled. It is as if
there had been an opening into Life itself and you had stepped

through. You are magnetized, pulled out of who you thought you were—and set free. You feel sensations greater than the impact of G's on your body when a plane comes out of a dive. It is an eruption eclipsing an orgasm.

No mirage or psychosis, this. Something fundamental has changed. A beacon has sliced through your life, and you feel an immediate, bodily connection to an aliveness you never knew existed, one that is both inside/*outside* you at once. There is no division of any kind. You are fulfilled and somehow complete.[19]

In the midst of this timeless experience, *you know immortality*. You know it; but you don't know *how* you know it . . .

There is a solidity to this moment and it becomes your touchstone for life. *It is your rock.* And you realize that nothing you do, nothing you know, not any of your activities or anything else in your life matter as much as—*This*.

It is what you have been seeking.

The next day I went running back
but it was gone—

Not the density though,
not the river pouring through my being,
not the root change in orientation

or the promises I made
to sing praises always . . .

o

The universal potential for awakening is our birthright. Many of us have had glimpses—moments so filled with awe and a sense of oneness, they can only be called holy. They show us that the awakening process is occurring in different degrees and in a variety of ways, all the time. Few of us will know the kind of illumination that so astonished the saints; but after any such moment of grace, we may want some kind of confirmation. We can find it in the lives of the mystics whose awakenings are called by many names—openings, illuminations, realizations—and come in many variations.

Like a great chorus, these mystics sing as one, and now, we'll begin to hear their voices. Some, like Teilhard, tell how they experienced a series of awakenings over a long period. Others speak of spontaneous openings to Mystery that lasted for minutes or hours; still others say days or months.

In fifteenth century India, Kabir had a direct experience of the greater Reality. What he saw—but not with his eyes—and heard—but not with his ears—went beyond the ken of intellect. His was the briefest of illuminations, but it gave him profound insights into truth, spirituality, and the nature of man that have made him one of the world's most beloved philosophers. He wrote of his awe at the unity he perceived:

> Everything is swinging: heaven, earth, water, fire,
>   and the secret one slowly growing a body.
> Kabir saw this for fifteen seconds,
>   and it made him a servant for life.[20]

For Blaise Pascal, the great seventeenth century mathematician and philosopher, the advent of the second *Fire* at the age of thirty-one was a religious conversion. A life-changing event, it revolutionized the focus of his writing and his work. He never forgot that night. After his death, a servant found the scrap of parchment he'd sewn into his doublet on which he'd written,

> On Monday 23rd November 1654, from half past ten til half past twelve, *Fire!*

Pascal called it his "night of fire" and described it as an encounter with God—but he was emphatic: it was not the God perceived by thought:

> The God of Abraham, the God of Isaac. The God of Jacob. Not of the philosophers and intellectuals.[21]

Hildegarde of Bingen, mystic, poet, artist, and physician, gave the *Fire* a voice:

> I, the fiery life of divine essence, am aflame beyond the beauty of the meadows. I gleam in the waters. I burn in the sun, moon, and stars. With every breeze, as with invisible life that contains everything, *I awaken everything to life.*[22]

Eight-hundred years later, Thomas Merton echoed her language of fire. He described the awakening that culminates what he called a "true education" as

> not so much a stable entity which one finds but a spark that was an event, an explosion . . .[23]

The spark is like the energy from the finger of God arcing toward Adam on the Sistine Chapel ceiling. Some people are struck by it and then forget. Others don't recognize what has happened to them; briefly stunned, they gather their will and go on their way. Many may be amazed and gratified by the experience but don't realize its significance, nor do they seek to find out. Still others may have had a major awakening early in life, but at the time, had no idea what it meant. If no one around them explained it to them—or if the church or conserving community dismissed their experience or made it wrong—they pushed it aside and never 'realized' it. Though many of this latter group go on to live good lives in admirable service to others, they have no idea of the gift they still carry within them. As I hear him, Jesus was describing these kinds of outcomes in the following parable:

> Behold there went out a sower to sow: And it came to pass, as he sowed, some fell by the wayside . . . . And some fell on stony ground where it had not much earth, and immediately it sprang up because it had no depth of earth: but when the sun was up, it was scorched; and because it had no root, it withered away. And some fell among thorns, and the thorns grew up and choked it, and it yielded no fruit. But some fell on good ground and did yield fruit that sprang up and increased . . .[24]

When he explains the parable to his disciples, he speaks of "hearing the word, the secret of the kingdom of God."[25] I infer, however, that he was not talking about hearing literal words but about *receiving and incarnating the energies of Love.*

To hear any parable differently tends to throw us into uncertainty, but uncertainty is a doorway to the new. Then a parable can be transformative.[26] In the earlier but lesser-known *Gospel According to Thomas*, Jesus tells exactly the same parable and immediately amplifies it by saying,

I have cast
A fire upon the world,
And I rekindle it
Until it burns.[27]

The mystery of this kind of *Fire* will land on many, but how it is received and whether it is lived or dissipates depends on a person's capacity to tolerate its power. This *Fire* has introduced a radically different mode of perception than thought—and intellect refuses to go there. A biographer described Father Bede Griffiths' own effort to bear it:

> The confusion that ensued with him between his rational mind and his spirit almost broke him. He sought out a retreat during which he fasted, prayed all night until tears flooded him and he had a tremendous breakthrough. . . . [Much later Griffiths said], "I was no longer the center of my own life."[28]

Vimala Thakar, the contemporary mystic from India, wrote after her awakening:

> Something within has been let loose. It can't stand any frontiers. The invasion of a new awareness, irresistible and uncontrollable . . . has swept away everything.

Within less than a year, the spiritual master Krishnamurti[29] confirmed her awakening and urgently implored her to begin to teach. She quotes his letter:

> Why don't you explode? Why don't you put bombs under all these people who follow the wrong line? Why don't you go around India? There is not time. . . . Go shout from the housetops, 'You are on the wrong track! This is not the way to peace!' Go out and set them on fire!

Krishnamurti's words ignited her to action and Thakar wrote her friends again:

> The burning ashes became aflame. . . . No words could describe the intensity and depth of the experience through which I am passing. Everything is changed.[30]

The Presence she'd encountered motivated her to become a servant to the people of India, and as a leader of the Land Gift Movement there, to speak all over the world.

How to Articulate the Presence that the Mystics Call God

No matter the nature of his experience, the mystic stammers. As we have seen, many try to express the gift of a spontaneous awakening by turning to the elements—earth, air, fire, hurricane, light, and water—which at least provide a common language for a consciousness impossible to describe. The late philosopher, Franklin Merrell-Wolff, was a professor of mathematics at Stanford and a rare example of the mystic who followed an intellectual Way. Very careful of words, he used the philosophical term, *"the Universal Self,"* but still added the image of a flame:

> Realization of the Universal Self is never . . . cause[d] . . . by the individual man acting in space and time. . . . His efforts prepare the Candle . . . but the Flame is lighted through a spontaneous act of Spirit.[31]

Later, he called the energies that suffused his body *"the Current"*:

> [It is] a Current of gentle Joy that penetrates through and through. . . . It appears as of the nature of a fluid, for there is a sense of "flowing through." . . . All over, . . . there is a quality that may well be described as physiological happiness.[32]

Being a scholar, Merrell-Wolff wanted to understand these joyful energies flowing in his body—and he worked hard to find out what would make them reappear. But the Current simply came and went. He could no more predict its arrival than St. John:

> The wind bloweth where it listeth, and thou hearest the sound thereof, but canst not tell whence it cometh, and whither it goeth.[33]

After many years, Merrell-Wolff found that if he wanted to remain in this fundamental relationship, he had to let go of trying to understand it. He learned, instead, simply to abide in the Presence of the Current, and after that surrender, experienced it as a form of Intelligence:

a ceaselessly flowing and self-contained stream . . . [one that] *com-prehends the totality that appears in the universe of objects* . . . [a] stream of nourishment.[34]

I tend to think that this ceaseless current is what Jesus meant when he said:

[I] will give you living water . . . . And the water that I shall give will turn into a spring inside . . .[35]

One of my favorite mystics, Mechtilde of Magdeburg, lived in Germany in the thirteenth century. Instead of taking an intellectual path like Merrell-Wolff's, she followed one that led her through her body. Mechtilde also wrote about a current. Her imagery described a body alive with what she called "*the Flowing*":

Wouldst thou know my meaning?
Lie down in the Fire
See and taste the Flowing
Godhead through thy being;
Feel the Holy Spirit
Moving and Compelling
Thee within the Flowing
Fire and Light of God.[36]

What a magnificent and earthy expression of the *Fire,* the energetic flow permeating reality! Carol Lee Flinders, a biographer of the mystics, comments:

Mechtilde . . . had absolutely no use for abstractions . . . . The astonishing concreteness of her imagery—its unembarrassed physicality . . . [are] intimations of an awakening into supreme joy . . .

Flinders also reminds us how this mystic's 'telling' also got her in trouble:

Asking herself at one point why she continued to write despite fierce censure, she said, "I cannot nor do I wish to write, except I see it with the eyes of my soul, and I hear it with the ears of my eternal spirit and feel it in all the members of my body: the power of the Holy Spirit. . . ." Describing the soul's relationship with God, she marvels at "the powerful penetration of all things and the special intimacy which exists between God and each individual soul."[37]

This is the passionate body. Its early formation is described at length in *The Dancing Animal Woman*. Heard within our everyday framework, some may pick up their ears at the phrase and imagine sex, but this is intercourse of a different sort: an ongoing and total engagement with life by what contemporary mystic Eckhart Tolle calls "the Joy Body." The passionate body is sensitive to ever-greater nuance—it is awake, alert, and streaming palpably with the Current. More than pleasure, more than happiness, the mystic's experience of the passionate body is one of incomprehensible aliveness; an intimacy with the Current—a continuum with it—fed by it, guided by it.

This is where her attention lies.

While most of us are being gradually introduced to this depth of reality, the mystic who encounters it consciously, finds herself radically changed. She will be forever different. As Franciscan Richard Rohr said, *"You can never go back."*[38]

> *The mystic sees and hears everything differently.*
> *The mystic lives in conscious communion with the*
>   *larger life/Life.*
> *The mystic's sense of identity changes.*
> *The mystic accesses life and relationship differently.*
> *The mystic is motivated differently.*

The Mystic Sees and Hears Everything Differently

Something happens to the mystic's perception after awakening to the energies of Love. The Rev. Ellen Grace O'Brian describes it this way:

> To have a direct experience of the Presence within which we have lived all our lives is like having lived in a dark room—and then the darkness vanishes.[39]

The Mystic Lives in Conscious Communion With the Larger Life

Mystics have found a way to walk like the shaman between the worlds. Along with the 'daylight mind' we all use, they nurture the 'inner dusk' *at the same time.* They know themselves to be separate persons, and simultaneously, experience a deeply felt bond with all of life. Teilhard's account, describes this communion:

> [He] felt that he was ceasing to be merely himself; . . . as though all the sap of all living things, flowing at one and the same moment into the too narrow confines of his heart, was mightily refashioning the enfeebled fibers of his being.[40]

In this experience of union, the boundaries of space and time dissolve, and the mystic feels a visceral sense of membership in humanity's long unfolding—past, present, and future—as did Teilhard:

> It was the soul of his entire race that had shuddered within him: an obscure memory of a first sudden awakening in the midst of beasts stronger, better-armed than he; a sad echo of the long struggle to tame the corn and to master the fire.[41]

The Mystic's Sense of Identity Changes

The mystic thus finds himself at-one with the rest of existence, bound to the hearts and souls of others. It changes how he perceives himself. That which was formerly 'other' he now knows to be *who he is*, and this under-standing *transcends* what we would call an identity.

The Mystic Accesses Life and Relationship Differently

You could say that the mystic senses something more like 'personhood' than an identity, and from within it, she accesses life in a much more intimate way. She listens, not with her ears, but with a self that is vast. These perceptions are not thought; they are known by a different means. Mechtilde's expression, "the powerful penetration of all things," reflects a so-called 'mental' processing that involves more than the thinking mind. Like Merrell-Wolff and Eckhart Tolle, she experiences this depth of Presence *in her body*. Mechtilde's invitation to "taste" and "feel" the flowing Fire is the only way she can express how she listens with *ears to hear*. But she is describing, not her body's, but what she calls her *soul's* perceptions. In fact, her entire being is her instrument.

I see it with the eyes of my soul . . . hear it with the ears of my eternal spirit . . . feel it in all the members of my body: the power of the Holy Spirit. . . .

We know in our hearts that something we may (or may not) have called 'soul' has always been present in us, but it has tended to be elusive. Yet if we turn back to the awakening we envisioned a few moments ago, what "poured into the room/ *into us*" was anything but intangible. *It had substance.*

> *The weight of You! Your density,*
> *The room, my heart, the universe*
> *—filled—*

We *felt* the substantiality of what flowed into us as we sat in the presence of a woman who was simply meditating. Moreover, in that moment, soul was more than an imagined static quality of *being*. It was action, too. *It moved.*[42] Soul was not a part, not an abstraction, not a separate entity conceived by the mind. Instead, we experienced it consciously *as ourselves*— the entire instrument *within which* and *with which* we were noting what was happening. We could not split ourselves into parts: outside or inside, noun or verb. This different sense of personhood included all that we were—thoughts, feelings, bodies, and more. So much more than the self we ordinarily knew, it seemed to be outside us:

> *The edges of me*
> *are gone—*
>
> *Where space was*
> *is filled to overflowing*
>
> *with*
> *Substance*
> *Presence*
>
> *—Thou—*

We under-stood: We were more than we thought.

The Mystic Is Motivated Differently

Mechtilde's poetry described how that power motivated her life. She took direction, not from her thoughts, feelings, or instincts but from the energies of Love:

the Flowing . . .
Moving and Compelling
Thee . . .

With a refined attention on the Presence in/around/*through-out* her, Mechtilde listened to Life with a larger self. She had learned to completely reorient her attention—away from the rule of ego and toward the Field of Presence that surrounded and permeated her. Her change of orientation was not unlike the way we shifted our visual attention from the birds in the Japanese painting to the shimmering gold field around them. Mechtilde *saw*: Nothing was split apart. Resting in that Field, she perceived everyone and everything as both self/*and peer*— as mystics from St. Francis to those of the Native American tradition have put it so beautifully: "Brother Sun . . . Sister Moon . . ."

Oriented to the Field—to the Current—Mechtilde, Teilhard, and the other mystics describe a world in which they are less concerned with identity because they are no longer in bondage to themselves. Instead, they remain exquisitely mindful of Presence and of the presence and needs of *any* 'Other,' be it person or creature, plant, river, or terrain. Living *as* this communion, they under-stand: The gift of awakening is given for the benefit of the whole, not just for oneself.

This is the transformation—the change of form. Most of us remain perched atop the three foundations at the threshold of this change. In these persons, Life has gathered and integrated the older form—I as an ego—within a larger consciousness that transcends it. But they had to cooperate.

Kenneth Woodward the religion editor of Newsweek observes:

In every spiritual tradition, getting free of the self is an ethical imperative. To 'love your neighbor as yourself' requires an extraordinary effort of self transcendence.[43]

It is no small accomplishment.

Every authentic spiritual Way insists that the mystic take personal responsibility for this essential and ongoing work. In this regard, Ellen Grace O'Brian notes:

> The sure indication of spiritual progress is the positive transformation of character. Visions, ecstasies, and philosophical insights that do not make us more compassionate, peaceful, and trustworthy people are just fireworks that fizzle.[44]

And so, each mystic turns—*as* the greater community—to serve it, and tries to learn what that service should be by listening with ears to hear. This is how each one cooperates with the power of Love, and at the same time, continues the work of claiming the realities that still live in the foundations of her soul. As the Buddhists put it:

> Before awakening, chopping wood and carrying water; after awakening, chopping wood and carrying water!

Why Does Awakening Matter

On his deathbed, the Buddha gave his last instruction:

> Make of yourself a light.

If we are to outgrow the kinds of perceptions and behaviors that have birthed the welter of conflicts in our Time, we cannot do it by relying on moral suasion, good will, trying harder, and problem-solving, alone. These ways are necessary, but they are not enough. Only the light of a Love that does not belong *to us* can set us free.

This light includes and takes us beyond science, beyond technological solutions, beyond a thinking process that splits us apart. If we are to transcend the ways we currently function, and instead, learn to cooperate with the greater Life, we need to tap the creative flow of the universe as an artist does. The painter Kandinsky counsels us to listen *inside*:

> The artist must be . . . deaf to the transitory teaching and demands of his particular age. He must watch only the trend of the inner need, and harken to its words alone.[45]

All of us are called to find a new mode of being in the world—to become artists of our own lives—and we need not do it alone. Every one of us has a direct connection to a resource beyond our personal selves that joins us with others and with Life. Mechtilde calls it soul.

This larger aspect of who we are quite naturally emerges as we deepen our practice. It offers a way of being *in* our lives that takes us past thinking—to what I am calling the soul process. The soul process is a way of listening, a living conversation, a courtship between the soul and the greater Life. It is a gentle turning of attention to what already lies within us/*within the universe*: the Creative, the Presence of Love. If we can learn to let the soul process be our compass—*and we can*—it can help to heal the divisions between the three foundations forever at war in our triune brains. And then, we just might make a small contribution to humanity's conscious emergence *as a people*—participants in the gradual awakening of Love.

The whisper then reminds us:

What is to give light must endure burning.

Victor Frankl[46]

Endnotes for Chapter 11

1 Source of Rumi's quotation unknown.

2 Attributed to Simone Weil (1909-1943), French philosopher, mystic, and political activist.

3 This is not light perceived by the eye but one that is inexpressible, what I call the *Light behind the light*. Artists from both eastern and western traditions have tried to express it with haloes or radiant fields surrounding a figure. In *The Book of Creation*, 5, Philip Newell calls it 'the light of life' referring to the same phrase used in John 8:12. Newell says, "It is to this light that we are called to be reconnected, both within ourselves and in all things."

4 Michael Washburn, PhD, *The Ego and the Dynamic Ground*, New York: SUNY Press, 1987, 130. *Author's note:* Washburn's text corroborates the experience of the soul's journey from a more 'bodily' perspective, an alternative view to the (more masculine) 'upward' imagery of transcendence found in earlier religious texts.

5 Isak Dinesen, "The Cardinal's Third Tale," in *Last Tales*, New York: Vintage Press, 1957.

6 Matthew Fox, PhD and former Dominican priest, has spent a lifetime trying to teach us that we all have *both* a scientist *and* a mystic within us. The author of many books and founder of two graduate schools, he was described by Thomas Berry as "the most creative, the most comprehensive and . . . challenging religious-spiritual teacher in America."

7 Evelyn Underhill, *The Mystics of the Church*, London: James Clarke & Co., 1925, 9. *Author's note:* Mystic wisdom lies at the root of the Jewish Kabbalah, the Muslim Sufi stories, and the Yoga Sutras; in the writings of Rumi, the haiku of Basho and Issa, the poetry of Han Shan, and the ecstatic writings of Kabir who straddles both Islam and Hinduism. Moses, the Psalmists, John the Baptist, and Teresa of Avila were mystics, as were Julian of Norwich, St. John of the Cross, and Hildegarde of Bingen. Many of our great poets are mystics: Walt Whitman, Hafiz, and William Blake; Jane Hirschfield, Rainer Marie Rilke, Emily Dickinson, Pablo Neruda, Wendell Berry, Czeslaw Milosz, and Mary Oliver. Poet and translator Stephen Mitchell and teacher Byron Katie are mystics, along with many of the great musicians and artists.

8 *Ibid.*, 11.

9 *Ibid.*, 10-11.

10 Exodus 3:1-14, condensed. Italics mine.

11 Just as a scene from a movie is projected out onto a screen from its source on a strip of film, one unconsciously projects a particular content of one's mind onto an external image, person, or group and then acknowledges its presence there but not in oneself. This is discussed further in Chapter 15.

12 In a lecture in Portola Valley CA, theologian Ed Beutner suggests that we learn as children from images rather than words. He read the tale of Humpty Dumpty and noted that in no place does the text refer to an egg, yet because the text has always been accompanied by a picture of an egg, we tend to believe that this is what Humpty Dumpty was!

13 2 Kings 2:11-12.

14 Pierre Teilhard de Chardin, SJ, *The Heart of Matter*, ed. N.M. Wildiers, San Diego: Harcourt, Inc., 1978, 61-74. In footnote 23, p. 79, Wildiers, notes: "That Père Teilhard himself appended to his autobiography the story of his first mystical experiences, shows that he wished the illumination that he had then attained to extend to what he had written." *Author's note:* An illumination is an awakening. Teilhard tells about these experiences in the third person as if they had happened to someone else, but they are his own story. Ursula King, Teilhard's biographer, further clarified in our correspondence the timing of Teilhard's expe-

riences: "You have used *The Heart of Matter* 61-74 as your source . . . but these texts were written at quite different times. Teilhard put into an Appendix to his autobiographical essay, *The Heart of Matter,* first, 'Three stories in the style of Benson,' written in 1916 and first published in 'The Writings in Time of War' (in not quite identical form). 'The Spiritual Power of Matter' written in 1919 on the Isle of Jersey was first published in the *Hymn of the Universe.* The fact that he appended them in 1955 meant that he thought them of great significance—but further experiences of his life augment the meanings of these texts by that time. He did have different mystical experiences, not all at the same time. I have written about this at some length in my book, *Towards a New Mysticism: Teilhard de Chardin and Eastern Religions* (1980)."

15 Pierre Teilhard de Chardin, *The Heart of Matter,* 63, 65.

16 *Ibid.,* 64.

17 Morihei Ueshiba, *The Art of Peace—Teachings of the Founder of Aikido,* compiled and trans. John Stevens, Boston: Shambhala, 1992, 5-7. Author's note: Ueshiba is known by the followers of Aikido as O-Sensei.

18 Richard Rohr, OFM, *Everything Belongs,* New York: Crossroad Publishing Co., 2003, 82.

19 This is a repeatable, verifiable experience in all traditions.

20 Frederic and Mary Ann Brussat, in a review of Robert Bly, *Kabir—Ecstatic Poems,* Boston: Beacon Press, 2004. Retrieved 2007 at *http://www.spiritualityandpractice. com/books/books.php?id=8652*

21 Carl Olson, Pascal's biographer, writes online: "The short life of Blaise Pascal (1623-1662) was one of intense intellectual brilliance, mystical vision and physical anguish. Pascal exhibited extraordinary mathematical and scientific abilities at an early age. On November 23, 1654, he had a 'definite conversion.' . . . Not long after this mysterious encounter with God, Pascal began writing notes for what he planned to be a thorough apologetic for Christianity . . . [posthumously] published as the *Pensées.*" Retrieved 2007 at *http://www.catholiceducation.org/ articles/catholic_stories/cs0011.html*

22 Ursula King, *Christian Mystics,* Mahwah, N.J: HiddenSpring/Paulist Press, 2001, 81-82. (My italics.) *Author's note:* Hildegarde was the visionary eleventh century abbess and a physician whose music, art, and written works have recently been recognized.

23 Cunningham, ed., *Thomas Merton: Spiritual Master,* 363.

24 Mark 4:3-8 and Matthew 13:3-23.

25 Mark 4:11 (Jerusalem Bible).

26 Luke 15:11-32. In a lecture in Portola Valley, CA, biblical scholar Edward Beutner said: "To be transformative, a parable needs to be seen as subversive: leaving the listener in doubt of his received wisdom or religious certitude and teasing him into doing some active thinking on his own."

27 Iyer, ed., *The Gospel According to Thomas,* 19.

28 Pascaline Coff, OSB, writes online: "Father Bede Griffiths (1906-1993) was a student at Oxford where he was tutored and befriended by C. S. Lewis. After an awakening, he later became an English Benedictine monk and researched the relationship between eastern and western spiritual traditions." Retrieved 2006 at *http://www.Bede Griffiths.com*

29 J. (Jiddu) Krishnamurti, the late sage from India, is known by his last name.

30 Vimala Thakar. All three statements quoted online. Retrieved 2005 at *http:// www.wie.org/j19/vimala*

31 Franklin Merrell-Wolff, *Experience and Philosophy,* New York: SUNY Press, 1994, 22. *Author's note:* Merrell-Wolff was a Harvard-educated philosopher and scholar, and professor of mathematics at Stanford. This is his personal record of transformation. His use of the term *Self* probably has not the same mean-

ing as that intended by Jung. *Self* is used by many disciplines to describe an identity that transcends ego. I understand *Self* as the inner/*outer* Presence of both tangible and intangible dimensions of Reality. The term *realization* used by Merrell-Wolff is also used by Underhill and similarly equated with awakening.

32 Merrell-Wolff, *Experience and Philosophy*, 20. *Author's note*: The Tao has also been described as the basic current that runs through all of existence.

33 John 3:8.

34 Merrell-Wolff, *Experience and Philosophy*, 344-345. Italics mine.

35 John 4:10-14, abridged (Jerusalem Bible).

36 Mechtilde of Magdeburg (1210?-1297?), "The Flowing Light of the Godhead 6.29," quoted in Carol Lee Flinders, *Enduring Grace*, San Francisco: HarperSanFrancisco, 1993, 43.

37 Flinders, *Enduring Grace*, 44-45. Flinders references Mechtilde's "Flowing Light," numbers 4.13 and 3.1.

38 Richard Rohr, OFM, lecture, St. Paul's Episcopal Church, Oakland, CA, February 2007.

39 Rev. Ellen Grace O'Brian, lecture, Center for Spiritual Enlightenment, San Jose, CA, Fall 2005.

40 Teilhard de Chardin, *The Heart of Matter*, 68.

41 *Ibid.*, 70.

42 "If they ask you what is the evidence of your Father in them, say to them, 'It is motion and rest.'" *The Gospel of Thomas*, Verse 50, in John S. Kloppenborg, Marvin W. Meyer, Stephen J. Patterson, Michael G. Steinhauser, *Q-Thomas Reader*, Polebridge Press, 1990, 141. Sometimes stated "a movement and a rest."

43 Kenneth Woodward, *Newsweek*, May 7, 2001. Woodward continues: "Indeed, most . . . theologians would argue it can't become a habit of the heart without the assistance of divine grace. . . . [To avoid pride, in particular], the mystics taught that love of neighbor must always take precedence over even the most intimate communion with God in prayer. . . . Similarly, Buddhist bodhisattvas are distinguished by their compassion, not their spiritual [experiences]."

44 The Rev. Ellen Grace O'Brian, Center for Spiritual Enlightenment, 'Daily Inspirations.' See *http://www.csecenter.org*

45 Wassily Kandinsky, Russian painter (1866-1944). Original source unknown. Retrieved 2007 from *http://www.wisdomatwork.com*

46 Frankl was the 20th century holocaust survivor known for his philosophy of meaning. Source unknown.

12 Learning to Live With Fire Inside

> But who can endure the day of his coming, and who can stand when he appears? For he is like a refiner's fire.
>
> Malachi 3:2

The energies of Love act on our minds, hearts, and bodies "like a refiner's fire"—words from Malachi that echo Rumi's "Burn all thought and expression away!" Both men imply that it is more than difficult to live with *Fire* inside. To befriend this *Fire*, we need to learn how to live in relationship to it. More accurately, we learn to live in relationship—all relationship—in wholly new ways: to live *as* the greater community of life.

After *Homo erectus* brought fire into his cave, he had to learn how to live with it. And although he'd gained a measure of comfort and convenience from that new power, he found that he also had a whole new set of problems! While in earlier times, his dwelling was cold, now it was often too hot for comfort. When in the past, the air he breathed was clear, now it was filled with smoke. Lungs blackened. People became ill. Some died. Flames and hot embers were a constant threat, and his children, once free to play about the cave, had to be physically restrained. Water boiled and burned fingers. The hunt's considerable efforts were wasted when food was cooked to a crisp. The presence of fire inside was not merely benign.

Nor is *Fire for the second time.* Although an encounter with the presence of *Fire* may be accompanied by intense joy, the newly awakened person is often surprised to find herself utterly disoriented. To her dismay, the awakening has brought with it not only a dawning of truth beyond her wildest imagination— but also an entirely new set of problems! Even though she seems to inhabit the same world as before, in the days and weeks that follow her experience, neither the world nor her responses to it are the same.

Reader Frankie Brogan wrote:

Oh, the pressures upon the human soul following such an awesome experience. I recall the hot, wild feeling that oppressed me. "Have I lost my cotton pickin' mind?" Yet I *knew* that my world had changed, that my place in it was different and that it would never be the same.

The ancient texts of many traditions have long been maps for this territory. *The Gospel According to Thomas* opens with Jesus' warning:

Let him who seeks,
Not cease from his search
Until he finds.
When he finds, he will be bewildered,
And, when bewildered,
He will wonder . . . .[1]

In Handel's *Messiah,* Isaiah speaks of leveling the mountains and valleys:

Make straight in the desert a highway for our God.
Every valley shall be exalted,
And every mountain and hill be made low;
The crooked straight,
And the rough places plain.[2]

In other words, everything is going to change! While it was a customary practice, in those times, to construct a new highway for the arrival of a king, we can also hear the passage to have an inner meaning: the making of a highway for the Power through our own tangled interior landscape. In this interpretation, the passage addresses the demands that a spontaneous awakening can place on the human psyche and body. In its wake can come sweeping changes in which everything a person has known himself to be—indeed, his whole reality—is being reorganized. Like the leveling of Isaiah's highway, what he's heretofore demeaned (and criticized in others) such as dependence or weakness or neediness, may be quite suddenly elevated; yet what he's held high, like his competence or the attributes that contribute to his popularity, are diminished. No wonder he's confused!

Evelyn Underhill referred to these kinds of upheavals as

a complete remaking of the human personality, *a re-forming* . . .[3]

This re-forming challenges the ancient, interior *"No!"* of our ancestors. While their solutions helped to control the discord between instinct, feeling, and thought—the discord remained. So does our own. Control isn't as reliable as we had wanted to believe.

The greater Love fashions a new kind of equilibrium, one far different from control. But Love can be a very difficult task-master. No one makes this so clear as Bede Griffiths. Griffiths was a twentieth-century Benedictine monk whose life and work in an Indian ashram married Christianity with the wisdom of the Hindu Vedanta. He once said,

The surrender of the ego is the most difficult thing we have to do.[4]

Because he used the older language of both these traditions, it can be quite natural for us to hear the power he describes in the quotation that follows as something existing outside of ourselves. For this reason, it is important to remember the experience of envisioning your own awakening as you read it—for the power that swept into the room/*into you* was outside/*inside* you at once. Griffiths wrote:

There was indeed something terrifying in this power which had entered into my life and which would not be refused. It had revealed itself to me as love, but I knew now that it was a love which demanded everything, and was a torment if it was resisted . . . I had wanted to keep my own will and to direct my own life; but now I had been forced to surrender. I had placed my life in the hands of a power which was infinitely beyond me and I knew from this time that the sole purpose of my life must be to leave myself in those hands and to allow my soul to be governed by that will.

I could never doubt after this that beyond all accidents of this life, behind all the pain and conflict, there was a definite power at work which was shaping human destiny. The pain and conflict arose from the resistance of the human will to this power, and this resistance in turn was due to our blindness. We were held captive by the material world, the world of reason and common sense; only when we had broken with the illusion of this world and faced the reality which was hidden in the depths of our being could we find peace.[5]

How human it is to resist! It seems so much easier than to surrender—especially if somewhere, way down deep, you think you're going to die if you let go! But ego doesn't die. No, if we've practiced how to stay, and keep using that practice as we face Love's many challenges, our awakening can take us well past the 'I' we developed during our childhood—past that old and partial self defined by the ancient, interior *"No!"* But now, we need to learn to *live* our awakening, and that involves developing a new kind of relationship between ego and the consciousness of Love. Even though ego cannot imagine such an Unknown, it still has to submit to what is clearly a greater power. Only then, can it relax its grip and learn to rest in Love's embrace.

The mystics' five inner changes—in perception, in the conscious awareness of communion, in the access of life and relationships, and in a different sense of identity and motivation—foreshadow our own changes after an awakening. We will examine them briefly in this chapter and more deeply in the chapters to follow.

Of his own inner revolution, Richard Moss exclaimed,

My *cells* were changed![6]

Should you, like Moss and Griffiths, be unexpectedly awakened, you will also have to learn to live with *Fire* inside.

Living With Fire Inside

You see and Hear Differently

You are likely to notice far more than before, and you also feel everything very deeply. You are amazed at a world that is *lit up*. You see what is before you, and words you've never used pour out of your mouth, unpremeditated: *"Glory! Glory!"*

You step out your front door each day and look around you, and the wind-tossed trees chatter in greengold—light language—leaving chance openings for blue. Another time, the salmon sun spreads out on the bay at sunrise, splashing color on the waves like a dare.

You enter a home, and see through the far window a cherry tree in bloom—and burst into tears. Or you are a passenger riding through a distant valley, and when the car rounds a bend, there appears before you a mountain range so green, the intensity of it shakes you to your core. You weep again. You may cry at beauty for the rest of your life. At every turn, the glory of creation reveals itself as *radiance*. Merton called it "a world charged with the presence and reality of God."[7]

Frankie Brogan described her own experience:

> I'll never forget how green the grass . . . how sweet the breeze, how tender birdsong. Nature just came alive for me. It was like landing in colorful Oz after being content with a black and white world for all those years.

But it is not just what you see that has changed. You may also feel as if your whole system is receiving far more input than usual, *and it is*. You are no longer buffered against life's onslaught of information, previously filtered from your awareness. As a result, your mind and body may feel jangled, as if every cell were cringing at the assault.

The awakening impulse—this Love moving through the entire human species like an evolutionary wave—is a *huge energy.* You will discover very quickly that trying to *understand*—which is a mental form of control—is no longer adequate to support the voltage coursing through you. At issue at every turn, is your whole bodymind's ability to adjust to its increase. Learning to tolerate and to accommodate the energy without becoming exhausted becomes paramount. You may find that there seem to be a series of learning curves: an influx of energy, then a period of discovering how to adapt, followed by a plateau; then, a new influx of energy. It hardly seems to be the benign bliss promised by the new-age spiritualities! Adds reader Pat Sullivan,

> or the kind guaranteed by 'old-age' revelations and conversions, either!

For some, driving a car—even being *in* a moving car—may be overwhelming. If you read the words of contemporary mystics, you will find that they refer repeatedly to similar difficulties. Franklin Merrell-Wolff wrote in his journal:

> Driving an automobile in traffic is particularly inimical. . . . To steer a way through the outer confusion requires objective concentration. I, at least, cannot move through these conditions with safety by giving only a peripheral attention to them . . . [and] the demand upon the vital strength is severe.[8]

Moss said of his early experience:

> I found at first I could not drive at all, and after that, I had to drive very slowly. I also had to use an internal dialog even to bear airports, and while I was in them, to walk slowly and just stay with my own breathing. In fact, the only way I could cope with the energy for months was by doing hours and hours of walking.

I wrote in my journal:

> The night after it happened, I was ablaze with the energy, but unaware of the extent of its impact on me. I went to my weekly volunteer meeting at Kara, the grief-counseling center. It being the end of the month, we filled out a routine report summarizing our activities: the clients we'd seen, the other related work we'd done, and totaled up our hours. I'd completed the form countless times and

spent fifteen minutes on this one, working as carefully as always—or so I thought. But at our next meeting, my supervisor was understandably irritated, and snapped, "You didn't fill out your report—you left the whole thing blank!" I was bewildered.

You don't realize, at first, the extent to which the call to Love is a call to live in so profound an intimacy with life-as-it-is. And Life's *'is-ness'* is immense! There are times your cells seem almost to soar; to vibrate like the highest notes of a violin in the hands of a master. Other times, you quiver in fear. Moss described this period of integration:

> That's the integral dance! You find yourself in the Current and you don't want to be out of it; and then it feels like so much, you don't want to be in it! *All the time!* Trust what's leading you. Don't listen to the negative intellect.

Your bewilderment and confusion may continue for some time. What is being fashioned in you is an acute and whole-bodied sensitivity to life. To tolerate the energies of Love requires that you step into a much larger self that is both exquisitely tender and at the same time, far more competent to bear this new reality. But you do! Little steps, at first—tiny primitive attempts to receive what is happening with gratitude—help you to embody this new consciousness of fundamental relationship *with everything*.

Colin Oliver expressed one of the small satisfactions that come with progress:

> It's a notable step when the everyday racy world (the market place) ceases to jangle the nerves with such persistence, but is included, welcomed in. As Rumi says, *What can you do? You have no shield.*[9]

You Learn to Access Life Differently

Little by little, you bend. It is a courtship. With no idea of what such a courtship entails, you learn to court the energy. You turn from what you *know* to what you *don't know* for guidance. You have to remind yourself to turn within and listen. You ask the Unknown repeatedly: *What shall I do? How shall I respond?*

Now I am undone.

Like a woman
newly blind,

turned for my life
toward a hand at my elbow

I cannot feel,
listening for sounds
I cannot hear

learning to rest
in something

New.

Like all those who have leapt any gap before you—you begin to see and hear in a different way. But you take in this strange new world and make it yours the same way you did as a toddler. You 'step back,' as you did then, into a larger perspective—one you cannot name. Even then, you may try to name it! Sometimes, in awe of what I was experiencing, I named it *God*; other times, *Glory* or *Radiance* or *Holy*. I also met feelings so deep, I could hardly describe them, but tried with words like *dread*. Other words came with the ongoing uncertainty, and I named myself *mystified* or *scared* or *helpless*. And yet, whatever the nature of the moment, I also whispered, *grateful*.

Richard Moss offers us encouragement:

> If you are conscious of something, you are bigger than it is![10]

Carol Lee Flinders suggested that the mystics viewed their long period of adjustment (which they called 'purgation') as a 'battening down' process in which they might balance the intensities of their ecstatic experiences:

> By imposing all manner of strictures on the external life, over which one *can* exert some control, they appear to be seeking to counterbalance the tremendous storm that is taking place within, which is not at all under the individual's control. The intense sobriety . . . is imposed to offset the almost unbearable joy arising within. *Purgation*

is the attempt to harmonize, or to align the whole person at the physical, emotional and intellectual levels, adjusting for the far-reaching changes that have taken place deep within.[11]

Moss gave a contemporary description:

There is an energetic change in you. Your nervous system becomes 'rewired' to some extent. The Great Self is engaging and penetrating your ego and it's like learning to process much higher voltage in your body. Let's say that your energy system was used to conducting '2000 volts' and now it's being required to conduct '200,000 volts,' instead. Your body is no longer buffered against that kind of power. It is engaging and relating to much more information than ever before—and is responding to it! This is a continuous process. Your organism keeps learning to handle and receive enormous amounts of information *all the time* and in the process is, itself, reorganized.

No matter what your preparation or initial response to *Fire*, after a spontaneous awakening, you are likely to need tending, spiritually. Moss wrote about how necessary this kind of care was immediately after his own awakening, for even though he'd been on a spiritual search for many years, he felt disoriented, nauseated, and overwhelmed.

My medical mind . . . offered a chain of distressing diagnoses: seizure, stroke . . . an adrenaline secreting tumor. . . .[12]

He left the place where he had encountered the extraordinary phenomena and walked back to the restaurant where he'd eaten an hour before. When he arrived, he found a friend sitting in the very seat where he'd had breakfast. A Jungian analyst, she took him to her home where she and her husband tended him gently for several days.

She dismissed [my medical concerns] . . . obtained holy water and lit candles that burned day and night . . . .[13]

After a while, she played The Messiah for him:

And every mountain and hill be made low . . . and the rough places plain.

It was healing.

Richard wondered, years later, if the intensity of his awakening had been because he was so young; for though he'd worked with a master and practiced diligently, he simply hadn't lived long enough to do enough of the necessary inner work to prepare for the powerful energies of Love.

In the book of Acts, Paul is said to have felt similar effects from a dramatic encounter with 'a light from heaven.'[14] Paul was not a spiritually inclined person but a soldier, and in this telling, he was totally unprepared for what had destroyed his worldview. Apocryphal or not, the story of his temporary blinding, his inability to eat, and subsequent need of his friends' care "for three days" (not to speak of the ensuing radical change in his life), demonstrates the overwhelming impact of a spontaneous awakening—and the deep need for trusted support. Moss clarified why it is important:

> Any system has to adapt to something new. If you had lived in a darkened room all your life and had never seen ordinary light, your first experience of it would cause new responses from the body. Then, as the body or system acclimates, the intensity of the response decreases. That is why people don't have these dramatic spiritual experiences after their first opening. Their system has acclimated.

Centuries earlier, John of the Cross also wrote:

> This love lasts together with its effect a long while . . . though not always in the same degree of intensity.[15]

We are not saints or spiritual masters, but we can learn from them how to tend the *Fire* inside. Often, they remind us to turn to the silence within. We may already have felt a great need for quiet, and in the months that follow (and routinely afterwards), we are likely to require protected time and space. Moss counseled:

> Rest in the energy. Simply rest.

Honoring the need for quiet becomes an ongoing, lifelong practice, honed in meditation in familiar surroundings at home, and particularly, on retreat. Retreat houses are not primarily designed for reading or activities—but for silence, meditation, and rest.

Your Sense of Identity Begins to Change

Moss recommended several other ways to acclimate to the energy, and the same suggestions can be found in the writings of other mystics, past and present. One of his most important statements referred to the necessity of being ordinary.

> You can't claim it with your ego. You have to integrate it—with naturalness, ordinariness, humility. You learn to access the person who is just preparing a meal, just driving, or just crossing the street.

Ego has a way of suggesting arrival, but we don't arrive: Waking up is not an end; it is a commission: We learn to orient to the Power and then commit to serve it. From long experience with the many traps littering the spiritual Way, the traditions stress the importance of this commission. They are understandably suspicious of an emphasis on radical awakenings, in part, because they are so tempting to the ego. For this reason, they've tended to cast a doubtful glance at mystical experiences and focus instead on their fruits. Priest and scientist Lorenzo Albacete describes the quality both he and the church consider the most important fruit of an authentic awakening:

> (The) sense of poverty before Mystery is called humility, and to me this is the most important sign of authentic religious experience. In the end . . . humility shuns all power, respects the demands of justice and shares with all mortals the challenge of death.[16]

Death is the constant reminder of our own ordinariness, and that ordinariness becomes an inner demand. We stumble after it—not knowing how to be ordinary—only how great is our need for the healing it brings.

In 1969, Rollo May wrote about driving a car in such a way that he was just driving.[17] The kind of car he drove wasn't important; it was *how* he drove! He didn't let his mind wander, or go on 'automatic pilot.' Instead, he did something quite ordinary: He began to notice the feel of his hands on the steering wheel, the touch of his foot on the pedals, the view outside his window, and the trees moving in the wind. I liked the idea so much, I began to try it, and as my attention to the experience of simply driving became increasingly refined, I turned the setting on the car radio from the news to classical music—then finally turned it off. May's example of driving was my first introduction to the practice of awareness.

It was Time. Alan Watts and Ram Dass had written spiritual books that had become best sellers, and the many philosophies of the East were seeping into our culture and kneading it like bread dough. Few of us realized the extent of the impact these Ways from the East were beginning to have on our lives. New to us, in particular, was the quality of attention they stressed— what Buddhism called 'mindfulness':

> When you are sitting, just sit; when you are peeling potatoes, just peel potatoes.

In the 1970s, '80s, and '90s, increasing numbers of people absorbed these novel ideas and began to learn to practice meditation. Before awakening, practices like these are a preparation. Afterwards, they become essential.

Meditation provides the necessary training in awareness to access life differently. As it hones your attention, *Something* begins to guide your life from within/*without*. You continue to ask, *How shall I do this? How shall I proceed?* and though you seem to be asking yourself, the responses come from both inside and all around you—from chance conversations with friends or strangers; in emails or what you pick up to read; on billboards or on bumper stickers; and in texts, sacred and secular. You are amazed. You keep paying attention to what life is offering in the moment in the hope of learning how to cooperate with it. You find that your cooperation requires a greatly increased capacity for discernment.

The Dalai Lama observed:

> Employing the faculty of *wise discernment* involves constantly checking our outlook and asking . . . whether we are being broad . . . or narrow-minded. Have we taken into account the overall situation? . . . Is our view short . . . or long-term? . . . Is our motive genuinely compassionate when considered in relation to the totality of all

beings? Or is our compassion limited just to . . . those we identify with closely?[18]

Because we tend to wear our own set of blinders, ordinariness suggests that most of us will want guidance in the discernment process. Others who are trained—not to give answers but to ask questions that illumine a person's own natural unfolding—can help us find perspectives we may not have considered before.

Ultimately, however, we each have to find our own way. On the other side of the gap, no spiritual advisor can tell you what is true for *you*. It is a creative journey—and your own. You live with tremendous unknowns, however, and as you proceed, you may occasionally find yourself looking, once more, for some kind of confirmation. You ask yourself, *Who else can tell me what their own experience of these astonishing things was like?* You might seek this kind of confirmation in lectures, in books, and in spiritual texts within your own and other traditions. Occasionally, you will be amazed to discover that many of these scriptures seem to be filled with wisdom *specific to this process.* You wonder: Were they originally expressed to guide people in this process of adaptation? Had you not been able to hear them from that perspective before? Or were they, like other kinds of wisdom, true at any level of understanding? You will probably never know.

You Begin to Live in Conscious Communion With Life

However, you may be even more astonished as you read these texts, for many of them—not all—seem to have come alive! The energy almost jumps off the page! And although you never felt it when you read them before, your body is now suffused by it.

The energetic Presence that radiates from awakened persons may, on occasion, be palpable in their written word. Reading the book of John can be an ecstatic experience. So can the some of the writings of Moss, Merton, and many others. I wrote in my journal:

When I was reading Merrell-Wolff last night, the Current was strong—as if it came in large loops—most of the time. There were sections of the book (I've started to note them in the margins), when it became much stronger but came in shorter kinds of waves. When I reflected on the experience, it seemed that these appeared when he was speaking from a very high place. It felt like a stunning recognition—as if the larger being-in-myself was telling me somatically, "Something universal is being spoken, here."

If you should ask a person who's had more years than you to explore the wonders of his own awakening, he is likely to confirm such moments. Your gratitude for these mysteries abounds. Little by little, you begin to trust: What you need (not what you want) is already there—part of the soul's ongoing courtship with Life. You are awed by the realization that the unfathomable Mystery is at your core/*at the core of everything*. Your life is filled to the brim with grace.

> *One day you under-stand that the Mystery at the heart of creation is Love, and that the Love you have been seeking has been there all along.*

You stand there and weep. Gratitude becomes who you are.

You also understand, in the deepest sense of the word, that Teilhard did not call its harnessed energies *"Fire"* without recognizing that—as with any transformation—*Fire for the second time* brings both boon and danger. The dangers are physical, psychological, interpersonal, and spiritual.

A story from the Talmud tells about four men who "entered the garden of Paradise" seeking union with the divine:

> Four entered the Garden. One went mad. One sickened and died. One became totally self-involved. And one, due to his humility, became a servant and light to his community.

The contemporary mystic Brenda Morgan, PhD, explained that while a mental breakdown, illness, or even death can be the consequences of a person's psyche, his upbringing, or his lack of familiarity with another culture's expectations and values,[19] they are usually the results of inadequate preparation for the energy:

When the soul receives an emanation, the nervous system responds. There must have been preparation—it's like an evolutionary preparedness. One must have cleared away enough 'debris' that the nervous system can receive it. Then the soul has to learn how to continue in that state, and how it can respond.[20]

Richard Moss clarified the dangers in the Talmudic story similarly:

First of all you must be prepared. If someone comes into the energy unprepared, it will destroy them. Therapy is a way of preparation: having to deal in depth with the psychological.

Both Richard and Brenda focused on the psychological danger. Brenda's term, "evolutionary preparedness," echoes the kind of under-standing that comes from excavating the three foundations of the soul. She is not only familiar with the human truths that lie in our minds and hearts and bodies. She also knows how easy it is to hide from them—and to see ourselves quite differently from who we really are. When she works with others to "clear away the debris," she, like the Buddhist teachers, offers both spiritual practices and therapy to help them integrate what they have found. Preparatory work like this can provide both the flexibility and "structural integrity" needed to withstand the energies' challenges to our programming—and to the ancient, reactive *"No!"* of our ancestors.

Absent the necessary preparation, the first three seekers in the Talmudic story may very well have been overwhelmed by the energies. As Moss made clear in his earlier statement, a humble heart and the surrender to ordinariness is essential for a relationship with a power which has left our hearts and bodies *so alive*. To learn to bear these energies in a whole-bodied way runs counter to every survival mechanism of the foundations. The foundations' tools are reactive: aggression, resistance, flight. Though these 'fight or flight' responses may be the survival tools we inherited, if we are to bear the energies of Love, we'll need to learn, instead, to *stay*. To stay when threatened— we don't contract in the old, time-honored ways. It takes all the courage, honesty, willingness, and trust we can muster.

As Lao Tse said:

A person with outward courage dares to die.
A person with inward courage dares to live.[21]

You Learn to Live as Relationship

The changes initiated by an awakening—and our need to adapt to them—also affect our relationship with others. This is where the dangers of a radical awakening become interpersonal. Our intimates may sense that we are somehow different but may not relate to it consciously. Nor are they aware of the affect of the energies *on themselves*. Moss said that it can be confusing to both partners:

> The longer you remain in the Current, the more sensitized your partner gets. He is dealing with a force field he cannot see or feel or touch. It's unbounding him, and his own ability to contain his 'stuff' is decreased. He puts out a little energy toward you and in you it's squared and doubled. Has he intensified his reaction or have you become more sensitized? *You don't know.* He may become very irritable. Your effect on him is like dissolving a sugar cube. By your very nature, now, you put him in hot water and *he doesn't want to be there.*
>
> *This is very real. Be still. Rest. Pray. Keep your body and heart open.* You will be learning about it as you go, carrying the authority of it, trying to communicate to each other about it. Right now you need your own calmness; the issue is how to protect yourself inside. You are like a newborn baby and as long as the surrounding energy is in harmony, you feel O.K., *but when you contract, it is violent.* Anger (your own) is like being hit by a Mack truck. And when you feel you have to defend against other people or groups or cars in traffic, it is physically and systemically extremely painful.

Our walls against pain, fear, and loss become, by definition, defenses against others. We cemented their construction in our earliest relationships. Therefore, it is quite natural—now that our protective defenses have become even further effaced by a radical awakening—that we feel most vulnerable in relationship, particularly with our intimates. In a body that is this alive, we are not numb. We *feel* our contractions.

> My body feels like someone had drawn the back end of a hammer over piano strings. I am totally jangled . . . . My heart is racing.[22]

The pain brought on by our defenses against others is truth's way of letting us know we are closed. This, I believe, is the "torment if it [is] resisted" Bede Griffiths referred to earlier in the chapter.

His statement demonstrates the importance of understanding how we contract—and we learn to understand the hard way! The pain of contractions like anger or anxiety or fear is *physical*: We feel severe pain in our necks . . . shoulders . . . low backs . . . and more. We have colds, pneumonia, and migraine headaches . . . We get heart attacks. Until we learn to practice alternative responses to our environment and the people in it, we are likely to hurt severely with every inner *"No!"*

All traditional spiritual practices are designed to override the programming inherent in the foundations of the soul. A well-known example is the phrase, "Turn the other cheek."[23] While Jesus' statement clearly means not to perpetuate violence, I hear it also, *as an admonishment not to contract*. The contractions of mind and heart and body impede our sensitivity to the energies of Love. Jesus' words—and his life—expressed the imperative to remain open to that Power and to *stay*, whatever life should bring.

Love is the power that guides a life lived *as* relationship. To remain in so intimate a communion with the mysterious Current—and therefore, with others in the greater community—our defensive contractions need to be removed. Spiritual practice is not about numbing. It is about opening our hearts even more.

And so we try to turn the other cheek: Instead of fighting physical or emotional pain, we learn to soften—and let go. We open our hearts and ask, *What do I need to feel? To amend? To under-stand?*—then, listen. Sometimes, we have to listen for a long time.

The child-in-us is afraid. So is the child in every other person. Our commission, therefore, is a never-ending labor of love. Spiritual practice instills increasing compassion for the needs and fears of the littlest child in all of us. It helps align the child's heart and body within a larger self—soul. The more we turn the other cheek by saying *"Yes!"* instead of *"No!"* the more we are able to listen with ears to hear—the more we can be guided, not by ego but by Love.

The *"Yes!"* to whatever Life brings is the Way to open to the energies of Love. *That,* I believe, is the deep and mystical root of the teaching, to "turn the other cheek." It is about "making straight in the desert a highway" in order to make a relationship with a greater Power.

The other more familiar interpretations about *social* behavior are built on that root—that bodily and very spiritual foundation.

You Are Motivated by Love

Mystics attest that after an awakening, something remains that continues to shape them from within. Gradually, they adapt to the joys and challenges of living with that *Fire,* inside. In the same way that led Bede Griffiths to discover he was "no longer the center of his own life," they learn to bend to a new Center, and the motivation of Love.

As we learn to say *"Yes!"* to Love despite our bodies' natural resistance, we discover a deeper connection to Life. And as our awareness of this connection grows, we no longer feel lonely and separate, but joined. We are living as relationship.

Endnotes for Chapter 12

1   Iyer, ed., *The Gospel According to Thomas*, 17.

2   The text of this chorus from Handel's *Messiah* is from Isaiah 40:3-4 (KJV).

3   Underhill, *Mystics of the Church*, 125. She is quoting Walter Hilton in *The Scale of Perfection*, a book that she describes as "a complete way-book of the spiritual life." Italics mine.

4   Bede Griffiths was intimate with many other disciplines, including Yoga and the work of Jung. This statement is included in his online biography at *http://www.bedegriffiths.com/bio.htm*

5   Bede Griffiths, *The Golden String*, Springfield, IL: Templegate Publishers, 1980, 117.

6   This and the remaining statements in this chapter by Moss that are not credited to *The Black Butterfly* are from a series of conversations.

7   Cunningham, ed., *Thomas Merton: Spiritual Master*, 78.

8   Merrell-Wolff, *Experience and Philosophy*, 8.

9   Oliver quotes Jalaluddin Rumi, *Selected Poems from the Divani Shamsi Tabriz*, trans. Reynold A. Nicholson, Cambridge: Cambridge University Press, 1898.

10 Moss has made this statement in lectures, groups, and conferences.

11 Flinders, *Enduring Grace*, 143. Italics mine.

12 Moss, *The Black Butterfly*, 18.

13 *Ibid.*, 19.

14 Acts 9:13-16. The book of Acts, probably written by Luke, contains stories drawn from many sources fifty years after Paul's letters were written. Luke significantly elaborates on Paul's own story detailed in Acts, probably to make a theological point. You may note also that this passage contains a lot of the same symbolism found throughout literature, e.g., Paul's blinding (like that of Lear and Oedipus), 'that he might see,' and the use of numbers such as Paul's need for care for 'three days.' Regardless of the culture, numbers such as '3' and '40' often have mystical significance in sacred and secular narratives whether it is days or apples or wishes or sisters. Likewise, '40' (as in 40 days and 40 nights) signifies 'a long time' or an important time set apart.

15 *The Collected Works of Saint John of the Cross* (revised edition), ed. Kieran Kavanaugh, OCD, Washington, DC: ICS Publications, Institute of Carmelite Studies, 462.

16 Lorenzo Albacete, *New York Times Sunday Magazine*, December 17, 2000, 32. Albacete begins by asking what it is the mystic or visionary has experienced: "Is it a reality outside the self, or is it the manifestation of something within? In the old days, psychiatric orthodoxy took the latter view, describing religion as a function of unresolved interior conflict . . . . As a priest and former scientist, I find myself . . . [thinking that if it] is an authentic contact with the transcendent Mystery, *it not only will but should exceed the grasp of science. . . .* Scientific rationalism is only one category of reason, and choosing to view it as the only judge of truth is a freely chosen prejudice." Italics mine.

17 Rollo May, *Love and Will*, New York: W. W. Norton and Co., Inc., 1969.

18 The Dalai Lama, *Ethics for a New Millennium*. Abbreviated from a quotation retrieved 2005 at *http://www.wisdomatwork.com*

19 There are many stories of contemporary Eastern sages who came to the United States utterly unprepared for the consumerism, wealth, and blatant sexuality of this culture. Because these things did not exist in their countries, their spiritual paths had not trained them in how to deal with such temptations.

20 The term *emanation* (also called a *transmission*) refers to the conductivity of a person with the extraordinary degree of openness and availability that results from exceedingly low self-involvement. This describes the gifted teacher and psychologist, Brenda Morgan, who made these comments in a conversation.

21 A selection from 'Thought for the Day' from *http://www.wisdomatwork.com* retrieved 2007.

22 From my journal.

23 Matthew 5:39 (KJV). "But I say unto you, that ye resist not evil: but whosoever shall smite thee on thy right cheek, turn to him the other also."

Fire For the Second Time

13 One-ing

Hear, O Israel: The LORD our God is One.

Deuteronomy 6:4

Your Sense of Identity Changes

There have been many attempts to express the mystery
of Wholeness and communion, and here, the language of
Deuteronomy names it *One*. Meister Eckhart coined the term
one-ing to express the unnamable unity that exists within/
among/between souls and the greater Life. It is an intimacy with
all that there is, the hidden and the seen. As you remember,
Teilhard de Chardin described his experience of this unity on
awakening:

> [He] felt that he was ceasing to be merely himself. . . . as though
> all the sap of all living things [were] flowing at one and the same
> moment into . . . his heart.

Like many others, Teilhard had realized something more
than what we call an identity; he felt himself to be a "man
whose soul was in instinctive communication with the unique
Life of all things." Such a passionate relationship with life/*the
Life behind the life*—can sound wondrous, but we may tend
to forget that we, too, are *already* bonded to Life and to one

another. When we awaken to this bond, it is not to some aerie-faerie consciousness. It is a physical, whole-bodied awareness: dynamic, earthy, and grounded in life/*in its Source*.

This is the paradox of the One/*the many*. All of us at our core/*circumference* are a continuum, a living family, past and present. In this unbroken lineage, we are modern/*primeval* human beings. And like our *Homo habilis* grandmother and every single newborn creature, we stream with the powers of the universe.

In those startling moments of the awakening we experienced together, we became conscious of the dynamic unity of One-ing. We had already begun to prepare ourselves for this kind of awareness by looking at the Japanese painting and turning our attention from figure to ground. Now, however, we also notice how the powerful energies of Love in us are drawn to the same power in another. Our allurement is not an attraction to the other's personality; it feels more like a current resonating between soul and soul. This potent magnetism brings us into a new kind of relationship with others—the living Communion at our root. Michael Washburn describes its nature in the language of transpersonal psychology:

> The power of the Ground is a magnetically attractive force. The ego is drawn to [it] . . . and to anything in which it is deposited or anyone from whom it emanates. . . . Spirit flows strongly to spirit and bonds therewith to form a union, a "mystical body" of ego-differentiated spirits. *Spirit is irresistibly drawn to itself as it meets itself in others and is thus moved to join in a higher life with others.* So powerful is this impulse for some integrated persons . . . that they value the spiritual whole more than any of its egoic parts. . . . [They are] so utterly devoted to spirit, that there is nothing they would not give, including their individual lives, *to contribute to humanity's collective life in spirit.*[1]

The allurement of Ground to Ground is compelling because this "collective life in spirit" is already present in us. Thomas Berry expresses it in terms of energy:

> In the late Paleolithic . . . and the Neolithic periods, we all lived in an ocean of energy. Physical and psychic forms of energy were intimately related. . . . There is a significant difference between physical energy and psychic energy. *Physical energy is diminished by use.* . . .

Psychic energies are increased by . . . the numbers of those who partici-pate in their activity. . . . Understanding, joy, spiritual insight, music, and the arts . . . are augmented . . . as they are communicated from one person to another.[2]

Although we may intuitively recognize the presence of these energies, our work today is to make it more conscious. We may never be able to give our collective life in spirit adequate language, but after a sudden awakening, we are intensely aware of it. This is where we begin to live in conscious communion with others and with Mystery.

We Can Consent To a New Kind of Identity

Whether or not we've experienced an awakening such as this, all of us can choose to live as members of the existing communion. We can remind ourselves, moment by moment, that we are part of the greater One: joined to the greater power; joined to one another.

What really matters is not the kind of awakening we've known. What matters is how we live our lives. How we live is not about being good persons. It is about living from the wholeness of *who we really are.* One-ing—being mindful of this unity—we know ourselves to be relatedness, itself, and learn to live *as* one another. We come to know *who we really are,* not by hoping to become enlightened, but through spiritual practice.

Practice Is the Essential Link to Living an Awakened Life

Spiritual practice is different from the public face of religion, although the great traditions have had long experience with it. Quietly and for centuries, the spiritualities and religions of East and West have developed systematic methods for awakening to a deep change of mind and heart. They've also found means of dealing with ego's many pitfalls along the way—like those encountered in the Talmud story. Teachers both within and outside these traditions have created countless systems for greater under-standing. These systems include a variety of practices such as meditations, prayers, rituals, and postures. They range from the use of *koans,* the practice of forms as in

Tae Kwon Do, the study of the yoga sutras, the *Bhagavad-Gita*, the *Koran* or the *Bible*, to present-day systems like Richard Moss' *Mandala of Being*.[3] Spiritual practices like these provide the means for yoking mind, heart, and body to the greater Life. They have always been part of the training offered in ashrams, convents, monasteries, and temples. What a tragedy—that except for those who chose the religious life—few were ever taught how to use them!

Episcopal priest James Blackburn acknowledges for the church:

> We have greatly underestimated the layperson.

Times are changing. We need no longer live a cloistered life to learn practices like these. If you should inquire about them, you will discover that there are as many paths to Life as there are persons. The renowned scholar of world religions, Houston Smith, observes that the choice of path and practice reflects a person's particular temperament. He suggests that the point is to live your own type to the fullest:

> It would be futile for us to try to convert [an]other into one's own type. It's like playing cards. You lead with your strong suit.[4]

Some will, indeed, work through a faith tradition. Others will work diligently at a program of recovery. Some will make a serious practice of service or meditation, yoga or the martial arts. Many will turn for guidance to a spiritual advisor, a spiritual director, a sponsor, or psychotherapist. Whatever Way you choose, each is an undoing; each, a world. Though you may spend a long time finding the path that is right for you, eventually, the day comes when it is helpful to make a commitment. As Gandhi said:

> If you are looking for water, it is better to drill one sixty-foot-deep well than ten six-foot wells.[5]

o

I had explored many different paths, and although I have always maintained the original practices that helped me to turn my life around, there came a time when I could no longer overlook two strong messages from deep inside me. Both had to do with the need for a spiritual community closer to my own roots. I had been away from active involvement in a church for many years, but now more than ever, I yearned for a place in which to serve and to celebrate—to express in community my gratitude for the privilege and joy of being alive. It was not only a social need. I also yearned for a sacred context in which to consecrate with others all of life's passages—its Beginnings and its Endings. I needed a community in which to grieve with others the shared loosening of lifelong bonds—the endless losses of children and friendships, partners and parents, beliefs, dreams, youth, life.

I longed for gesture and symbol and ritual, not realizing that this was my body's yearning. In my marrow, they were legacies from the Time when there were no words at all: from the ritual mating dance of snakes, to the nesting flight of hawks, to the chanting, dancing, and drumming of my earliest ancestors.

Ritual bridges difference. It bridges time and space. Scottish archeologist Graham Ritchie once told us about an ancient Paleolithic burial site he'd uncovered in Vedbeak, Denmark. When he excavated it, he found the remains of a deeply moving ritual: There, a grieving Neanderthal mother had laid her dead infant in the embrace of an outstretched swan's wing and buried him.

The soul of this primeval woman spoke her profound hope and heartbreak across time and space and species—and we felt her grief and her love as our own. She had lived among the first humans to become aware of death.[6] 100,000 years later, her helpless act of consecrating her loss in symbol and ritual spoke '*more than the words*'—precisely what I'd tried to avoid in the dream of the freezing infants.

I realized, then, that what my body yearned for was the *communal* recognition of this timeless and sacred bond: a bond with those I knew and those I didn't; with persons present, past, and yet to be born. All this was absent in my culture's rituals of New

Year's Eves and tailgate parties and the emptiness of Christmas shopping. I needed a community that embodied our belonging to all of Life—its *joignance* and its beauty.

As I listened to my body's messages, I decided quite spontaneously one day, to inquire at a local church. For twenty years, I'd slipped in unnoticed at Christmas and Easter to see with the eyes of my primal grandmother the wonders of celebration, there. In this place, every human body seemed a chalice for the current—the living water—in symbol and ritual, yes; but also in dance and mime, drama and art, and the resonance of song and trumpet and drum. This church had long allured me, but I had resisted its pull on my soul. Now, however, it seemed the right place in which to sanctify mysteries such as these.

I knew that, for me, it was no longer a matter of belief or denomination. I under-stood that I belonged to a communion of being greater than any tradition, but now, I wanted to live that one-ing in community. When I brought my yearning to the door of the church, I was invited to join a small meditation group there. A few days later, I sat for the first time with the people who would become my companions, friends, and teachers in the years to follow.

Why Do a Path and a Practice Matter?

How tightly we tend to hold to our perspective! How powerfully our brains' programming presses for our own survival, regardless of others! This root bondage to self is so deeply ingrained that, as Ursula King previously told us, Teilhard felt our only hope for genuine human community lay in the transforming power of Love:

> The fire of love may be the only energy capable of extinguishing the threat of another fire, namely that of universal conflagration and destruction.

We Have Mis-understood Love

Most spiritual paths work in us to refine a different kind of love than we've been taught by our culture. This Love is a genuine compassion that rises when the inner 'debris' is cleared away. One of the most important challenges to my journey was the following quote from Native American priest and therapist Anthony De Mello. He said love stems from awareness:

> How few understand what love really is, and how it arises in the human heart. It is so frequently equated with good feelings toward others, with benevolence or nonviolence or service. But these things in themselves are not love. *Love springs from awareness*. It is only inasmuch as you see someone as he or she really is here and now and not as they are in your memory or your desire or in your imagination or projection that you can truly love them, otherwise it is not the person that you love but the idea that you have formed of this person, or this person as the object of your desire, not as he or she is in themselves. The first act of love is to see this person, this object or this reality as it truly is. And this involves the enormous discipline of dropping your desires, your prejudices, your memories, your projections, your selective way of looking . . . a discipline so great that most people would rather plunge headlong into good actions and service than submit to the burning fire of this asceticism. When you set out to serve someone whom you have not taken the trouble to see, are you meeting that person's need or your own?[7]

We can develop a practice of awareness within our existing relationships. Every intimate relationship—if consciously engaged—has the potential to be a significant spiritual path. How late in life I came to understand that the deeper purpose of marriage was to learn how to love! This was its sacramental nature! (I speak here not only of marriage, but also of other deep commitments to relationship made before a community.) We may take a vow to love one another in a formal ceremony, but I believe we deceive ourselves if we think we begin a committed partnership in love.

Loving takes a lifetime. In the west, we've had few models for relationship rooted in anything other than power. Nor have the fantasies and distortions of love dispensed by the media helped us in our long-term commitments. Until we can move past the kind of intimate relationships the world has thus far put into common practice, we will continue to confuse physical desire and emotional neediness with the kind of love that De

Mello speaks of. But we can use a spiritual practice to develop our awareness.

Twelve-step programs articulate the relationship between this kind of growing self-awareness and how it becomes integrated:

> There is a direct linkage among self-examination, meditation and prayer. Taken separately these practices can bring much relief and benefit. But when they are logically related and interwoven, the result is an unshakable foundation for life.[8]

If we make the choice to *see* our distortions rather than project them onto others, we will have taken a first step towards greater insight. But insight is not enough for true acceptance and genuine commitment. We need to take these aspects of ourselves in our arms! To embrace them is a sacramental act.

It may be helpful to remind ourselves that every new form holds within it the remnants of what had come before it—whether it is the spine of a vertebrate, a story, a religion, or a self. We can learn to embrace those qualities on the other side of the duplex and let ourselves be who we are. Then, our relationships with others will be transformed: No longer based on power, they will have become a way to participate in the unfolding mystery of Love.

You Live in Conscious Communion With the Larger Life/life

A new kind of foundation is required to support the energies of Love—a different kind of conscious relationship. Thus far, in our inquiry, you have had an opportunity to experience the subtle differences between having a relationship to your thoughts or to your feelings or to your sensations—but the spiritual work of conscious attention is of an entirely different order.

In our daily lives, most of us tend to follow the many forms of 'thought' that move like ghosts across our mental screens: the words . . . feelings . . . images . . . and sensations that quite automatically determine pleasurable, fearful, or aggressive reactions. We realize that this is how our minds work! On the other hand, a spiritual path teaches us how to develop the softest, least aggressive quality of attention and turn it gently away from the self-centered focus of 'my' thoughts, 'my' feelings, 'my' sensations and memories—and towards an orientation that is not about 'me,' at all.

The intent of this turning is to bring us into a different quality of relatedness, one that results from giving our attention—not to these objects of consciousness—but to something that is *not an object*.[9] It is not unlike looking between/*beyond* the branches, the leaves, and the birds in the Japanese painting, and seeing, instead, the shimmering field that holds them. With skilled guidance and practice, we learn to make the essential internal shift of attention from figure to ground. We 'step back' and bring a refined quality of attention *to awareness itself*, and not to the 'thoughts' that have so enchanted us and kept us captive.

To Become Life's Intimate, We Become Aware of Awareness

We give the fullness of our attention—"all our heart and all our mind and all our strength"[10]—to the Field that holds what usually occupies us. 'Stepping back,' we let go of the thoughts, feelings, images, sensations, opinions, and desires that have helped to create a separate identity—and drop into the embrace of a more profound Perspective. This Perspective is at the heart of every spiritual and religious tradition. It consists of a relationship with a different kind of referent: an unnamable Mystery, a Depth of Being that includes our ordinary way of thinking *and transcends it*.

To put it another way, we experience the difference between having a relationship to *thoughts* about love . . . or to *feelings* of love . . . or *sensations* we associate with love—*and come into a quality of deep relatedness with Love, Itself*. An endnote gives Teilhard's description of the quality of attention needed for this kind of communion.[11]

Gradually, we learn to give our attention to the energetic Field instead of to its contents. We 'drop in' to the depths of ourselves. It can feel like going into a veritable abyss. We don't avoid our fear of this unknown—we feel it—and finding guidance in the words of St. John, quoted earlier—"though formal reason tries, it crumbles in the dark"—we *stay*. We settle into the darkness of this abyss repeatedly, rather than flee it out of fear, or discomfort, or a need for certainty.

We become clay for the Potter. One day—if we are damp enough, innocent enough, spontaneous enough—we may be surprised to discover that, like Bede Griffiths, we are no longer the center of our own lives. The larger Life 'behind' the life we know and everything in its embrace—is our conscious Core and Context.

In a statement that represents the crux of spiritual practice, Ken Wilber, the respected philosopher and theoretical psychologist, sets the practice of meditation squarely within this framework of life/*the larger Life*:

> If we—you and I—are to further the evolution of mankind, and not just reap the benefit of past humanities' struggles; if we are to contribute to evolution and not merely siphon it off; if we are to help the overcoming of our self-alienation from Spirit and not merely perpetuate it, *then meditation—or a similar and truly contemplative practice—becomes an absolute ethical imperative*, a new categorical imperative. . . . Meditation is simply what an individual at this present stage of average-mode consciousness *has to do in order to go beyond that stage.*[12]

Wilber alludes to the crucial difference between a singular focus on self-improvement and that of surrendering to a Power/*Process* greater than ourselves. Call it Spirit or Evolution as he does, or Love, Compassion, Life, Consciousness, or God—we orient to something much greater than we are, and remain open to the continuous nourishment of that Presence, the "living water." We give it our undivided attention—particularly as we relate to another person. It is from *that* Wholeness that we serve, not out of an anxious sense of pity or a noble desire to do good.

Conscious Communion Takes Energy

It takes a vast amount of energy to stay attuned to these subtleties—far more energy than is needed for thought. To sustain a conscious relationship to the greater Reality—to remain attentive, attuned, and responsive to it—requires discipline. This quality of attention demands significant physical and psychic energy; and our ability to increase the energy available to us is honed in the practice of meditation.

Energy and attention are deeply entwined. As Thomas Hand, SJ, cheerfully instructed his meditation groups:

> Where attention goes, energy flows!

The Practice of Attention Contributes to One-ing

By engaging in one of the many practices of attention—among them, art, contemplation, yoga, a martial art, meditation, or prayer—we begin to recognize that these energies are both *generated* and *grounded* in us at the same time. They are generated by attention; they are grounded as they become embodied. The very nature of spiritual practice brings us deeper and deeper into our bodies. "Chopping wood and carrying water," we continue to thaw out *more than the words*.

We let go. Letting go, our bodies relax and become supple, like those of little children. Such a bodymind is not contracted like those of the freezing infants in my dream; it is wide-awake and listening. Only a soft body and a vulnerable heart are sensitive enough to attune to the needs of a world filled with persons and species so very different from ourselves.

The Dalai Lama says that such a body is our more natural state:

> Look at this body. It is soft. It functions well with a gentle mind. If aggression were natural, then why is the body less functional, and why are there more illnesses when a person is aggressive and angry? Jealousy and anger are *part* of our mind, but not the dominant force of our mind.[13]

With practice, the awakening bodymind develops this kind of structural integrity. Attuned to its Ground, it becomes strong/ *vulnerable*—tender enough to be exquisitely receptive to the larger life. A person anchored in this quality of awareness is innately sensitive to our common bond. I hear this kind of sensitivity expressed in the story of the woman who merely touched the hem of Jesus garment, and *he knew it*.[14] Apocryphal or not, it is an unforgettable image that conveys the other side of Moses' *Fire*: the acute sensitivity we need to live in Love—in intimacy with others/*with the divine*.

This sensitivity is not all happiness and light. A body this alive feels more of everything: more delight, joy, compassion— and also more pain. It is the price we pay for Consciousness. We cannot have a sensitive body and at the same time inhabit one that does not, at times, hurt, particularly when we contract. Says Moss of the alive:[15]

> When we harden our hearts, it hurts.

The yearning for a conscious relationship with Life has been my doorway. When I've wavered, I've been aided by words like these of Rumi's:

> The breeze at dawn has secrets to tell you
> Don't go back to sleep.
> You must ask for what you really want.
> Don't go back to sleep.
> People are going back and forth across the doorsill
> where the two worlds touch.
> The door is round and open.
> Don't go back to sleep.[16]

If we don't go back to sleep, we will feel an ever-increasing intimacy with all there is—our companions in the wider Embrace. *Every* relationship is sacred, and as we learn to live from within this growing awareness, we turn to a handful of so-called strangers and know them intimately. We know the ancient redwoods in the same way; the stone cliffs, the meadow, and the light shining on the river. We are rapt at our kinship with a blazing world. It is lit up from inside.

I wake before five every day, now. There is something sacred . . . waiting . . . in this pre-dawn time. Each morning, when I peer out my window into the darkness, I see the eerie glow of two faint headlights from a truck parked in a distant meadow. Some unknown person comes every morning to put out grain for the cattle pastured there. How many thousands of years we've tended our livestock in the dark! What a human act! Now the new moon is cresting the pond where they water—a shining obsidian mirror. My candle flickers and illuminates each facet of the tiny crystal bowl that holds it. The headlights, the flame, and the moon are the only lights I see, yet everything, *everything* in this darkness—is brightness.[17]

Journaling offers another way of trying to express the experience and the mystery of one-ing. Still, the questions we asked at the beginning of our journey together remain:

Who am I? What is Love? What is God?

Questions like these can only point the way toward what we seek. But as our practice takes us into deeper and deeper kinds of awareness, it demonstrates to us that we are loved *in our very Ground*. We under-stand that, quite aside from the love of particular people in our lives, we are simply—beloved, bathed in the unseen depths of Existence. We begin to recognize that our own love and the greater Love are not separate, but that we and Love are *one-d*. Then, a final question arises:

What am I to do?

The world's traditions reply as one. In Bali, we saw their response dramatized in the ritual of *Prasad*. There, men and women parade to the temple carrying baskets heaped with offerings. Dressed in festive silken garments, they offer *Prasad*— their gift to the Master. The gift of *Prasad* may be fruit; it may be flowers; it may be service to an organization. Every kindness done for another is *Prasad*.

But what is important is this: Whatever is offered or whomever one serves, it is a conscious offering—*not to the other person but to the Master*—to God, to Brahman, to Love, to the unfolding Creative of the universe. The celebrant in the ritual is not the Master. He only represents that greater Reality, but the spiritual message is nonetheless vividly expressed in his action: He receives each gift of *Prasad*, blesses it *and gives it back—distributing it to all of the people*.

All of the people. *All* of life. *All* of the time.[18]
Then Love loves. That is *It*.

What Am I To Do?

We ask again, and again the traditions respond in unison, this time, through the words of the Buddha:

Hatred can never cease by hatred,
hatred can only cease by love—
this is an eternal law.[19]

Both the Buddha's words and rituals like *Prasad* remind us how we may serve life—by giving our selves to love/*Love*.

This becomes our motivation. We work 'inside' to work 'outside.' In our innermost work, we pray to embrace the rifts that need mending: our differences with others, but also the divisions within our own hearts—the love/*hate*, strength/*helplessness*, independence/*dependence*—whatever inner/*outer* conflicts challenge us at the threshold. We offer our embrace in service to a love that is growing in us/*a greater Love that is vast*. We turn and offer it to the world. It is our blessing, our work, our worship. By grace, the abyss is filled with love; by grace, we receive our divinity; by grace, we offer it up.

At a Zen retreat center on top of Tassajara Mountain in California, there is a simple dirt path bordered by plants and trees and an occasional handmade bench. The path winds among scattered small cabins, a vegetable garden, the springs, the *dojo*,[20] and the river. Walking at night, there is only the silence, some rocks to mark the way, and here and there on the ground, an oil lantern and a vase of flowers. It is as if some unknown persons had left gifts there as they passed.

To celebrate life and beauty, to relieve suffering, to leave a small marker for one another on the path, that is what any of us on the spiritual journey can do. We are all beginners. We walk. We listen. We serve. Walking, that is all, and this is the nature of the *Fire*: that those who walk are treasures. We love them, not for what they've been or done; we love them simply because they are there. We love them because they are walking along the same winding trail worn smooth by many others—all of us walking toward a horizon where the Unknown waits. We love them because we know it is Love itself that holds the dead and the living together as One; Love that gathers up and holds hearts that have been broken, and in the breaking, opens them wide. We love them because we know that in some mysterious way, it is also our own love—broken, offered, and given back.

Loved, We Love

Out of the felt reality of being loved comes the fruit of our self-giving. Heart and soul and thought and action unite to give it form. Trusting, we listen to the depth of each moment and our "*Yes!*" is simply this:

> *We learn to embrace our authenticity until it becomes one with our gift.*
>
> *We repeatedly offer who we are to the Power—and are offered back to the world.*

From the perspective of the greater Love, it is the little acts of love that are beautiful: the *Prasad* of each to the other, as unanticipated and as holy as a fistful of dandelions proffered by a little child. Sometimes, the simplest act carries the whisper farthest.

o

At midlife, when I was feeling most confused and lonely and afraid, my twelve-year-old son labored in secret in the back yard. While I worked long days in a high-tech company, he sawed and chopped and hauled brush to carve out the interior of a huge bush along the fence line. When he was finished, he asked me to close my eyes and led me outdoors by the hand to see his gift. On the far side of the garden, he stopped, then told me to open my eyes. When I did, I saw we were standing in front of a dense bush. I didn't understand. Then he pulled aside a single branch and my jaw dropped. It was a doorway that had covered a hidden opening.

Inside, he had made me a bower. It was a spacious enclosure: a leafy dome overhead, the ground below swept bare. In the center, he'd set upright a small log and smoothed its cut end for a seat. The hut was a holy place, a verdant haven from the world's demands. I went there often, for in that interior space, I felt safe and quiet and more at peace. It was no bush on fire, just an ordinary plant; but opened, and with the debris cleared away, it was my sanctuary—kiva, temple, and green cathedral.

o

What we offer isn't intended to make us larger. It gives increase to others. It may be our presence, undefended. It may be the gift of our goods, thus depleting our possessions. It may be an offering of our creativity, thus opening us to criticism. It may be our talents or our time. It may be our safety on behalf of another, or a different kind of risk that leaves us vulnerable. Whatever form it takes, the gift of our selves is a spontaneous movement of soul reaching to soul, an outer expression of the unfathomable Communion in which we live.

Then Life Flows Through

The depth of this truth is a far cry from the saccharine 'God is love' of the bumper stickers. It points toward the Mystery, the one-ing of love/*Love*. Michael Washburn describes it as a sacred attraction:

> The power of the Ground begins to disclose its innermost nature as . . . the *dynamic essence of insight and affirmation of others.* . . . It manifests its character as . . . spontaneous spiritual attraction, the impulse to spiritual intimacy. . . . Under these conditions, the ego is completely at one with the life of spirit . . . reaching out to bond with

others, spirit to spirit. . . . The power of the Ground is the . . . outflowing heart of compassion . . . pure spiritual power that embraces and confirms others, irrespective of their merits. . . . It shows itself to be *luminous love, consciousness in search of communion.*"[21]

It is this reality that is becoming conscious in us—a Consciousness in which *you* and *I* and *we* are one. In this One-ing, we participate in a larger, more complex set of relationships—what Jesus called "the Kingdom"—where there is only the eternal *"Yes!"* of the universe.

Endnotes for Chapter 13

1 Washburn, *The Ego and the Dynamic Ground*, 246. Italics mine.

2 Berry, *The Great Work*, 167-171, condensed. Italics mine.

3 Richard Moss teaches a powerful practice of orienting to the ineffable (what I have called the Third Beginning), in his workshops called *The Mandala of Being*. He also explains his methods in depth in his most recent book, *The Mandala of Being—Discovering the Power of Awareness*, Novato, CA: New World Library, 2007. See *http://www.richardmoss.com*

4 Houston Smith, interview, *East/West Magazine*, Mt. View, CA, January 2004.

5 A selection from 'Thought for the Day' from *http://www.wisdomatwork.com*

6 It is generally understood that awareness of death dates from the Paleolithic period and that the Neanderthals were the first to be aware of it. See Swimme and Berry, *The Universe Story*, 274.

7 Anthony de Mello, SJ, *Awareness*, New York: Random House, 1990.

8 *Twelve Steps and Twelve Traditions*, New York: Alcoholics Anonymous World Services, 1952, 100. *Author's note:* This text describes the philosophy and practice from which all Twelve-Step programs have emerged.

9 Language and grammar trip us up here and insist on such things as nouns and referents like "something" for "that" which is not an object!

10 This is my understanding of the first of the two commandments Jesus taught: *"You shall love the Lord your God with all your heart and with all your soul and with all your mind."* See Mark 12:29-31, Matthew 22:40, Luke 10:25-28.

11 Teilhard's description of the nature of this union is included in the editor's footnote to the quote, "Someday, after mastering the winds, the waves . . ." in Pierre Teilhard de Chardin, SJ, *Toward the Future*, tr. Rene Hague, New York: Harcourt Brace Jovanovich, 1975, 87. Hague's footnote reads: "As early as 1917, in the very middle of the first world war, Père Teilhard felt himself called to give living expression to this ultimate form of love in God: 'The true union that you ought to seek with creatures that attract you is to be found not by going directly to them, but by converging with them on God, sought in and through them. It is not by making themselves more material, relying solely on physical contacts, but by making themselves more spiritual in the embrace of God, that things draw closer to one another. . . .' (*Writings in Time of War*, 143, 197). (Ed.)"

12 A selection from 'Thought for the Day' from *http://www.wisdomatwork.com* (Second italics mine.) Retrieved 2005.

13 The Dalai Lama in a speech at Stanford University, January 2006.

14 Mark 5:25-34 and Luke 8:40-48.

15 'Alive' is used here in contrast with the way Jesus used the term, 'dead,' in his statement, *"Let the dead bury their dead."* Luke 9:60 (KJV).

16 Jalal al-Din Rumi, *The Essential Rumi*, tr. Coleman Barks, New York: HarperCollins, 1995, 36.

17 From my journal.

18 Familiarity with my own tradition helped me to recognize the great truth at the root of *Prasad*. It is visible in the work of Mother Theresa; heard in the story of Jesus' feeding of the 5000; and made concrete in the church's ritual of communion. Each of them is a *koan*, each fathomless.

19 A selection from 'Thought for the Day' from *http://www.wisdomatwork.com*

20 The *dojo* is a term used in Japanese martial arts that refers to a formal gathering place for students and teachers in which to meditate and to conduct training.

21 Washburn, *The Ego and the Dynamic Ground*, 128-129. Second italics mine.

14 Living in the Kingdom While Living in the World

Between me and God
there is no between.

Julian of Norwich[1]

An awakening offers, if only for an instant, confirmation of the fullness and the glory of a seamless reality we may have previously only imagined. Like a great *"Yes!"* it breaks us open, inviting us into an intimacy with Existence that *is* living in the Kingdom.

We *all* live in the Kingdom every day of our lives. It's just that, most of the time, we may not be aware of this realm where "there is no between." We may discover its *inward* aspect in meditation. But busy with our lives, we may not recognize that the extraordinary moments that seem so rare in the *outer* world are also part of the experience of the Kingdom. And they are happening all the time.

In her writing, Teresa of Avila tried to describe what life was like when one lived "grounded in the soul instead of in the mind."[2] Grounded in the soul, we inhabit the deepest form of the inner/*outer* reality; what Jane Hirschfield called "liminal space." This reality is undivided: It is center and circumference, here and there, past and future.

Four centuries after Teresa lived, Edgar Mitchell, the sixth astronaut to walk on the moon, had an epiphany as he hurtled home through outer space. Years later, he tried to tell an audience about the breadth and depth of what he'd experienced. To do so, he tapped the wisdom of the mystics, saying:

> It has been said that to know ourselves we have to know the universe; but to know the universe, say the mystics, we have to know ourselves.[3]

His words have a way of turning our worldview inside out. Colin Oliver painted the same radical change of perspective in his lovely poem, "In The Vast Sweep of Heaven."

> Inside the person the secret
>   and inside the secret,
>   curled north to south, the country.
>
> Inside the country the lair
>   and inside the lair,
>   curled head to tail, the wolf.
>
> Inside the wolf the womb
>   and inside the womb,
>   curled nose to knee, the child.
>
> Inside the child the heart
>   and inside the heart,
>   curled east to west, the stars
>
> in the vast sweep of heaven.[4]

Not being astronauts or poets, it can be difficult to try to express the revolution of being "grounded in the soul"—the Unity where inner and outer are no longer separate. I found myself repeatedly bogged down when I started to write this chapter. I was struggling to be clear in my use of concepts like 'self,' 'other,' 'God,' 'soul,' and 'Kingdom'—but my *bodymind's experience* could not separate them. Much as I'd hoped to delimit the words; much as I wanted to express what was soul and what, our true Self; what was Ground and what, Heaven—I could not tease apart these subtleties with thought. Eventually, my mind simply had to give up.

I remained completely entangled until I decided to trust the experience of my whole self and let the words fall where they may. Then, amazing things happened. As I'd finish a section, various references either 'occurred' to me like a lightning bolt, or arrived like a gift in the mail from others. Each reference confirmed, not my concepts, but the fullness of actual experience. I'd written, for example:

> Called out of us, the soul rises in awareness. While it has always been within us, it now seems to be 'outside' us too, encompassing the self we have always known.

The same day, reader Frankie Brogan sent an email with these lines by the Irish poet and philosopher John O'Donohue:

> The soul is not simply within the body, hidden somewhere within its recesses. The truth is rather the converse. Your body is in the soul, and the soul suffuses you completely.[5]

Yes.

When I try to feel into the mystery of soul in myself, I reflect first on the three foundations, and how they have helped me to symbolize the way we've all evolved. It is easy for me to see how each of us began in infancy as a body-consciousness, then developed more complex feelings, and eventually began to reason. But as I grope my way into the ephemeral nature of soul, it isn't discrete like the first three. It's almost as if it were a vast membrane enveloping all three foundations—yet it is more.

In my experience, soul is not something we have; it is more like who we are—*together*. Grounded in the soul, we are no longer merely separate individuals. We are also a *We*: my soul/*Soul*. And if I/*We* listen *as* soul, it is a living bridge to others; a way of relating that is complementary to knowing. My colleague Susan Neville calls it a "deeper pattern":

Recently I dreamt about a woman who, when she bent down, had a cockleshell dangling from her neck. Where the image of a cockleshell came from I had no idea, but it was such a prominent detail, I looked it up to confirm my view of it. Two weeks ago my daughter came home from college. Sitting at the table one evening, what did I see—a simple cockleshell strung on a piece of string around her neck. When these things happen, I feel connected to the world in a very strange way. These images speak another kind of truth. I feel in touch with a deeper pattern that I don't understand but that I trust.

Soul lives in relationship with reality-as-it-is, not as we conceive it to be. Beyond the honeycomb of thought we constructed as toddlers; beyond the language that filters what we receive from our surroundings; beyond the limiting divisions between me and you, subject and object, time and space, cause and effect, there is a seamless set of transactions between the worlds—inside/*outside,* here/*there,* me/*you,* 'reality'/*the greater Reality.* These transactions go unnoticed most of the time. But those who walk between the worlds like the shaman, *see* differently. Now Thomas Berry's koan becomes clearer:

> [For the human species to evolve, we must descend] far back into the genetic foundations . . . to the shamanic dimension of the psyche.

Everything in the universe—including each one of us—is a dynamic field of energies that interacts with everything else. Berry called this reality "a ground with many centers." The Buddhists named it "InterBeing." Philosopher George Jaidar[6] called it the "soul process." In this mutual transaction, the greater *"Yes!"* has always been said *to* us. Our part is to *live* our *"Yes!"* in return. I call that kind of response *faith.*

We Can Develop a Different Kind of Faith

Faith is different from belief. Belief, as I tend to define it, is a belief *in* something. Faith is a way of life. Better said, it is a way of *being life.* Being life, we are integral to the whole.

Faith doesn't know. It inquires. The soul feels its way into each moment, as if asking, *What now? What now?*—then listens for a sense of what is needed. The Rev. Mark Goodman-Morris adds:

This is not the unconscious prayer to a projected God you want him to be, but the God of the universe that loves us.

Faith is a radical surrender of knowing—evolution's change of mind. Faith doesn't keep God in its pocket like a lucky talisman. It is a *vulnerable* position. Faith refuses to reduce Mystery to an object the mind can label with words like 'God,' or 'the unconscious'. . . 'Jung's Self' . . . 'the universe' . . . or 'nature.' The fullness of reality cannot be compressed in this way! To have a creative relationship with the larger Life, we cannot live according to old thoughts, habits, or beliefs—or relate to it as an object of consciousness.

The kind of faith I'm trying to express is a way of engaging life creatively by going beyond a mind that is already made up. It requires that intellect be engaged as needed, but that it no longer dominates. Such a faith presupposes that our minds serve something they cannot name or understand. And that depends on a radical shift of orientation from figure to the larger Ground. With this orientation, we're no longer the ones who live our lives. We are lived-through.

William Sloan Coffin wrote:

I love the recklessness of faith. First you leap,
and then you grow wings.[7]

When I can dare this kind of recklessness—and it is not always—it allows me to enter what Jaidar called the soul process. This process takes place in the here and now when I stand empty of memory and empty of my plans. It is in moments like these that I feel most vulnerable and exposed, and sometimes even quite terrified. *How do I know* that a particular choice is the right one? I don't.

And yet . . . and yet . . . when I *live* in this way, I'm never more myself, never more fulfilled—and once in a while, act in ways I might never before have conceived.

The Ad

In the middle of a night several years ago, I heard an abrupt inner command: *"Put an ad in the paper! Say this!"* The ad's copy followed, fast and furious. I couldn't tell you now whether I was awake or asleep, but this was more than just one of my 'ideas.' It arrived whole: a detailed ad for a course that I'd never envisioned, never even considered. I sat up and scribbled the instructions on a pad by my bedside. They were very specific. When I woke the next morning, this is what I saw on the yellow Postit™ before me:

> MINING YOUR LIFE FOR MEANING
> How to Discover the Meaning of Your Own Life
>
> How do you discover the meaning of *your* life? Does it consist of a slide show of people, places, events, a series of jobs or merit badges earned? Learn how expressing your own inborn creativity can deepen your experience and increase your awareness. This gathering is about living your life and writing about it. Small group, safe, supportive environment. You need not be an experienced writer to join. . . .

That morning, I typed up the ad exactly as it had come to me, added dates, and sent it by email to the editor of a weekly newspaper for which I'd written occasional columns. Then, I telephoned a local daily with the same copy. When I asked what the ad would cost, the operator's reply was "$300"! I hastily withdrew it! Embarrassed, I called my former editor: "I had no idea how much the ad I emailed would cost! I'll shorten it!!"

"Don't worry, Anne," he shot back, "we'll give you a free display ad for next week's issue and send it to our sister paper too." I was astonished at his generosity—and yet I wasn't, for I had once heard said:

> When it is Time for something to happen in the universe, the action is as easy as a hot knife through butter!

The next day, however, my mind began to argue. *Just what do you think you're going to do in this course, now that you've put an ad in a paper?* I had no idea. It was now Saturday and the ad was to run Tuesday. I tried all morning to sketch an outline—

and failed. On Monday, I went to my studio, having completely forgotten the ad! As I turned on the computer, I saw the Postit™ note on the desk. Twenty minutes later, the plan for a complete ten-session course had laid itself out on the screen before me.

The ad drew nineteen replies. As I talked with the first person who called, I wondered to myself, *what I should charge?* (I hadn't even thought of the fee!) When he asked, I responded with the first small sum that floated into mind; I'd done no math in advance. The course was filled in a day. Since then, I've never advertised or sent out fliers, nor have I changed the fee. Word of mouth has filled two yearly offerings six months in advance for several years. 'I' had nothing to do with it. 'I' didn't come up with the idea for the course, create its overall design, or even try to fill it. I am still amazed.

o

The long story of life is filled with acts of faith orders of magnitude greater than this: There were no instructions at the tide line for those first living things driven or called to make their perilous way out of the sea onto dry land. Bit by infinitesimal bit in that new habitat, *all* forms changed: among them, how those proto-amphibians were to breathe, to hatch, to nourish and protect themselves. We have seen how radical changes of form like these accompany any genuine transformation. Whoever first carried fire home in his hands had to transcend a built-in instinct to flee it. This amazing human creature could not have known the consequences of his actions beforehand—only that he must listen to some strange inner suggestion and follow it to its conclusion. By following his call, he was serving the universal flow of the Creative. I suspect that some form of faith exists in the cells of all the earth's creatures whenever they are poised on the threshold of Life's transformative moments. But do I, who am so reliant on knowing, dare to enter the unknowns of the Time in which I live? Am I willing to live in uncertainty without guarantee of success? These are the kinds of questions I ask myself all the time.

The poet W. S. Merwin writes from this edge of unknowing, and lends encouragement with a different kind of metaphor about a butterfly:

> It is said that the monarch butterfly can fly 2500 miles in the fall from Maine to Mexico and arrive, not tattered, but as fresh as if it had just come from the chrysalis. The achievement is magnified by the fact that a migrant monarch anywhere along the route will be *three or more generations removed* from its most recent ancestor there. The individual butterfly had never been to the place before and never could have learned the way. *It knew it—its knowledge part of a guiding inheritance,* along with the aptitude for transforming itself from an egg into a caterpillar and from a chrysalis into an adult able to fly.[8]

Surely, if a butterfly has a guiding inheritance, so do we! We are all heir to the gift of a creature's body—its connectedness to earth; its ability to live in concert with life. If we are to follow that whispered guidance as part of our *species'* long migration from body, to heart, to mind, *to soul,* we need to listen with all these aspects of ourselves. *They* are the tender connection we have with Life. We may not know what or where that connection is, but we can trust that—like the butterfly's—it was long since built in.

> *There is an Intelligence, a Love within which we are enfolded, a larger Field in which we live.*

We live in a "ground with many centers," a field where everything penetrates everything else. Within things, within us, between and among everything that exists, this Intelligence lies deeper than feeling and sensation can access, beneath and beyond the reach of thought. Invisible, unnamable, this "Ground of all Being"[9] *supports* the three foundations of the soul. They are made of it, dug deep in it—this true Foundation of our lives.

We are not used to relying on anything so subtle as this, but this deeper Foundation is only subtle as long as it is an *idea*. It becomes very real *when we learn to act in concert with it*. Then, we engage what Parker Palmer calls the "reliable truth."[10]

Zen Buddhists call this truth "the Tao"—the Current that runs through all of life. Jesus called it "the Kingdom."

Once in a while, like sunlight breaking through an overcast sky, the nature of this Kingdom makes itself known as a present/*eternal* reality. To bring that kind of reality to life, only stories will do. For the remainder of our journey together, we'll turn to story (and finally, to poetry) for glimpses of this unseen mystery. If these slender shafts of light reflect similar moments in your own life, I hope you will share your stories with others, too; for it's only when *all* of our stories are told and embraced that the dynamic nature of the Kingdom is revealed. Then the radiance shines through us, *together*.

The Chair

High noon on a beastly hot day at a harbor in British Columbia, and the sun is relentless. I walk alone on the quay by the water; to my right, a parking lot and below on my left, a few sailboats hanging low in the marina. It is low tide and the barnacles bake on the heavy black pilings. A small dock floats at the foot of a long ramp that leads up to the quay. Because of the waning tide, the ramp is steeply pitched between low water and the quay above it. Half way to the top, an elderly woman pushes a sailor's wheelbarrow uphill.

The going is rough when you try to bring bulky duffel bags, boating equipment, and uneaten groceries back to land from a boat. I watch as the wheel of her overloaded cart keeps catching on the evenly-spaced cleats along the ramp. Each time it hits a cleat, the cart bangs the side of the wooden railing and tilts precipitously over the water. The woman keeps trying to right it, but it gets stuck, again and again.

I run to help her, and together, we work our way up the ramp with the awkward load—banging rails and cleats, fighting gravity. By the time we're near the top, she is gasping. I yank the wheelbarrow up the last few feet to the quay alone, then turn to give her my arm. She is clearly weak and exhausted, and whispers, "My husband told me to wait for him . . ." she gasps mid-sentence and points a limp hand . . . "near that dumpster in the parking lot." She needs to sit down, but there is no bench, no grass, no curb, and no shade by the stinking dumpster; nothing but melting blacktop, radiating heat waves and row after row of parked cars. The sun is scorching as it bounces off all that hot steel and chrome.

The old woman looks frail. She stands in the sun, bent and alone, waiting for a husband who is nowhere in sight. I lean down, put my face close to hers and say—partly to her, partly to God—*"We need a chair!"* Then I turn toward the parking lot.

A small pickup truck is making its way toward us, laden with furniture. Roped upright atop the load like a throne on a dais is a small wooden chair.

Fear shouts, *Don't be foolish! Don't even think of it!* I gulp, then step into the middle of the lane and hail the truck. One of the two young men rolls down his window on the passenger side and looks inquiringly. I smile and try to swallow, but my mouth is dry. "I'm wondering: Are you just coming into the lot or are you leaving? This woman is not well and needs a chair to sit on. I was hoping you might be coming in to park, and that we could borrow your chair for a while." They smile, but say no, they are leaving—and drive on. I wave them off, thinking, *Well, I guess that wasn't the thing to do;* then, look down to the far end of the lot. *But maybe the boat rental shed over there can spare a chair.* There is still no sign of the woman's husband, so I explain my plan to her, then turn and lope toward the small clapboard shed. Despite my pleading, the three people in the rental office are not *about* to give up a chair! I step out the shed's screen door, disappointed and empty-handed, and shade my eyes against the glare. Squinting, I look through my lashes across the baking asphalt and what do I see? An elderly woman hobbling across the lot, propped on either side by the two men in the pickup! One pushes her wheelbarrow with his free hand; the other has the wooden chair slung over his arm. When I reach them, they explain, "We decided to bring her over by this bush where there was a little shade. We'll leave the chair here for her and come back and get it later."

o

The wonder of it! I'd been amazed by other confluences in my life, but I'd never acted on them before. This time, I was pushed over the edge of my hesitation by a book I'd been reading on vacation, a gift from a friend the previous week. The timing of the gift was impeccable. Its author George Jaidar stressed that *when we trust just long enough to act, we discover the cosmos can be trusted, too.*[11] I had barely begun to make it my priority to live in this kind of relationship with Life, but Jaidar made clear that such a commitment demanded more than lip service. One had to enter the soul process by acting. So when the chair appeared, I moved *fast!* Only later, did I realize that Jaidar's words reflected a *spiritual* interpretation of the passage from the Sermon on the Mount we examined *psychologically* in Chapter 6:

> Everyone who hears these words . . . and puts them into practice is like a wise man who built his house on the rock. . . . But [he] who hears . . . and does not put them into practice is like a foolish man who built his house on sand.[12]

It was by acting in response to the inner/*outer* whisper that I actually came to trust the Kingdom. No longer an abstract idea, it became a present reality. From that day on, I knew I was not alone; that life (and I-as-life) could be trusted, and that what was genuinely needed was available—arising in the instant of need. I came to see this mystery as a mutual unfolding, having nothing to do with me as a separate individual but with *Us*—the Communion of Existence.

Endnotes for Chapter 14

1 Julian of Norwich. Source unknown.
2 The well-known saint from Avila, Spain, Teresa (1515-1582) wrote three books, of which the best known is *The Interior Castle*. Source of her statement unknown.
3 Edgar Mitchell, from a speech at a conference at the Institute of Noetic Sciences, 2004.
4 Colin Oliver, "In the Vast Sweep of Heaven," Clare, Great Britain: Unpublished. Used with permission.
5 John O'Donohue, *Anam Cara—A Book of Celtic Wisdom*, New York: HarperCollins, 1998, 49. O'Donohue echoes Meister Eckhart's phrase, "Your body is in the soul."
6 The late George Jaidar is the author of *The Soul*. See discussion later in the chapter and publication data in endnote 11.
7 William Sloan Coffin, *Credo*, Westminster: John Knox Press, 2003.
8 W. S. Merwin, *The Ends of the Earth*, Washington, DC: Shoemaker & Hoard, 2004, 180, Condensed. Italics mine.
9 The name that theologian, Paul Tillich, gives to Mystery is the "Ground of all Being." It combines *Ground*—which resonates (like Thomas Berry's coined words) with the moist earth of *adamah* and the *kiva*—and *Being*, which carries overtones of the transcendent. And there is no way to objectify it.
10 Parker J. Palmer, *The Active Life*, San Francisco: Jossey-Bass, 1991, 44.
11 George Jaidar, *The Soul*, New York: Paragon House, 1995. "The soul process" is his term.
12 Matthew 7:24-26 (NIV).

15 How to Enter the Kingdom

Not until all is given
Comes the thought of heaven.
When the mind's an empty room
The clear days come.

Wendell Berry[1]

If we are to hear the story of the chair in Chapter 14 and the stories that follow it with 'ears to hear,' we shall need to release the mind's grip on its old images and ideas, and let it become "an empty room." All religions have consistently offered lessons about this necessary change of mind, but it is likely we have heard them (and perhaps even Wendell Berry's phrase), with the minds of the three foundations. These ways of perceiving can only lead us astray by throwing us back into our old identity—the one with concepts for everything. Tai Chi Master, Richard Farmer, says:

> For me, as the layers of ego fall away, all that seems to remain is the existence of love in the silence, and the falling towards it within me.[2]

Though the messages of countless sages, poets, teachers, and philosophies are similar to one another, I am most conversant with the Judeo-Christian tradition. I've therefore, chosen examples from several of Jesus' statements about what he called "the Kingdom." How people ordinarily *hear* these statements range from ideas about an afterlife to the more abstract kind of perceptions developed by academics (see the endnote for an example).[3] But to consent to a new *kind* of "identity"—as relatedness or as soul—we have to let go of these kinds of mental concepts, and the first to go is the concept of cause and effect. My expression of need did not cause the chair to appear. Neither do I believe in a puppeteer-God who had it all planned and pulled strings. That is an older way of listening.

In teaching about the Kingdom, Jesus challenged three other concepts: those of space and of time, along with our belief that we are separate and independent selves. In the first example, he tied the three together:

> The Kingdom of God is within you.[4]

The meaning of this passage hinges on the choice of a preposition. Episcopal priest and scholar Jim Blackburn explained that 'within you' is a translation from the Greek, *'entos,'* which also means 'in your midst' and 'all around you.'[5] This single choice of preposition, *'entos,'* basically means *'in, around,* and *between!'*

Entos blurs our concepts about space, but Jim has more to say about its use in this passage—and he is emphatic: "*Entos* is a plural word. 'Within you' does not mean a personal, isolated indwelling. *It indicates a group!*"

The group is doubly important, here. These seven words— "the Kingdom of God is within you"—deal with more than the concept of space. They also address our perception of identity; and the group is closer to the mystery of who we are *as* relationship in the inner/*outer* Kingdom.

Before exploring how we can actually experience this larger so-called identity, it may be helpful to look at one more passage in which the concepts of space and identity are again, entwined. In the following selection from the *Gospel According to Thomas,*[6] Jesus first separates the Kingdom from our ordinary ideas about space:

If your guides claim
That the Kingdom is in the sky,
The birds of the sky will be there before you.
If they say it is in the sea,
The fishes of the sea will be there before you.
The Kingdom is within you and without you.[7]

He then immediately answers the basic human question of identity: *Who am I?* in his next statement:

When you know yourselves, you will be known.
Then you shall know that you are
Sons and daughters of the Living Father.
But if you do not know yourselves
You are in poverty and you are poverty.[8]

In this stanza, Jesus implies that there is a deeper level to know about ourselves. He suggests that *who we really are* has to do with our relationship to Mystery (personified here as the 'Living Father'), and that our poverty *is in not knowing ourselves deeply enough*. This message is similar to his statement in Matthew, quoted in Chapter 9:

If salt loses its saltiness, how can it be made salty again? It is no longer good for anything . . . .

Without saltiness, salt has lost what it really is—its 'salt-ness.' In chapters 8 and 9, we saw how our contractions contributed to the condition of self-avoidance. This time, we hear his metaphor from a spiritual perspective (rather than the psychological perspective in the earlier chapters), and the term *Self-avoidance* is capitalized, for Jesus is saying that the 'salt-ness' of who we *really* are—is Presence.

Because the presence of Presence is inexpressible, it is often communicated the way the four blind men described an elephant—one view at a time.[9] In his teaching, Jesus circles this issue of Presence from every angle, and each time he speaks, gives us a different perspective—a 'snapshot.' In this example from Matthew, he says:

Where two or three are gathered together in my name, there am I in the midst of them.[10]

To understand 'I' in this way is not to hear him talking about his personality, but about what lies at the deepest dimension of who he is. As I hear the passage, he is saying, "There am I/*Presence* in the midst of them." He is also emphasizing the importance of seeing our own identity differently, and makes clear that this ineffable Presence is registered by "two or three gathered together"—*the group*. He further qualifies his statement by saying that a group will know Presence *if it is practicing focused attention*—e.g., "in my name."

I think what he means is this: We are unaccustomed to discerning the sacred bond of Presence in our everyday lives. These energies are easier to detect in group meditation because the group's unified attention helps to amplify them. This might sound strange to a non-meditator; but those of you who've had longer experience meditating with others may remember that, at first, you probably weren't aware of anything at all like 'energy.' You may have even wondered what people in the group were talking about! But as you honed your capacities for attention in the group, your awareness of the presence of Presence grew.

Our capacity to register this energetic Presence is like the tiniest seed of a wild mustard plant[11] that gradually spreads throughout an entire field. It begins as the subtlest of hints and slowly becomes a palpable expression of *who we really are—together*. In the teaching from Matthew—"where two or three are gathered together in my name, there am I in the midst of them"—I hear Jesus insist that if we are to enter *this* kind of Kingdom, one that exists in the here and now, we have to *live* as relationship. And we need to do more than think it. To understand the way we belong to each other and to Life, we have to *do* it—turn our attention to the presence of Presence.

We are all members of an awakening species and an awakening earth, all capable of attending the presence of Presence. If we consciously attune to this subtle reality within/*among*/all *around* us, we will witness our true personhood as One: as individuals/*the group*/*Presence*/*Life*. When we rest in this kind of awareness, we are joined. And there is no between.

Then, when we are threatened, there is the possibility of choosing a different way to respond—rather than go to war.

Some readers may grow concerned about these kinds of interpretations because they don't fit within traditional teachings. In this kind of situation, I am aided by the words of Sarah Bagley:

Truth loses nothing upon investigation.[12]

The purpose of our investigation has been to seek a common denominator in the hope of transcending our differences. To that end, we've been attempting to listen to familiar and unfamiliar teachings in what may seem to be an unusual way. To hear texts in this manner does not mean one is abandoning one's tradition any more than Thomas Berry abandoned the priesthood by calling himself a "geologian." On the contrary, Baptist minister and journalist Bill Moyers described this common denominator as the root of all religions:

Every religion rises from within. Each one expresses a lived human experience.[13]

Historian Evelyn Underhill concurred:

Each great religious tradition . . . originate[d] in the special experiences of some soul who has acted as the revealer of spiritual reality.[14]

People from every tradition—as well as many who stand outside traditions—have described their own dynamic introduction to that root religious experience. Called by many names over thousands of years, it is a *felt energetic connection between human beings and the greater Life.* As Berry told us in Chapter 13, "we all lived in an ocean of energy during the Neolithic period." In later periods, it was seen to be a connection to Brahman, to the Tao, to God, to Jesus, or to other spiritual leaders. In our Time, we may also extend that awareness of connection to all of creation.

Although anyone who meditates regularly in a group is likely to experience Presence, a sudden or spontaneous awakening *radically* unlocks it. An awakening such as this is an abrupt introduction to the energies of Love, and it can change a person forever. This first exposure can be electrifying. It may feel almost like being 'plugged in'—plunged into a spaciousness/ *timelessness* that has no limitation. In this kind of awakening, the energies of Love break through our contractions, and ego comes face to face with a Power that far exceeds its own. In such a moment, our everyday minds become consciously aware of an unquestionable truth that is One. It has been registered physically, mentally, emotionally, and spiritually—and there is absolutely no way to prove it.

Though some have been 'once born,' rarely do the rest of us experience this kind of breakthrough into Consciousness without first knowing great suffering. It can be a very dark time—a period of disillusionment or emptiness, despair or terror, in which a person seems to reach the very bottom of himself. The endnote gives several examples.[15]

Then, unexpectedly, comes the flash of *Fire,* and in its wake, he is left radically alive. This sweeping shift of referent— from the personal to the universal—has been called a death and rebirth; but in Love, it refuses to be labeled. When this new Consciousness is born, it *will not* be divided. Jesus describes such an undivided mind in the *Gospel according to Thomas*:

> When you make two into one
> And what is within like what is without
> And what is above like what is below,
> And when you unite male and female in one
> So that the male is no longer male
> And the female no longer female . . .
> Then you shall enter the Kingdom.[16]

T. S. Eliot offers a sea image for this seamless reality, and calls it his "beginning":

> . . . Out at sea the dawn wind
> Wrinkles and slides. I am here
> Or there, or elsewhere. In my beginning.[17]

Eliot's "beginning" is the fundamental change of mind revealed in a spontaneous awakening. We can *approximate* it, however, by turning our attention to what I call the *third Beginning*. This Beginning is different from the first two—childhood and the childhood of the race—in that it doesn't represent a particular stage or time. Rather, it is a complete change of orientation.

Changing the orientation of our minds is real spiritual practice, and all of us can learn how to do it.[18] It is not unlike the way we turned our attention from the figures of the birds to the gold in the Japanese painting. To orient to the third Beginning, we turn *away* from the programming inherent in our three foundations by giving our attention to the immediacy of the present moment—sometimes called 'the Now.'

Once more, the analogy of the dancer can be helpful. As we saw earlier, the dancer first prepares by stretching, then turns her attention to the music. Once she is well in her body and attuned to the music, *then,* she can begin to dance. Likewise, if we have learned in our practice to drop deeper into ourselves than thought, we can turn our attention to the precise moment in which we are living, and *stay*. In this liminal space, we are fully present/*in the present*. Then, we can begin to dance *with Life*—and all kinds of transformations are possible.

Andrea, a young entrepreneur, stands in her kitchen early one morning, still angry with her husband for not walking the dog before he left for work. She doesn't have time to take the dog out. She's unprepared for the management meeting she's leading at nine, and has a proposal to write for a client. Her anxiety is sky-high but she also knows an alternative to a body wracked with tension. She has learned how to become completely present to the moment. She turns her attention to that third Beginning, stands very still, then takes a few deep breaths and 'drops in.' Leaving her thinking behind, she lets her mind drop down, down—into her body's awareness. Andrea chooses to be in the moment-at-hand—not to relive what happened this morning or anticipate what is to come. She *stays*—fully present—with no idea of what will occur, then listens inside and asks . . .

In a flash, she feels her body's response and the hot tears well up and spill over. From the perspective of *being*—being at the Beginning—Andrea has tapped some old feelings. Painful as they are, she stays. When she realizes they belong to the child-inside who'd felt too responsible and often left behind, she lets go. Her anger is gone. She is at peace.

Learning to orient to the third Beginning is a practice we can rely on in any situation. It can transform feelings, attitudes, and behavior in a moment. This is the way to peace.

Without conscious attention to an entirely new orientation, we remain at the mercy of our programming, deep in the triune brain. No matter what kind of awakening we have experienced—gradual or abrupt—it yields no fruit. Rather, we are like the seed scattered by the sower that has fallen by the roadside—with *"no depth of earth . . . scorched . . . and because it had no root . . . withered away."*[19] Through the practice of meditation, Andrea had long since prepared the soil of her inner garden. Well-rooted in her self, all she had to do in the moment—was to 'drop in.'

Life offers beauty, joy, and opportunities. It also offers cranky children, clothes driers that break down, and difficult moments in relationship. Harder to accept are the violence, cruelties, and the abuse of power rampant in the world around us. At such times, we learn to 'drop in' and to be with whatever is happening. Rather than judge it, we turn the other cheek and stay. We become acutely aware of the intangible moment-at-hand, and then give it the most refined quality of attention: We soften our breath, become very open, alert, and relaxed. We don't try to make an object of a moment by thinking about it. We are just present to it. *We are it.* It is our Beginning, too.

And that is why it's important. At the cusp of every moment, we are not the person derived from past experience—not caught in the net of our own convictions. In this kind of orientation, we are brand new. We are pure potential, and in this sense, stand at the Beginning of *ourselves*. This is so different from the threshold of our collective lives—a threshold of conflict between certainties! The third Beginning is a state of complete uncertainty, a creative threshold: an opportunity to respond in a new way. If we stay, remain exquisitely attentive, and listen to Life with ears to hear, we are more than who we think we are. We are grounded in the soul. Unencumbered by memory or by anxiety over the future, we are *awake*.[20]

Poet Colin Oliver describes such a mind as

> one that is open and not stitched up with knowing.

Knowing—thinking, defining, judging, opposing—keeps us from entering the inner/*outer* Kingdom. But when we stand at the third Beginning, we are simply *here*—what T. S. Eliot called *"The intersection of the timeless with time."*[21] In this ineffable moment, ego is disabled. It has no power.

Disabling the ego is the work of the spiritual Way. Ego cannot function in the present—only in past or future. But the Power called by so many names—God . . . the Buddha . . . Atman . . . the Tao—*only acts in the present moment.*

Long before Freud, the various traditions of East and West offered teachings and practices like this to confront our programming. In another of his many snapshots of the Kingdom, Jesus suggested we "become as a little child." In *The Gospel of Thomas*, he offered a metaphor for how to enter the kind of Kingdom he called "the place of Life." When his followers asked him how to go there, he responded:

> An old man, heavy in years,
> Will not hesitate to ask a baby, seven days old,
> About the place of Life.[22]

In another passage, he used the same image:

> These babies being nursed
> Are like those entering the Kingdom.[23]

The sweetness of their reply is moving to me:

> They asked: "Shall we enter the Kingdom?
> We are small."[24]

A baby has not yet differentiated a 'me' separate from others, nor does it divide 'now' from 'then,' 'here' from 'there,' 'past' from 'future,' 'beginning' from 'ending.' But there is a crucial difference: When we stand at the third Beginning, we are *"like a child" but we have not regressed. We make meaning out of our experience*; a baby does not. In this deep, liminal space, we are *aware*.

Psychologist Ken Wilber goes to great lengths to differentiate the mental processing that is 'pre-rational' from that which is 'post-rational,' and states categorically that "genuine mystical or contemplative states are not to be seen as regression to infantile states . . . as did Freud . . . [nor should one] elevate prerational states to some sort of transrational glory . . . [as did] Jung. . . . The higher developments do indeed lie beyond reason, but never, never beneath it."[25]

We Can Change Our Minds

The function of spiritual practices like these is to 'break the mind'—to break ego's grip on the mind's distinctions so we can open to a larger kind of awareness.[26] Our way of thinking requires contrast. Surely, intellect identifies shades of grey, but in order to name what it has experienced, it often wobbles on the razor's edge of opposition: above/*below*, male/*female*, self/*other*, mine/*yours*, friend/*enemy*. Each polarity excludes the other—and when ego sticks to the label it has chosen, it 'creates a world' based on exclusion. The ills of our planet are rooted in this kind of opposition.

The 'breaking' of a mind made up—a mind that knows *what* things are and *who* one is and *how* one is supposed to act—happens whenever circumstances force a collision between old ways and the New. But as we learned from the Chinese symbols for crisis, these collisions can also be opportunities. When we are open enough to see and hear these conflicts differently, they bring us to the creative threshold.

In human history, there have been major social, global, or cosmic changes that caused widespread transformations. The taming of fire eventually transformed a young humanity driven by instinct into more evolved creatures who used words. Much later, during the formation of the earliest tribes, the demands of group life forced radical changes in social behavior and added a repertoire of subtle feelings to human awareness. In the Neolithic period, some huge cosmic force—probably an ice age—caused the hunter-gatherers to leave their way of life entirely, and build homes.

Many of our sacred stories come out of collisions like these between old and new Ways. These stories hold the wisdom that emerged from those conflicts and contributed to the ongoing unfolding of the human mind. The Buddha's teachings are an example: They helped his people develop inner ways of coping with the radical social changes confronting them. The second Appendix amplifies these examples to show that catastrophic change may seem destructive from one view, but from the larger perspective, be very creative.

In our own chaotic Time, whatever degree of stability, sanity, and compassion we can offer to the violence and suffering on this planet, we will develop by living from an entirely new orientation. From this orientation, *we take responsibility for the quality and direction of our attention*: We soften our focus, remain alert, and drop deep into ourselves. We let go of any kind of aggression in mind or heart or body. Then, we turn our attention to the third Beginning—the immediacy of the present moment.

It is the necessary change of mind.

Essential to any transformation of consciousness is the development of a greater objectivity than we already have.

When we stand on intellect's foundation as an ego, we don't have the objectivity to *see that we don't see.* Our ongoing awakening, however, offers the possibility of a much larger perspective: a radical inclusiveness that embraces what intellect's divisions have torn apart. But beyond this threshold of transformation is a gap! A chasm! And to leap it—to fly—we have to let ourselves fall from the comfort of what we know. We have to let go and drop from our thinking mode into something we cannot turn into an object—like the golden field in the Japanese painting.

This time, however, we give our attention, not to a piece of art, not something we can visualize, not to a "graven image" as the Old Testament warned.[27] No, it has to be something the mind can't seize on—something like 'the Beginning of the moment.' If we can take that leap,

We become conscious of Consciousness, itself.

To bring this perspective to bear on our thinking is the essential shift of attention needed in our Time—a turning away from a bondage to self and toward the Ground of Being—and there is no way to conceptualize it. If through practice, we learn to maintain this quality of attention *at the same time* we are using our minds in the usual way, we will find that we are walking between the worlds—not unlike the shaman. It is not an easy task, as the Sufi teacher, Llewellyn Vaughan-Lee, reminds us:

> It requires strength of character to be able to live in different worlds [and they can] evoke different shadow dynamics . . . [It] requires a greater responsibility and awareness than we have been used to . . . and we need to be continually attentive [so neither] the ego or shadow co-opts part of the experience for itself.[28]

We don't do it alone. The art of living in different worlds is not a one-way street; it is a state of relatedness—a one-ing of attention to/*and from* the larger Consciousness. Our everyday minds can't 'comprehend' (from the Latin: *seize*) or 'explain' (*flatten out*) what living *as* relationship looks like. (I love these dangling roots on words! They say so much about our ordinary point of view!) This way of being neither seizes nor controls. *It receives.*

So doing, we develop a qualitatively different kind of relationship with a mystery that goes well beyond definition. Merton simply names it *silence.*

> There is in all things an inexhaustible sweetness and purity, a silence that is a fount of action and joy. It rises up in wordless gentleness and flows out to me from the unseen roots of all created being . . . .[29]

This silence—"the mind's empty room"—is not the kind of emptiness our intellects define. This emptiness is full. *Emptiful*. To me, the word I coin is resonant with the word *beautiful*.

To enter *this* kind of Kingdom, we shift our attention from the mind's knowing and drop into what seems like emptiness inside. Then, we begin to dance with Life. We ask, *What now?* and are amazed to discover that the emptiness *is* full! New possibilities, all kinds of new responses to the situation at hand, rise out of the stillness within us—another way that spiritual practice 'breaks the mind.' When, instead of reacting from our gut, we drop in to the silence and ask, we are offered spiritual gifts just waiting to be received: courage, reverence, awe, patience, restraint, gratitude, and more . . .

Sometimes, this is how I experience it: In the middle of a spat, I 'step back' from wanting to be right, then ask from some place deep in my body, *What now?* What rises is usually a response that is exactly right for the occasion! I don't think up this response; *it is offered*. In this situation, what might rise in awareness is forgiveness. If I am feeling stubborn or afraid, the suggestion might be willingness or courage. When I'm trapped in judgment, what occurs to me is compassion. All of these responses from the "empty room" are nonviolent; all of them, a softening. And any one of them—if I receive *and act on it*—returns me to the present moment.

The silence—Merton's "fount of action and joy"—is the silence of Consciousness itself. Ego cannot function here. We cannot be grateful or forgiving and remain guilty or angry about the past. We cannot trust and at the same time, be anxious about the future. Asking, we become grounded in the soul. It is a kind of prayer.

The ancient words, *"Ask, and it shall be given you . . . knock, and it shall be opened unto you"*[30] now hold new meaning for me. By shifting my attention and resting on this Ground, I am, for a period of time, freed from judgment and living in the Kingdom.

Then Love loves and things are seen to happen very differently.

The Vacuum Cleaner Store

Off the plane and on the road before seven-thirty in the morning, I am alone, and driving along the freeway from the Burbank, CA airport to visit my daughter. I'm feeling so delighted at the prospect of some quality time with her! After a few miles, something leads me to turn my attention to the mystery of Presence. I drop in. (This is a dangerous thing to do when driving! It is not my usual practice, but I include it—with apologies—because it offers such an easily communicated example of the Kingdom.)

Ordinarily, I'm pretty tense driving on southern California highways and more than a bit fearful—the drivers here can be aggressive and their speed, very fast. But today, alert, yet resting in the Presence, I am aware of a difference: *How pleasant the drive seems! How courteous the drivers, how measured the tempo of the morning rush hour! We're all just flowing along easily, no one tailgating, no one cutting in front of me.* It feels utterly remarkable.

I've driven this freeway countless times, and as I slow to take the Topanga Canyon exit, I turn east—in the opposite direction from my daughter's home. Continuing along the road, I feel slightly uncertain and wonder whether I might have missed the correct turn. *No,* I say to myself, *I could drive to her house in my sleep!* Reassured, I drive on. The surroundings still seem a little unfamiliar but I never quite know—so much of the landscape here can seem the same. *And after all, it's a foggy morning. Things don't ever look the same in the fog . . .* Further along, I really begin to wonder: *Have I just not noticed this group of houses before? Or that intersection?* I keep watching.

Almost ten miles east of my daughter's home, I notice a sign for a large Sears Roebuck shopping center, and I know I've never seen *it* before! Indeed, I've gone the wrong way! I decide to call my daughter and drive into the main entrance of the huge Sears parking lot. It's so early, the lot is completely empty. Still, I make five very conscious choices: At the end of the entrance lane in front of store, there's an option to turn left or right. I choose the right turn and shortly afterwards, there is another intersection. At this choice point, there are easily five-hundred empty parking spaces fanned out to the left, another several hundred straight ahead, and hundreds more to the right. I decide to turn right. Fifty yards further, I see a long empty row at the far boundary of the lot, right next to Topanga Canyon road. As I approach it, a space half way down the row and facing the road I'd been driving seems just right. I make a left, then turn right into the space, pull on the brake, and ring my daughter.

"I've taken a wrong turn on Topanga. It's probably ten miles out of my way."

"Oh, mom, have you by any chance noticed a Sears Roebuck out that way?"

"Why, yes! That's where I've stopped to call you."

"Mom, would you mind doing an errand for me? There's a tiny little vacuum cleaner repair shop right across from Sears on the other side of Topanga Canyon Road. I made the trip over there early this morning, but they weren't open yet, and we really need the part they fixed today. Could you pick it up for me?"

I glance up and peer through the fog. "Why hon, it's straight across the street. My headlights are shining right on its door."

o

On this morning, *I did not know*. I'd been lost; I'd made a mistake, and had no idea of what I was doing, or that I was so far out of my way. Only after the fact, did I realize I was learning the language of Love. Lost, mistaken, and 'out of my mind,' I'd been at the Beginning of the Moment.

Later, when I told my daughter how the morning had unfurled, she said, "Mom, you have the whole universe behind you!" I replied, "So do you! Everyone does!" Physicist and philosopher David Bohm has a way of describing this kind of orientation:

> If [a person] thinks of the totality as constituted of independent fragments, then that is how his mind will tend to operate, but if he can include everything coherently and harmoniously in an overall whole that is undivided, unbroken, and without a border, then his mind will

tend to move in a similar way, *and from this will flow an orderly action within the whole.*[31]

Such "orderly actions" occur all the time when we live *as* relationship at the Beginning of the moment.

Bohm continues:

People create barriers between each other by their fragmentary thought [and] each one operates separately. When these barriers have dissolved, then there arises one mind where they are all one unit, but each person also retains his or her own individual aware-ness. That one mind will still exist even when they separate. . . It's actually a single intelligence that works with people who are moving in relationship with one another.

Another philosopher, Martin Heidegger, uses different ter-minology to describe what happens to him when he lives in the same way:

Where is the boundary of the body? Every body is my body.[32]

You Are Motivated Differently

We mistake our perception of the Whole, however, if we limit our idea of the Kingdom to that which occurs between human beings. When we live *as* relationship, we are woven together with everything in existence.

Poet and clay artist, Robin Begbie, writes:

I watch
I listen
I feel
the movement of the wind and water
the colors of the earth
the animals
the birds
the people
our connection to each other[33]

As relationship, we no longer look at our surroundings as a set of objects 'out there.' With softened gaze and gentle focus, we see from every point of view at once and listen with ears to hear. The voice of Lao Tse sings the beauty of this mystery:

Who will prefer the jingle of jade pendants
if she once has heard stone
growing in a cliff?

Brother Sun, Sister Moon, gopher snake, dolphin, whale, stone, river, and star; from this perspective, we celebrate every aspect of the larger Story that we are—together. Subjects among subjects—'animate' and 'inanimate'—we are all abiding in the Field.

We also discover ourselves to *be* the Field. Contemporary mystic and spiritual teacher Eckhart Tolle is definitive:

> If you don't know yourself *as* the Field of Presence, you are unconscious.[34]

We under-stand that in this shared Consciousness—this 'ground with many centers'—*everything* is involved; and that the Presence which is *'entos'* binds together creatures, events, and phenomena—even the printed page.

The Snake (2)

Although I wasn't in town for Don Bisson's[35] day-long lecture, I listened to his taped words two months later as I drove across San Francisco Bay to care for our newborn granddaughter, Chloe. I was strangely impacted by the C. S. Lewis story he told about a little boy who had been cursed. The way he told it, the boy's skin had been turned into scales like those of a snake, and every time he tries to tear off a layer of ugly, scaly 'snake skin,' another layer appears beneath it. Layer after layer he removes, and still, there's always one more underneath. Surely, he is cursed. Then, the Lion appears to the boy and says, "Let me peel off the last skin for you."

Bisson says that Lewis considers the Lion a Christ-Consciousness figure[36] and asserts that it is always the Lion who removes the last skin—we cannot do it ourselves. His story goes on to say that when the Lion actually pulls off the last skin, it penetrates deep into the boy's core and hurts more than the loss of any of the other layers. The boy suffers terribly. Then, the Lion tells him to bathe in a particular well, and although the water stings at first, it soothes and heals him—washes him clean of the debris that had obscured his tender connection with the depths of *who he really is*. With Being.[37]

Listening to the story, I remember the words of Meister Eckhart:

> A man has many skins in himself, covering the depths of his heart. . . .
> Go into your own ground and learn to know yourself there.

Later, when I reflect on Eckhart's words in the light of the story, I realize that in my own soul work, I've been peeling off layers like snake skins for a very long time. It has been especially painful in recent months, but I realize there is nothing more I can do. By nightfall, however, I am feeling desperate, and though it is not my usual practice, I get on my knees by my bed like a little child and surrender to the inner Lion—to Love. I don't even know what to ask; only that the last layers of defense be peeled away.

As the week goes by, I notice that a mild depression has fallen over me like a fine gray silk. It feels like impending grief. I go out to the garden at dawn and step down into the stone tub to meditate. Immersed neck deep in the warm water, the first whisper I hear is a statement Richard Moss had made to a group, years before:

> You lay your ego down; you lay your self down before God; you *lay your point of view down* . . .

Once more, I discover it is not I who surrenders. Love surrenders me. *Point of view . . . Point of view . . .* The phrase becomes a mantra and then a link in a long chain of associations: *I lay my world view down . . . beliefs down . . . lay my dreams . . . my yearning . . . my hope down . . .* Time passes, and then from out of nowhere—"*I lay my secret down!*" I am shocked. *What secret?* Some time later, in the silence of this most silent question, the truth arrives, and only when it is finished with me, do I understand: I have spent a lifetime refusing love.

Time to lay the secret down.

Late that afternoon, I pull up behind a little gray car parked along a curb. Inscribed on the top of the license plate holder are the words, *"I'm not spoiled . . ."* and at the bottom, *"I'm just loved a lot."* Maybe it's because of their playful nature that the words slip past my deeply-held beliefs and hit me like a ton of bricks. Could I even imagine what it would feel like to live inside that kind of confidence? Could I let it seep into my body, rattle around until it got comfortable, and take up residence— maybe even stay? I drop into the Beginning of the Moment and am shocked when a new and unexpected question rises: *Could I tolerate the pain of letting love in?*

"Yes!" I cry to the Lion. And as it begins to peel away the too-tight skin of self-protection, an old and frightened identity falls like a tattered garment in a heap at my feet. It is the only self I have ever known.

> Not until all is given
> Comes the thought of heaven . . .

Perhaps a child's secret is the last thing to die. I think, in our heart of hearts, we tend to feel insufficient. Many of us judge our very human-ness. What a terrible burden! Little do we know that we are enough as we are.

By evening, I begin to feel a new kind of peace inside, but Love is not through with me yet! Two days before, I'd taken some books off the shelf to lend a woman who'd asked about dreams. After she made her choice, I put the rest back except for one by the Jungian, John Sanford. I had read it more than twenty years before, but this time, when I leafed through the table of contents, one title caught my eye. Now, after dinner on this most amazing day, I stretch out on the couch to follow up on the chapter that had intrigued me, "Body, Soul, and Wholeness."

An hour or more goes by. Then I start the next chapter. As bedtime approaches, George gets out of his chair and exclaims, "Oh, look!" but I'm in the middle of a page and deeply absorbed. He tries again, "Look, Anne! Look here!" I put the book down and get up to look where he's pointing. On the floor at the foot of the couch—on the same day the 'snake skin' has begun to fall away from around my heart—is a gray baby snake: soft, shiny, smooth-skinned, and a little over a foot long. She is curling and extending her body, struggling to make headway on the slippery oak floor, and getting nowhere.

How did she get in? Neither of us knows, but we work together to help her escape. We gather her slithering body onto a piece of paper, but she keeps sliding off. Clearly, she is trying to escape *us*! I finally suggest, "Maybe, you could try to pick her up with your fingers?" (Not that I would do it!) With only the slightest hesitation, George takes her mid-back between thumb and index finger. I run ahead to open the door, and as he goes out, call after him, "Oh, please, find her a nice soft place in the garden!"

When the dust settles, I return to the couch and begin to read where I left off. In the next paragraph, Sanford mentions a snake for the first time. He goes on to describe how the snake has come to be associated with both condemnation and healing:

> Today we tend to associate the serpent with evil, largely because of the story about him in the Garden of Eden. Christian theologians have interpreted this story in terms of the origin of sin and evil. . . . Ancient man however did not see the serpent as evil, but rather [because it sheds its skin] *as a symbol of the renewing, transforming energy that lies at the heart of life.* Even early Christian theologians did not all agree that the serpent in the Garden of Eden embodied evil . . . [but] *believed the serpent carried out the divine purpose of bringing consciousness to mankind, rather than introducing evil.*[38]

The images of the snake and the Garden of Eden had introduced my silent slide show, *The Evolution of Stress*, from which this book is derived. Nearly thirty years after that same conference where I also first saw Teilhard's words, "Fire for the second time," on a poster, Sanford's paragraph brings me full circle.

Entos

That Life gathers up and offers in proximate relationship all these facets of a greater Under-standing leaves me in awe! The Kingdom—the mysterious way that life is held and organized—

had revealed in a single day a series of inner/*outer* events that echoed the story of the boy with 'snake skin.' They began with Moss' injunction, "You lay your point of view down." Next, came the child's secret, followed by a more healing perspective on a license plate—"I'm just loved a lot!" Later came the question, "Could I tolerate the pain of letting love in?" The day ended with the appearance of a living snake in our home, and finally, Sanford's summation of the snake as healer, the snake as a bearer of consciousness.

The wonder of Life's *"Yes!"* to us! The density of this Kingdom—this Field of flowing energies—the greater Reality, palpable and pregnant and holy! Mark Goodman-Morris called it *grace*. In a letter to his college-bound daughter, he gave her his blessing:

> Grace upon grace. Grace is one of those tricky realities that I didn't quite get until I was in my thirties, but I know I was bathed in it from birth. So are you. Grace is what gets you through. Grace is what lifts you up. Grace is what surprises you. Grace is what happens when the right person, the perfect words, the timely touch, the unexpected silence or sorrow, reaches down to that place just below your soul and embraces you and you realize you are nothing and everything at the same time. And this grace is available all the time. All the time.

There is so much more going on around us than we are able to see or feel—a fullness to existence that we will never understand. To name its revelations 'synchronicity' can barely hint at its majesty. To call our stumbling upon it 'intuition' scarcely touches the edge of the holy garment that enfolds us. This Life behind the life we *know* is more than what we think—more than we can symbolize. It is more than nature, more than physics, more than Jung's Self or the material universe. When we rest in this deep Communion—in the Kingdom—we are Home. And like Philip Newell's tapestry of creation "shot through with silk," it is shot through with God.

Endnotes for Chapter 15

1   Wendell Berry, excerpt from 'The Clear Days,' in the series of poems titled "The Country of Marriage," reprinted in *The Selected Poems of Wendell Berry*, Washington, DC: Counterpoint Press, 1998, 96.

2   Richard Farmer is the founder and principle Instructor of the international Rising Dragon Tai Chi School and offers extended courses in the service of living that philosophy. See http://*www.soulmoves.co.uk*

3   The following statements summarize an 'academic idea,' this one, a consensus by 76 internationally known scholars from a broad spectrum of traditions who reached agreement on the definition of *Kingdom*. Primarily faculty members of mainstream American and Canadian universities and schools of theology, their research confirms that in the Judeo-Christian tradition, it was blasphemous, even idolatrous, to utter the name of God. It was therefore common practice to refer, instead, to *the Kingdom, Heaven's Imperial Rule,* or *Heaven's domain*. "Normal Israelite and Judean usage avoided the name of God, for which the term *heaven* was substituted. . . . As a gospel especially concerned with relations to Judaism, Matthew adheres to the use of *Heaven* in place of God's name." Robert Funk, *et al*, *The Five Gospels*, 195.

4   Luke 17:21.

5   Jesus was a Jew who spoke Aramaic. Greek was the first language in which his words were written down. The complex meanings of the Greek word *'entos'* accurately reflect the same complexity in both Aramaic and Hebrew. Just as the galley proofs of this book were being edited, a book by Neil Douglas-Klotz, PhD, clarified this point:

    "Both Aramaic and Hebrew have only one preposition that must describe both the relationship 'within,' (as in 'within my interior, emotional life') and 'among' (as in "among my exterior social community"). . . . The way [Semitic people] experience[d] the inner self . . . correspond[ed] to the way [they] experience[d] the community. . . . We Westerners have been raised to see individual and community, as well as humanity and nature, as separate. Previous cultures were not so inflated with the idea of control, or so disconnected from their environments." Neil Douglas-Klotz, *The Hidden Gospel—Decoding the Spiritual Message of the Aramaic Jesus*, Wheaton, IL: Quest Books, 1999, 18, 86.

6   Some will interpret Thomas' Gospel to be Gnostic. The Gnostics focused, in part, on personal self-knowledge. But as we see in this and the next selection, the Gospel of Thomas maintains a connection to the *entos* language which stresses the importance of the community. This is very different from the more independent, self-orientation of pure Gnosticism. Current research asserts that ". . . the Gnostic myth is not explicit in the Gospel of Thomas . . . [and] Gnostic tendencies are not sufficiently dominant [in it] in any case . . . ." John S. Kloppenborg, et al, *Q-Thomas Reader*, from the Foreword, Santa Rosa, CA: Polebridge Press, 1990, viii.

7   Iyer, ed., *The Gospel According to Thomas*, 17. Italics mine.

8   As I hear it, 'poverty of self' also comes, in part, from saying, *"No!"* to who we are. This version of the stanza is from an unknown source, different from the one at the end of Chapter 7. Italics mine.

9   In the story, one blind man grasped its trunk and said, "An elephant is long and snake-like." One felt the elephant's leg, others, the flank or the ear. Each described the elephant differently. None saw it whole.

10 Matthew 18:20. Douglas-Klotz's research also augments our understanding of the phrase 'in my name:'

"The Aramaic word *shema* (as well as its Semitic root ShM, or *shem*) can mean light, sound, name, or atmosphere. . . . [Regarding] the admonition of Jesus to pray 'in my shem' (usually translated 'in my name') . . . according to Middle Eastern tradition, in the words of a sacred scripture or the words of a prophet, all possible meanings may be intended." Douglas-Klotz, *The Hidden Gospel— Decoding the Spiritual Message of the Aramaic Jesus*, 19.

11 Matthew 13:30-32 (NIV). "The kingdom of heaven is like a mustard seed which a man took and planted in his field. Though it is the smallest of all your seeds, yet when it grows, it is the largest of garden plants and becomes a tree, so that the birds of the air come and perch in its branches." Also found in Mark 4:30-32 and Luke 13:18-19.

12 Sarah Bagley was deeply involved in the women's rights movement in the nineteenth century. Her words, spoken in 1846, are inscribed on a granite marker at the Lowell, MA Historic National Park.

13 Bill Moyers in a lecture at De Anza College, Cupertino, CA, 2005.

14 Underhill, *Mystics of the Church*, 11. See also Thomas Berry, *The Universe Story*, 190 which states: "The spiritual experiences at the center of the traditional civilizations were communicated through sacred revelations that took place in the depths of the human unconscious and were awakened by inner dreams or outward experiences, and found abiding form in sacred scriptures. . . . These revelations appear in the Rishi or Seers of ancient India . . . in the experience of Buddha in Bodh Gaya . . . the illuminations of . . . Zoroaster . . . the biblical prophets, in the Christ appearance and the Pauline Epistles."

15 The Buddha wrote of the suffering he endured just before he awakened, as did many saints such as Augustine. In a conversation, Moss cited several contemporary examples, including teachers of consciousness like Eckhart Tolle, author of *The Power of Now*, who suffered a long and painful clinical depression; and Byron Katie, who wrote of the depths of her despair in *Loving What Is: Four Questions that can Change Your Life*. Few, if any, of those who have radically awakened are spared suffering. The Dalai Lama is an example of that rare person who has become fully awakened through a rigorous, lifelong training within a religion that comprises both philosophy and practice. I cannot speak to an awakening that is drug-induced. However, it is my understanding that most such experiences, intense as they may be, neither cause a partial, much less the complete "remaking of the personality" such as Evelyn Underhill and others describe. Richard Alpert is an exception. Though he experimented with LSD in the 1960s, he went on to India and studied meditation and yoga with a Hindu teacher who renamed him Ram Dass, ('servant of God'). He has since led a life of devotion and service to others.

16 Iyer, ed., *The Gospel According to Thomas*, 24.

17 Eliot, "East Coker," Four Quartets, *Collected Poems 1909-1962*, 183.

18 For example, Richard Moss has developed a rich set of experiential methods for learning to live from this inner orientation—and particularly, for discerning the patterns of behavior that keep us from resting there. The practice is easily learned in his various group offerings, worldwide, and the methods are also explained in depth in his most recent book, *The Mandala of Being—Discovering the Power of Awareness*, Novato, CA: New World Library, 2007.

19 See the parable of the sower in Chapter 11.

20 The great traditions have consistently reminded us to 'wake up.' This was Jesus' repeated admonition to his disciples in Mark 14:32-42. Bach's familiar Chorale, *Sleepers, Wake, (Wachet Auf)* is based on his parable of the wise and foolish virgins (Matthew 25). We also hear it in Paul's letter to the Romans 13:11: "[I]t is full time now for you to wake from sleep." In some traditions, the term *awake* is reserved for only the highest state of consciousness, sometimes called 'consciousness without an object' or '*samadhi* without support.' But I am using it here to denote *everyone's capacity to stand at the third Beginning—the Beginning of the Moment.* If we want to contribute what we can to the increasing consciousness of the world, it becomes crucially important that we each offer our own awareness, as we learn—one by one and together—to be fully present to Life.

21 T. S. Eliot, "The Dry Salvages," Four Quartets, *Collected Poems* 1909-1962, 198.

22 Iyer, ed., *The Gospel According to Thomas*, 18.

23 *Ibid.*, 23.

24 *Ibid.*, 24.

25 Ken Wilber, *Sex, Ecology and Spirituality*, Boston: Shambhala, 1995, 206, 235. In this immense integration, (853 pages), Wilber documents what he calls the "pre/trans fallacy." See also Ken Wilber, *Eye to Eye*, Boston: Shambhala, 1990.

26 Joel and Michelle Levey discuss the practice of balancing these opposites in *Living in Balance: A Dynamic Approach for Creating Harmony and Wholeness in a Chaotic World*, foreword by the Dalai Lama, Berkeley: Conari Press, 1998: "Paradox is a great teacher. . . . You . . . learn the most about living in balance through the times you get out of balance . . . [and] discover [that it] grows . . . both [through] the experience of being *in balance* and that of being *stretched* out of balance. . . . Balance is really a verb—something you lose and regain over and over—[It is a] balancing *process.*"

27 Historically, among the Hebrews, there was a need to address the issue of using pagan idols and images. The pagans, as I understand the word in this context, were those who had multiple gods and goddesses (or those who had not yet let go of them in the process of becoming aware of God as the Unity described in Chapter 13, "One-ing.") Best known is the warning in the Ten Commandments: "Thou shalt not make unto thee any graven image, or any likeness of any thing that is in heaven above, or that is in the earth beneath, or that is in the water under the earth." Exodus 20:4 (KJV). See, also other texts, e.g., Leviticus 26:1 and Deuteronomy 4:16.

28 Llewellyn Vaughan-Lee, *Alchemy of Light, Working with the Primal Energies of Life,* Inverness, CA: The Golden Sufi Center Publishing, 2007, 118, 121. Vaughan-Lee, PhD, is a Jungian and a Sufi sheik. For consistency, the verb tense has been adapted by the author. See *http://www.goldensufi.org*

29 Thomas Merton, "Hagia Sophia," in Cunningham, ed., *Thomas Merton: Spiritual Master*, 258. Excerpt.

30 Matthew 7:7 (KJV).

31 David Bohm, *Wholeness and the Implicate Order*, London: Routledge Publishers, 1980, xi. Bohm also made significant contributions to the field of neuropsychology. In the quote, I have replaced the word *man* with *a person*. Italics mine.

32 Martin Heidegger, *Being and Time*, tr. John Macquarrie and Edward Robinson, New York: Harper Collins, 1962. Quoted online by William Cornwall, retrieved 2007 at *http://www.bu.edu/wcp/Papers/Comp/CompCorn.htm*

33 "Connecting," unpublished poem by Robin Begbie. Robin is a New Zealand-born poet, potter and clay artist now living in Northern California whose work is widely known. See *http://www.redfoxart.com*

34 Eckhart Tolle, contemporary mystic and spiritual teacher, in a lecture at Berkeley, CA, late 1990s.

35 Don Bisson, FMS, is a Marist brother, a supervisor and trainer of spiritual directors, and a widely respected commentator on the interrelationship of spirituality and psychology. I have used Bisson's version of the C. S. Lewis' story from a lecture in 2000, Portola Valley, CA, in which he referred to the boy's skin as 'like snake skin.' The original story can be found in C. S. Lewis, *The Voyage of the Dawn Treader*, New York: HarperTrophy, 1952, 109.

36 Theologians differentiate between Jesus, the man of history, and the Christ Consciousness of the ages.

37 The two symbols of the snake and the well resonate throughout history. The snake in the Eden story tempted Adam and Eve to *know*. I relate it to the snake's genetic template in our bodies and minds: the cold and paradoxical passion/*violence* of the reptilian brain encountered in the first foundation. I hear the symbol of the well, among many of its other echoes, as the healing 'Source' that lies beneath the first foundation and from which our roots drink; I also hear it as the 'living water' to which Jesus refers in John 4 and 7, as well as Merrell-Wolff's 'Current.'

38 John A. Sanford, *Healing and Wholeness*, New York: Paulist Press, 1977, 44-45. Italics mine.

16 Harnessing the Energies of Love

*The great poets of tragedy, such as
Shakespeare or Aeschylus, never leave us
with a sense of meaningless horror and disaster.
Out of the darkness shines an intense ray of
hope and beauty, which owes its brilliance
precisely to a clear-eyed acceptance of the
terror of the story.*

Helen Luke[1]

When we know from our own experience that we live in the mysterious Field of Presence, we begin to dwell in it, consciously. Trusting, we take one small step at a time and try to live each day as it unfolds. The day may bring joy; it may bring sorrow, but our intention is to live in concert with *what is*. That kind of wholeness includes the darkness—and in that darkness, *"God shines."*[2]

The unfolding of Life operates, not by clockwork, but through birth and death, and it is here we come face-to-face with the necessary depths of our surrender. That surrender is an embrace of the darkness: what is hidden, what we fear, what we hope to avoid. These dark realities—be they dread, death, pain, or grief—live very close to our core. There God shines.

How do we harness for God the energies of Love?[3]

As Helen Luke tells us, the shining "owes its brilliance precisely to a clear-eyed acceptance of the terror. . . ." We may have to let go many times in order to accept something difficult on our spiritual journey, but we can't surrender what we don't *'have'*—what we haven't yet made conscious.

All too often, we are not conscious of our fear.

Love asks that we look fear and suffering in the eye and that we walk the human path of grief. It also reminds us, even as we stream with life, to give ourselves up to our dying. With every surrender, every letting go, ego dies a little—and each time, we taste the meaning of the adage, "Die before you die!"

Help us to know our fear.

Terror

Six vultures slam into the wind. I am rapt at their intensity as they swoop in an ever-narrowing orbit so low, their wing tips seem almost to graze my window. From a distance, they are beautiful—a barely discernible wobble differentiating them from the graceful red-tailed hawks. Close in and intent on their target, however, their flight is foreboding, menacing. I shudder as they sweep faster and faster in a long ellipse from the very edge of the house to the far end of the freshly-mown field. The feathered fury continues unabated until, as if on cue, all six fly to the dying pine in the middle of the field and land on its bleached and broken branches.

The birds are so huge they almost seem to fill the tree. I watch, astonished, as three of them spread their wings and hold them wide. They stand like statues facing the wind: three dark totems in ecstatic pose, three with wings folded. In a short while, a solitary vulture flies down to a thicket in the gully at the end of the field, then another . . . and another . . . High in the tree, one remains unmoving. As if guarding the sacrifice, it extends its wings like a black-robed priest at an altar.

I want to intervene, beat back the onslaught near the tangled underbrush where the deer and other creatures hide their young. The urge to protect reminds me of my grown children, busy with their lives. They still flow through my far-ranging thoughts many times a day. Perhaps, a mother used to years of casting a net of awareness shaped to the well-being of her children never reels it back fully. She may not *tend* the net the way she did, but it is always there, flapping about . . .

The next morning, it is almost dark as I wash my face and look out the window—too dark to make out an unfamiliar shadow in the field, small and round. Curious, I get the telescope, balance it on the edge of the tub, and focus. There! A plump California quail hen squats all fluffed out next to the dirt path. Her eyes are partly open—tending her net even as she sleeps—and her beak points due north. Poking out from underneath her wings are four little heads, all facing south— two chicks tucked in on each side, their bright, black eyes wide open. After about ten minutes, as if on signal, all four jump up and scoot for cover under a low manzanita bush near the old stone tub. The hen opens her eyes, looks resigned, and follows. An hour later, the whole family is still foraging in the stubble of mown hay. There are seven chicks now. The cock, his black plume curved forward from head to beak, must have been sitting on the other three.

There is such a look of pride in California quails! They make me smile. Even scurrying stiff-legged at top speed, their posture is upright and formal. The chicks, fluffy inch-and-a-half copies, strut about just as importantly, like tiny Charlie Chaplins. The adults call and cluck as they scratch at the exposed earth, and the little ones respond with a high-pitched cheep.

I step out the door on my way to the stone tub to meditate, and they *whir-r-r-r!* loudly, scattering towards the manzanita. The garden is morning-damp and glowing; the scents of jasmine and lavender mingle with the sweet smell of freshly mown hay; a tangle of Spanish sage and native gaura bend to an unexpectedly cool June wind. I am reminded of the whispered beauty that first captivated me in the underground church of my childhood, and whisper to myself, *Oh! It is this joy, my heart's gladness for all these things, my own love*—for the quail, the trees, the light, as they all break into my awareness—*this is the love I sought!* But Love asks more than this.

I drop my robe, descend three steps, and sink down into the warm water until my head is at ground level; then close my eyes. Mind offers snippets of thought that blow by like leaves in the wind: the grievous news in my email this morning from a friend in New Hampshire—a great ecologist dead, struck in the prime of her life by bacterial meningitis.

How did it happen? . . . My fear rises automatically. *Will it happen here?* . . . *To me?* . . . *To those I love?* . . . My heartbeat speeds up. I shudder, remembering that my friend had also written about neighbors, less than a mile away: two professors killed by teenagers who'd broken in. "I bought a key for the front door," she added, "we've never locked it in all these years. This morning, I locked myself out because I'm not used to needing one. What is happening to our world?"

I watch my mind continue its endless loop: *I used to live there! It was our home.* I observe and comment: *Fear again . . . It's 7:15 in the morning and I'm already immersed in fear! I've rejected every thought that's passed! How can I believe that I love Life if I can't remain open to a death with its own timetable and not seek to protect against it?* I step back and observe further: *Hmmmm . . . Self judgment.*

Finally, I let go. Thought dissolves and after a while, I'm just breathing . . . There is nothing to differentiate the interior space from the larger Space . . . the body's prayer from the larger Prayer . . . a self from the vast Stillness . . .

Loud squawks and a beating of wings from under the dense manzanita next to me break the silence. I recoil instinctively, then turn my head toward the sound and come nose to nose with a red-tailed hawk just landed four feet from me after bursting out of the bush. His posture is erect, aggressive, and he stares at me fiercely, lightning flashing from his yellow eyes. An infant quail wriggles in his shining black beak.

He turns, spreads his huge wings and lifts off, then lands on a low branch less than thirty feet away. The furious beating of wings disturbs some pine needles in the crotch of the tree and they flutter to the ground. I watch, stunned, as he pins one of the chicks I had just taken into my heart firmly against the branch with one claw and kills it swiftly with a slash of his curved and powerful beak.

In the midst of the shock, practice reminds me to take it in—and breathe . . .

I've noticed that except for three occasions, hawks fly with their legs tucked under them. But when they are mating, their legs trail behind them as they dance in the air, their distinctive calls a medley with the wind. In their courtship flight, their claws hang empty, but later, when they build a nest together, they carry single long pieces of straw as they fly back and forth across the field. It is a beautiful sight, these graceful, soaring birds, tails glinting gold in the sun, trailing long grasses. This time, high over the pale gold field, the hawk trails in its claw a limp baby quail.

Even as the quails still cluck and search for their missing chick under the manzanita, I watch the hawk take food to its own young high in a far-off tree and wonder at the gift of the teaching:

The energies of creation and destruction are One.

It is a larger truth than mine.

I am amazed by the ongoing transaction between the inner and outer worlds, the same themes, inside as out: the maternal protection of the young, a flurry of fear, the breach of sudden death. At the same time, a growing awareness has shown me how I avoid my fear, how swift I am to turn away from horror and pain, and how much more easily I accept the things I prefer, or admire those that bring me pleasure. In this brief moment, however, the resonance between inner and outer worlds has revealed the unavoidable law of life: that it is not split, but seamless. This larger truth reminds me not to identify with any part of a divided consciousness—neither the good nor the bad—nor to congratulate myself on small successes or denigrate myself for failures. It suggests, once more, that I orient to a deeper/*higher* Ground—one that transcends these very human judgments.

I am grateful for the morning's courtship between my daily self and this vast mystery. At the same time I'm shaken, for I also know it as an abyss. I cannot keep myself—or the people I love, the creatures I bless, or the plants—safe from harm. *That is law.* Yesterday, the vultures flew low. Today, the hawk. Tomorrow . . . what? Can I embrace life *as* loss and call *that* Love? Can I admit so human a helplessness before these mighty powers at work throughout the universe and in my cells—powers I cannot even imagine, much less name?

Love lies like a river of Fire at the bottom of an abyss. Can I face certain annihilation and remain this tender? Something from the abyss says *that* is a faith far deeper than my own.

Love is One. In Love, embrace and release—giving and receiving—are not sequential. They are one act.

Death

It is a beautiful day, clear, sunlit, the October wind stiff and cold and blowing so hard the seagulls seem to hang motionless in the sky. George reins in the small sloop's mains'l and keeps it close-hauled as we head east on Maine's Penobscot Bay. There are four of us in the little boat, heading out Eggamoggin Reach on blustery waters.

The sharp slice of the prow through the whitecaps hones my attention. Along the sloping meadows of the mainland, bright red and orange maples dance with yellow birches. There are small houses, mostly white, and scattered among them, weathered gray and red barns. The cold, the beauty of autumn colors, and the shapes of the buildings long engraved in genetic memory sing my body awake.

In the wind shadow of a large island, the gusts suddenly slow and toy with the sail. It luffs, shifting direction—one way, then another. It is uncertain, navigating the ocean's waters. One minute, we're breezing right along; another, and we're becalmed; the next, our little boat is tossed by gusts so strong, the buoys clamor for attention and we wonder if we'll survive! In the relative calm of *this* moment's wind, I look into the distance toward Deer Isle Bridge.

Something white is moving strangely on the water, maybe half a mile away—maybe more. "Look! Over there—what is it?" I ask the others. It is a very unusual sight. Someone wonders aloud if it might be a trapped bird. George's hand is on the tiller and he changes course, heading toward the commotion. In the light wind, it is a slow process of tacking back and forth. Closer, we see that it *is* a bird—a large white gull, flapping its wings and tugging at something in the water. "Is it a catch?" We're all asking at once, now. "A fish?" "Maybe the bird's caught in a net!" "Is it tangled in a lobster line?"

The gull's body jerks awkwardly. There's clearly a struggle going on with an equal force beneath the water's surface. The wind picks up just enough to allow us to tack directly toward it. Then we see.

Floating next to the flailing seagull is another gull, its head and upper body submerged. Its white tail points straight up at the sky and it bobs aimlessly, rising and falling on the waves. Its mate—whose commotion had drawn our attention half an hour before—is tugging at the dead gull's head and neck, using her beak in every way she can to try to pull the carcass upright. I feel immense anguish as I watch the stricken bird try to make sense of the senseless; as I witness her efforts and her many wiles to right a grievous wrong.

After a long time, the exhausted gull paddles a few feet away and looks back at her mate, as if dazed and bewildered. Once she has rested, she returns to her task and tries once more to do the impossible. Under drooping sails, we, too, bob aimlessly on the water. Wordless, we witness her defeat; and in hers, we witness our own.

May we not turn away from our dread.

Pain

While I was writing Chapter 14. "Living in the Kingdom," my intention had been that the chapter you are now reading would be about pain and death. However, everything I'd written, thus far, had come from my own body's experience. I found myself wondering, *How can I write about these difficult subjects when I've had no such experience of my own?* Life gives its answer in a matter of weeks. Half-finished with the chapter, I become aware of something quite subtle in my upper abdomen. There are no symptoms, no pain, nothing palpable. But I have spent a long time living deep in my body, and I know that what I'm sensing is unusual. I give it a few days, then call my doctor: "There is some kind of presence in my upper abdomen."

"That's a little different. We don't ordinarily hear that kind of description," she replies, "but come on in." I go to her office, but she, too, can feel nothing. Wise woman, she orders the tests anyway. They show two tumors in my pancreas.

Many of you know well this kind of shock—the possibility of a malignancy. You know, too, how your terror explodes when you first approach a surgeon's office for assessment. It is the same for me when I go to the clinic a few days later. The sign on the doors seems to shout: *"CANCER CENTER!"* I'm not at all ready to take it in.

Panicky, I step into the lobby alone while George parks the car. As I walk down the hall, a young man sits by a floor-to-ceiling window and plays quietly on a classical guitar. Further on, a woman in a long skirt is seated by another window, singing in a hushed voice and playing an Irish harp. I feel a surge of gratitude and thank them—then hide briefly in another alcove to wipe away my tears. *Somebody cares.*

The doctor recommends surgery but I resist. I've heard far too much about the dangers of pancreatic surgery, and I have old, old memories of hospitals. My panic rises as I remember the eyes of strangers staring at me over white masks, a tray of knives, and long needles in my arms and legs when I was four.

The surgeon's schedule, however, allows time for me to adapt to the idea, and in that interval, many people offer their wisdom. When I talk with Richard Moss, he reminds me that any inner 'stories'—what he calls hidden beliefs or ideas—will make me resistant to what life is offering. He suggests that, whatever they are, they need to be seen and felt, and offers a prayer as part of my practice:

> May I not bury my stories
> May I not deny my fear
> May I only turn to my gratitude . . .
> gratitude for the fear itself.

During the weeks that follow, I say the prayer, finish Chapter 14, and begin to work on the next one. I find myself upheld by the very things I'm writing about: faith, the Ground, the Kingdom, the greater Communion. The tales of the chair, the vacuum cleaner store, and the snake help to remind me that I am part of something greater, and that I'm deeply connected to life. Each tale is a revelation of a need met by Love.

The same Love, present in the people around me, buoys and sustains me.

The day arrives. It is, as the surgeon had warned, a 'big surgery,' and he removes three quarters of my pancreas and all of my spleen. It goes well, but the next night in my hospital bed, I sense once more something inside me that can't be explained. With only this strange inward sensing to guide me, I call the nurse, "Something is wrong!" It is ten o'clock. They don't believe me. I call again. Six hours later, they discover a drop in blood pressure. I have been hemorrhaging internally. I remember two orderlies running my gurney at top speed through the hospital corridors in the middle of the night. I remember how abruptly the nurses tilted the head of the gurney to the floor. Strapped in and hanging upside down, I'm told that this position will send blood to my brain. I slip in and out of consciousness as they give me the gift of other people's blood. Pint after pint after pint.

In the days that follow, I remember pain that is absolute. Physical pain is *root*. It brings you to your knees. But I had been prepared. On the day before surgery, Richard had spent time with me in sacred meditation. Later, he talked about accepting the long months of helplessness ahead—and how to meet pain. Step by step, he showed me how to counter my resistance: to soften the quality of my attention and let go of the thoughts that come unbidden with the waves of pain—*Oh no . . . stop! . . . Please stop! . . . I can't bear it!*—words that calcify fear and keep it god. He taught me again how to release any breath that was in the least way aggressive.

Richard showed me how to apply to pain what he'd taught us all along: the quality of attention that allows us to *live* life and not avoid it.

"Don't avoid the sensation of pain," he said. *"Stay with it . . . Meet it as it rises with the most exquisite receptivity . . . the softest breath possible . . . Keep your attention right on the pain . . . Don't turn away. Then offer it up with gratitude."*

Pain becomes my teacher. As each wave rises, I remember his words about how to submit; how to offer up my helplessness before the Infinite. It would not have been possible without the long practice of attention in meditation. Even now, each time the pain comes, I contract, first, out of habit: I tighten my body, resist the pain and gasp, *"No!"* Then, I remember.

When the next wave of pain comes, instead of pushing it away in fear, I create a space for it. In the same way I once stretched out my arms to embrace the most unlovable qualities in myself, I open to embrace the unlovable in life. My fear is fuel for the *Fire*.

I breathe in . . . and bring the gentlest breath to meet it. I breathe out . . . and let go of the contractions in my body. The breath touches my pain softly and becomes a caress. Breath meets the presence of pain with gentleness and my body opens and lets it in.

I say, "Thank you!" and I mean it. Each time, a miracle occurs. The pain dissolves and in its place is Stillness. In its place—Peace.

The gentle surrender of my body's breath to what Life is offering in the moment becomes my yoke. It is the harness that binds me to Presence.

I am grateful for a good prognosis. Months later, however, I discover something else that has lived all along beneath my awareness—a veritable bulwark against Life's wholeness. Whether or not we all presume in our hidden hearts a protection from death, I surely did. I discover it—many months into the long recovery process—only after the grieving begins. I don't know why I am grieving, only *that* I grieve. I weep and weep and weep.

One day, the truth arises: *There is no safety from pain and death, no going back to the secret invincibility I'd always relied on.* No wonder I grieve! I tell my friend Shirley, "I don't like it! I want my life back!" She says to me, "This *is* your life." Shirley under-stands. She lives with non-Hodgkin's lymphoma. But I don't want to hear what she says, and push it away.

In the night, however, the dreamer offers the same message: "Let go!"

I dream we're going to set the house on fire and burn it down. We take out everything except some bed pillows and their cases. I think maybe we should keep them, but am told, "No, let them go; we will get everything new."

On waking, I go outdoors to meditate. A dream allowed to rise in meditation can unfurl its living truth in poetry. Poems, I find, have a life of their own, and often their endings surprise me. This one is no exception. Out of the dream's image of a burned down house—what I hear as ego's false structure—comes a poem with an unexpected gift: a condition of being completely undefended and trusting. It offers me a vision of freedom, an image of openness and intimacy with life that I shall never forget. This is how the poem ended:

. . . But once her house had burned down,
she could see
through its charred timbers
that the moon and the stars
had always been there.

She could walk like a ghost
through its walls,
and let the breeze
blow through her
like a cloudless sky.

Although there are moments when I *can* let go, there are many others when I just plain struggle. On those occasions when I find myself on the edge of an abyss, it helps me to remember the old, old dreams of falling, falling into some kind of endless depths. I realize, now, that in these dreams, I am falling into a chasm that is already inside me: the depths of the life I am living/*the depths of the Life behind the life.* When I allow the silence of *that* kind of death; when I see how its embrace informs and enlivens everything; when I am able to acknowledge its Presence in my mind and heart and body and soul *and take it in*—then, I can say, *"Yes!"* to Life from all my foundations.

For that moment, however brief, I stand under the two great commandments: "You shall love the Lord your God with all your heart and all your soul and all your mind;" and "You shall love your neighbor as yourself."[4] When the first is embodied, it has the same meaning as the second. They are one law.

There is no transformation until the loving begins.

When I am surrendered, there is a peace in me, a simplicity and a patience I cannot explain. My sleep is untroubled, my days, quiet. Something has changed deep beneath my awareness. If I were to try to express what is different, I'd say that these must be the moments when I am resting in the reliable truth, the Ground to which I was called by the very first whisper in my childhood—the song of the soul seeking its true Foundation.

Grief

When my beloved friend, Ann Plaw, was dying, I went to her bedside often and listened to her as she faced the ending of her life. "I don't know how to do this," she whispered. "There's nothing to tell me if what I'm thinking or feeling or doing is the right way. Nobody gave me any lessons." While I sat with her, I reflected on the enormity of what was going on inside her. I knew that her admission came from a deeply lived journey: one in which she'd learned that her life was not something to be controlled, but to be surrendered, one moment at a time.

Ann first entered the nursing home against her will, and as any of us might, found herself living Dylan Thomas' words, "rage, rage against the dying of the light."[5] She *didn't want* to be there, and fought so hard that by sheer grit, she was able to go home after a stay of only two weeks. But the day came when she asked to go back, grateful for the loving care she had received there. Many of the patients who surrounded her suffered from dementia. I was awed when she told me, "You know, I've come to realize that I'm part of a new community, now. Some of us may be less able than others, but we're all members, here. No one's better than anyone else." It was a triumph.

A living humility radiated from her despite a natural tacking back and forth between resistance and acceptance, fear and faith; despite some days that went worse than others. Ann had learned how to face the many calamities in her life by working a rigorous spiritual practice, step by step. Each step was a surrender; each strengthened her faith. Now she demonstrated the depth of her humanity. She didn't settle for easy answers. Instead, she asked the hard questions, turning them over in her mind and answering as truthfully as she could.

"Who am I really?" Her responses over a period of more than eighty years had been a gradual awakening to what was true in her, and what, facade or false premise. Bedrock to her, bedrock to her questioning was the desire to be honest—with herself, with others, and with God. There was no Self-avoidance. Had she settled for prescribed answers and limited them to "I am a mother . . . a professional . . . a seamstress . . . a child of God," there would have been no further search. She'd have been off the hook, saved from the hard work of claiming her authenticity. Doubtless, she was guided by the wisdom of her spiritual practice, but she didn't allow *any* distilled answers to let her check off a question and say, "Done!" No. Her inquiry went deeper: "Who am I, now," she asked, "in this bed with only a bedside table and a small locker of my own things with me—my world bounded by a hospital curtain? Who am I, here, where no one knows the work I've done, the children I've borne? Who am I really?" For the last time, Ann struggled with the human questions that had shaped her living: *Who am I? What is Love? What is God? What am I to do?* Then she added a final one: *How do I weigh the value of my life?*

Love is a warrior. In previous years, Ann had learned how to let go of attitudes and behaviors, relationships and belongings, activities and beliefs that did not square with an honesty that increased with every investigation. Now, as she entered the last six months of her life, she made a more fundamental surrender. She told her friends, "I saw that life would have its way—over my body, my lifestyle, my freedom to move about." In this harness, she lost her hearing, then her sight, then her digestive ability. Breathing, itself, became difficult. She met each new challenge, initially, with an attempt to compensate. But all the hearing devices and special foods, all the medicines and skilled helpers could not put my friend back together again.

What Is a Life Well Lived?

Those of us who loved Ann understood that decades of learning to surrender did not make this one easy. But when she began to put that discipline into practice for the last time, we saw before our own eyes how it worked. She began with an honest recognition of the truth of her situation, and an admission of complete defeat. She asked the Unknown for help. She let us in. We watched her take each step on her Path, faltering at first, then clear and forthright, following her own light.

Ann made an unqualified acceptance of each of her losses, trusting that the resolution of her work would be accompanied, as it had in the past, by a sense of completion and peace. She allowed herself to grieve each loss until she eventually stood naked before life, as vulnerable as a turtle without a shell, yet with an amazing strength born of facing her truth. We watched her show us how this stage of life is lived: not with platitudes and intellectual assertions, but with a deep and ultimately graceful assent to life-as-it-is that is whole-hearted.

While I was mourning Ann, the whisper uttered a single line: *Love is born of grief . . .* Was it true? I had no idea. The rest of the words came later:

> *Love is born of grief.*
> *Not the love we seek as consolation*
> *but a Love that embraces all things—*
> *that does not judge them right or wrong;*
> *a Love that is not locked into a morality*
> *which provides certainty*
> *in an uncertain existence.*
>
> *Love has to do with*
> *a quality of compassion*
> *and a lightness of being*
> *that comes of letting slip from one's shoulders*
> *all the expectations and all the protest—*

first the heavy armor,
then the sturdy cloaks,
and finally,
the last soft silks—
garments that have been, for us,
a "No!" to what life has offered.

How Do We Harness for God the Energies of Love?

'Harnessing' speaks to our ego: We want to hold on to the reins, to harness the energies of Love, ourselves—but 'we' cannot do it. Soul work turns that very human yearning on its head. We've been invited, instead of trying to control life's contradictions, to embrace them—the good, the bad, the wanted, and the unwanted—and to be grateful for even the most hideous things. When we respond to Love's invitation in this way, the reins slip through our fingers. The rest is grace.

The Buddha said,

> You cannot travel the path until you have become the path itself.

Thus, comes the mystery of one-ing: Harnessing is a reciprocal process. As our hearts open, we, in turn, are harnessed by Love. This paradoxical Love dwells within/*among/all around* us when our hold on life is loosened and we have no idea who we are. We ask, *Who am I?* and find in the lack of any answer, the seeds of an epiphany. Jesus described it in a parable:

> The kingdom of heaven is like treasure hidden in a field. When a man found it, he hid it again, and then in his joy went and sold all he had and bought that field.[6]

As I hear the parable, the man stumbles on the Kingdom quite by accident and is awed by the experience. No longer ignorant of the treasure that lies in his own depths,[7] he is momentarily humbled. For the first time, he has seen his own insignificance before the vastness of Mystery, *and he wants this relationship more than anything else.* He also recognizes that he is not ready to claim it. In the upwelling joy of his awakening, he sets aside his desire to hold onto the treasure, and instead "hides it," not so much from others, as from himself—for he has much work to do and he knows it. He has to buy the field.

It is a costly purchase. To buy it—to respond to the root question, *Who am I really?*—he must relinquish more than his possessions. As in Lewis' story of the boy with snake skin,[8] he has to release his grip on everything he's used to define himself—his desires, beliefs, accomplishments; even his family, his lifestyle, and his religion. Each is one of the 'many skins covering the depths of his heart' that have kept him in bondage to ego. He lets them go—and still, he stands at the gap. "What is left?" he asks. He does not know; and this time, face to face with the abyss, *he knows he does not know.* Giving up, giving in at last, the man turns to what Lewis called the Lion and asks, *"What does the Lion need?"* The Lion then strips him of the 'last skin,' the unknown barriers to his core and leaves him naked.

When we ask the Lion to remove the last skin, we see the many convictions we don't even know we are strangled by: the longings and beliefs about ourselves and others and life we once were afraid would drive love away and leave us all alone. Stripped of our deeply embedded self-protection, we stand before Life as we really are.

We feel naked. Profoundly humbled. It may seem more like humiliation at first, but in time, the Lion's wound/*blessing* becomes humility—a bringer of peace. It is in this context that I understand the parable.

Humility is the sole requirement for the Kingdom; the only stance that allows an authentic relationship with God; the only one that permits us to live in harmony with others, and with the whole community of life.

How do we harness for God the energies of Love?

We love the very face of God we fear.

When asked how to befriend God, Hafiz, the beloved poet of Islam, replied:

I hold the Lion's Paw
Whenever I dance. [9]

True humility makes us fearless. In Love, we hold the Lion's paw.

Love asks for an open and spacious heart. It lies behind what is broken and what seems empty. It comes through a relinquishment of safety and a relinquishment of power. Love brings us to our knees to bring us Home. Then, yoked more firmly to Presence, we tap the simplicity of our inner, aboriginal, and holy selves. From this deep and tender connection with life, we under-stand:

> It is not the preservation of our own life
>   that matters.
> The Life matters—all of the life on this planet.
> All of existence. For all Time.

To live in harmony with the rest of existence, we dismantle the barriers to Life our inner divisions have created. Alone and together, we learn to stand at the Beginning of ourselves and let slip from our shoulders

> *all the expectations and all the protest—*
> *first the heavy armor,*
> *then the sturdy cloaks*
> *and finally,*
> *the last soft silks . . .*

Then the spiritual honey is freed to flow from our core. Long bound in a honeycomb of mental compartments, the power of Love is released.

> Then, for a second time in the history of the
> world, humanity will have discovered Fire.

Love is not something we do. It stands revealed as who we really are. Walls fallen away, we find ourselves in communion with everything—in communion with Being itself—*I AM.*

This is Presence.

Endnotes for Chapter 16

1   Helen Luke, *Dark Wood to White Rose,* New York: Parabola Books, 1989, xi.

2   The full quote by Meister Eckhart is at the beginning of Chapter 2.

3   In this chapter, the interpretation of the phrase, "harnessing for God the energies of love," is my own. At least on the surface, Teilhard's attention in this essay is on the physical and psychological sublimation of sexual energies/desire. But I think that neither his life nor his tradition would disagree with the kind of surrender that is the focus of this chapter. His biographer, Ursula King, supports this inference in "Rediscovering Fire," *Earthlight Magazine*, Fall 2000, 15: "The living fire which animated Teilhard, . . . summed up by him as a heart of fire, was 'a fire with the power to penetrate all things, and which invited a surrender to an active feeling of communion with God through the universe.'" See also Appendix I: "The Issue of God."

4   The two commandments Jesus taught are found in Mark 12:29-31, Matthew 22:40, and Luke 10:25-28.

5   Dylan Thomas, "Do not go gentle into that good night," *Dylan Thomas: The Poems*, London: J. M. Dent & Sons Ltd., 1971.

6   Matthew 13:44.

7   The version of the same parable in the earlier *Gospel According to Thomas*, 109-110, reads:
>   The kingdom is like a man
>   Who is ignorant of the treasure
>   Hidden in his field. When he dies,
>   He leaves it to his son, who sells it,
>   Being unaware also of the treasure within.
>   The buyer will come.
>   Discover the treasure while plowing. . . .
>   He who has found the world, and riches,
>   Should then deny the world. . . .
>   The world is unworthy of the man who finds himself.

8   See Chapter 15 and the story of the Lion in C. S. Lewis, *The Voyage of the Dawn Treader.*

9   Hafiz, *The Gift*, tr. Daniel Ladinsky, New York: Penguin Compass, 1999, 57. The great Sufi master Hafiz (c.1320-1389) is the beloved poet of Persia, and of the Sufi wing of Islam.

Presence

COMMUNION

If [all] are faithful to their own calling . . .
communication on the deepest level is possible.
And the deepest level of communication is not
communication but communion. It is wordless, it
is beyond words, and it is beyond speech, and
it is beyond concept. Not that we discover a
new unity. We discover an older unity. My dear
brothers and sisters, we are already one. But we
imagine that we are not. And what we have to
recover is our original unity. What we have to be
is what we are.

Thomas Merton
Spiritual Master—The Essential Writings, 229
From his last talk in Calcutta, just before he died

Llanthony Abbey, Wales

Presence

Love has taken away all my practices and filled me with poetry.

Rumi 1

Who am I? What is Love? What is God?

To step into the silence of Llanthony Abbey is to enter a hallowed world. A green carpet rolls down its aisles and out through stone arches to the meadows and hills beyond. Without walls, what once seemed dead is filled with life, and the sky holds everything in its embrace.

When all is fallen away, we stand and see with our whole selves. The One Reality rings with its beauty and pain, and our joy resonates with the joy of the universe.

Rumi sings our song:

There's nothing left of me.
I'm like a ruby held up to the sunrise. . . .
    It has no resistance to light.²

Emptied of all that is partial, we are a sanctuary for the heart's conscious light. There, bound by neither time nor space nor walls of self-definition, we find the gentleness at root, the forgiveness upwelling, the many beauties of being human—the truth of who we are.

In an ancient text, the *Upanishads*, it is written:

> This little space within the heart is as great as this vast universe. The heavens and the earth are there, and the sun and the moon and the stars; fire and lightning and wind are there, and all that is now and is not yet—all that is contained within it.[3]

In this embrace, Life lives us—and we are overflowed.

Then, there is the possibility of love.
Then, there is poetry.

o

In the Field—4:30 a.m.

Even under the bright moon
Orion gleams.

Andromeda's pinpoints
bathe this little chair
with light from a past so deep,
humanity had barely stirred.

Two owls begin comment, an antiphon.
By day, the red tailed hawk
will watch
from the same hollow pine.

And in the stillness, the dazzling dark,
Presence
brighter than moonlight.[4]

In Presence, my soul sings poetry. It always comes as a surprise. I see an old stone pine leaning in a field and the soul whispers, *There is a time when the trees are singing . . .*

What does that mean? I ask, but she doesn't say. So I stop going where I thought I was going, sit down, and listen . . . Her words rise, singing the depths of Love, whispering Wholeness.

o

The Singing of Trees

There is a time when the trees are singing,
      when they are
      hollow with their own
      Presence

and the hushed sounds that blow through them
      as they stand there
      witnessing
      and singing

are like breath on old pipes
      or wooden casks.

It is then I know the past is never sealed:
      that all the loves, the wrongs, the dreams,
      the shattered hopes,
      the horror of everything dead—

It is these that sound the deepest tones,
      the root of the chord
      on which the whole Song rests.

The soul sings of a Love that is infinite. She declares that *everything* is needed for its intricate work; that Love leaves nothing out—not you, not me, not past or present, nor light nor darkness, nor truth nor sorrow. She reminds us, as she did in a long-ago poem, that if we are to be free, Love needs most of all, the things long buried at our Beginnings.

o

The Despised

It was a small house,
a few cramped spaces—
walled off and
without light

It is no wonder
she was misshapen,
confined there and
unlamented

Nor in that darkness
was it any wonder
she hadn't known
she'd built herself
a prison

But once her house had burned down,
she could see
through its charred timbers
that the moon and the stars
had always been there

She could walk like a ghost
through its walls,
let the breeze
blow through her
like a cloudless sky

I heard the poem's echo in the silence of Llanthony Abbey.

Love unfolds in silence. Ego rests in its embrace. This Field is not partial; everything that appears in it is received with loving care.

Love coheres. It is an energy that unites. Love alone joins us to existence by that which is deepest in us. Then, all of creation is shot through with light:

o

Dinner

Tonight,
when we sat down to dinner,
our work done,
white corn, basil,
cucumbers and red tomatoes
picked fresh from the garden
—a feast on blue pottery plates—

I reached across the cherry wood
glowing in the evening light
and held your hand.

We looked out over the hills together
and watched long shadows
deepen the rolling pasture's curves,
a summer sky turn gold.

One slender beam of light
crossed the room
from a high window in the west
and caught the crimson rose
wide open and floating
in a black clay bowl
on the table before us.

For a moment,
        everything was a living fire.

Poets and sages celebrate this silent Presence in verse composed of what we can see and touch and feel. In Sodo's haiku, it is a hut.

> in my hut this spring
> there is nothing
> there is everything[5]

And in M. C. Richard's poem, a garment.

> I put on my poet's shirt
> and birds fly through.
> Birds perch in me and
> their throats tremble.
> Their high singing builds
> in me like a listening love.
>
> Clothes are the sheaths
> of my being—so many old dreams of
> changing dress, unable to decide . . .
> what to wear?
>
> Now the dreamer is at rest:
> she wears the nest, the eaves
> and orchards. Wears the tall pine
> of the white-throated sparrow
> in the city walk-up—the gutters
> and sills—understanding a language
> she does not know, hearing the inaudible.[6]

Wearing her poet's shirt, Richards photographed a gleaming pottery bowl she'd fashioned and laid at the tide line after the clay was fired. One small bowl on the wide, wet shore—an earthpoem whispering an inaudible: "adamah/*Adamah!*"

Beyond, within, and *all around* the clay bowl, the hut, the poet's shirt—the Emptiness that is full is not these. It is small/ *It is greater than the universe.*

> *The luminous universe is not God. It rides on the utter-*
> *ance of that Mystery like a leaf on the current of a river.*

When we attend the Current that lives us, we drop into the depths of Presence. From within this heart of life, we *see* others in a different way. We see Who they are, and loving them, love at the same time, More.

o

Taking Soundings

At dawn,
he knots a ball of white string in fathoms,
ties it 'round a granite rock the size of his fist,
and rows his dinghy across the windless water.

Low tide. Nothing moves
until he drops the rock
overboard
and a hundred silver circles
spread across the shining surface.

Seeking the ocean's depth,
he paddles back and forth,
    back and forth
    between the islands and the dock:
    drops the rock, pulls it up,
    examines the string,
    lets the rock slip from his hand and
    plunge once more into the silence.

Warming my hands
around a brown earthen mug,
I watch my husband from the kitchen window.

The wake behind his boat
streams out in a wide **V**
like an ermine cape
trailing behind a King.

When you see one you love
grapple alone with what is given,
whether he works in a field
or on the wide water,

you see how small he is.
You see his Majesty.

The soul drinks from the soundless sound of the Current, a stream of giving and grace. There, her attention rests. She calls to Existence—deep calling to Deep:[7]

Who am I? Who are You? What is Love? What is God? . . .

The whole surround responds—overtones from the past, echoes of the present, calls from the future—*all of the voices* breathing infinite relationship. In this Communion, our bodies resonate like organ pipes. Animated by life's energies, they ring Presence.

In the Field of Presence, we drop into the depths of another person like a rock on a string. Our souls make inquiry—not of the person—but of the Infinite. Taking soundings, we know another *with* ourselves/*in* ourselves/and *as* ourselves—for they *are* ourselves.

o

Love is more than we think, more than we feel. It is the silent Song that powers our lives and knits the universe together. Attuned to its energies, the soul knows that Love transcends individuality, transcends time and space, transcends the boundaries of life and death—and that sometimes, the palpable Current confirms the living mystery and presence of all the awakened and their secret work of Love.

Endnotes for Presence

1 Rumi, "Buoyancy," in Coleman Barks, *The Essential Rumi*, 104.
2 Rumi, "The Sunrise Ruby," in Coleman Barks, *Ibid.*, 100.
3 *The Chandogya Upanishad* (8, 3), seventh century BC.
4 The poem arrived whole as I meditated outdoors under a full moon before dawn, a day before the pancreatic surgery described in Chapter 16.
5 Yamaguchi Sodo (1642-1716).
6 Mary Caroline Richards, abridged from "Poet," *Imagine Inventing Yellow: New and Selected Poems*, Barrytown, NY: Station Hill Press, 1990, 3.
7 Psalm 42:7.

The Song of Love

Who loves, loves Love
And loving Love, creates a circle so complete,
There is no end to Love.

St. Bernard[1]

You are loved.

You are accepted, held in a vast embrace. There is nothing in you, nothing of character or tendencies, race or sexuality, accomplishment or failure that is not held, not needed. You are a child of God. That which you deeply are is deeply wanted.

You are not alone, not left to your own devices.

There is more going on than can be seen. You belong to an activity that is beyond comprehension. Trust it.

You are known.

That which you have sought is seeking you. That which you want to offer to life is greatly needed. You may not yet know what it is, but it is exactly the right gift and only yours to give. Give it.

You are part of a great leap of loving such as the world has never known.

You have work to do. Begin it. Get on your knees and say to the Great Lover, "do what you will with me!" and mean it.

Leap into the day and learn what it is to open your heart, to be mad with desire for the One Love, mad with passion for the One Moment.

There is only one ancient and forever work of art: the slow fashioning of Life and the gradual flowering of Love. Find your Way. Find your practice. Find your companions. Give your life to Love.

The world sings in its many voices, *"Do you love me?"* It stumbles across your path a hundred times a day in its beauty and its suffering. Respond. Every moment of self-forgetting is an offering; every act of self-giving, a tongue of *Fire*.

Be bread. Be broken. Let go of what you know. Do all you can to find in your heart what your mind can't comprehend. Moment by moment . . . place by place . . . person by person . . . wound by wound . . . Dance! Fall! Fail! You will be busy, but not with the busy-ness of the world.

In the heart of you lies Love. Without your opposition, it shines through you. You have only to let yourself be held in the larger embrace, let yourself be loved, let yourself be known as you are—*and you will be lit up.*

Thomas Merton said, "There's no way of telling people they're walking around shining like the sun."[2]

You are a shining.

You are not only the small being who wants to be safe.

You are Love.
You are Life.
You are Light.
You are Fire.

Go shining

Endnotes for The Song of Love

1   St. Bernard of Clairvaux (1090-1153), known for his series of sermons on love and his book, *On Loving God*.

2   Thomas Merton, "Conjectures of a Guilty Bystander" in Cunningham, ed., *Thomas Merton: Spiritual Master*, 145.

Appendix I
The Issue of God

Someday, after mastering the winds, the waves, the tides, and gravity, we shall harness for God the energies of Love . . . .

In this book, I have tried to stay true to Teilhard's quote and at the same time, encourage you to draw your own conclusions about what 'for God' means (or does not mean) to *you*. Teilhard chose to use religious language for what he understood as mystery—but mystery is deeper than any religion! Religions have helped us to grapple with what we can*not* understand by providing words and symbols, even though they were inadequate to the task. Inevitably, these words have become calcified and loaded.

As a result, for many of us, any reference to God is problematic. Either the idea doesn't square with our intellect or it conjures up too much that disturbs us. Some find it difficult to swallow the long history of aggression, competition, and control manifested by many of the religions. I deeply respect these concerns. However, to leave mystery out of the equation is a mistake the modern world has made. It avoids the unknown.

No one has ever found an adequate word for mystery, not even the Buddha or Lao Tse or Jesus. However, the languages these masters spoke shaped their minds in ways that made them very different from our own. Scholar, Neil Douglas-Klotz, suggests that languages like ours that separate inner from outer, cosmology from psychology, and divide human life into mind, body, emotion, and spirit have prejudiced us in the West. There are other equally valid ways to view the world! He helps to unveil the richness of Aramaic, the ancient language of Jesus. Like the other Semitic tongues, Aramaic reflected the notion of a continuum—a single community that included everything from planets to what we would call the voices of the subconscious. In these languages of the Middle East, the known and the unknown lived together, and a single word might encompass many different shades of meaning. This perspective was very different from that of the Greek mindset—bent on distinguishing one kind of thing from another.

Jesus called the great mystery he experienced in his life 'abba,' and the Greeks translated *abba* to mean 'father.' Their translation propelled the notion of a 'father God' into Western culture. Douglas-Klotz reveals that *abba* had countless other meanings, and adds, "in the words of a prophet, all possible meanings may be present."[1]

> The word for "father" (*abba*) can also mean parent, ancestor, or founder [and is based on a root] which points to all movements [in nature or in the cosmos] that seek to complete themselves or find an end. . . . This root also helps form the root of one of the words for love in Hebrew and Aramaic. [As] used in the Lord's Prayer, it can refer to parenting in the cosmic sense . . . which is beyond gender . . . and indicates a process . . . that begins in unity and gives birth . . . to new forms.[2]

All of us are part of an awakening process that is giving birth to just such new forms. That process is mysterious. Our own mindset was shaped by the Greeks, however, and prefers definitive answers. It tends to replace mystery with efforts at social change, personal growth, education, and democratic values.

This raises an essential concern. Surely, we need overarching values that speak to all people, but those values can't be just social or scientific or intellectual theories. They have to have heart, entail a depth of feeling, and involve service to others, particularly those who are suffering or in need. In our endeavors to do good, we have, indeed, created some magnificent ways to serve others! Many of our efforts, however, have thrown the baby out with the bathwater—and we need what we've discarded—if only for one reason: in order to see ourselves right-sized.

Problematic for me in these efforts is an ever-growing sense of human power and hubris. No doubt, many of our social or self-improvement programs are helpful, but they often lack the humility with which to engage the dilemmas of our world. This becomes a major issue for those who are anti-*anything*—anti-war, anti-poverty, anti-global warming—for such a position can quickly become yet another ideology. To be against something throws us automatically into an argument with *what is*—and the self who has answers is so adept at polarizing! We align with the 'right' side or the 'right' answer and make the other 'wrong.' Left to its own devices, the mind's view of the world hijacks our emotions and propels us into further dividing ourselves: between strong and weak, straight and gay, have and have-not, liberal and conservative, Christian, Muslim, and Jew. It is tearing us apart.

I believe that to be right-sized, we need to view our lives against a backdrop that dwarfs us. We need to make the humiliating surrender to that which we *can't* answer: the truth of our human vulnerability and need; the ultimate problem of our own impending death; the ugliness in the world that we can*not* fix; and the dangers we face that are beyond our capacity to solve, *at all*. It is this despair—the hopelessness, powerlessness, and ultimate terror of non-being—that we need to have *lived* in order to serve with any measure of humility. These unknowns represent some of the vast mysteries that take us from a stance of thinking we know what to do, thinking we know what the word 'God' stands for, thinking we can solve our problems if we just try harder—and begin to humble us enough to live as members of creation who offer their service as peers. Then, we have walked in the shoes of those we're trying to help—by walking in our own.

To that end, I believe we have to live our lives in relationship to the unknown as well as to the known—and you simply can't name mystery! The word *God* (or *Brahman, the Tao, Atman* . . .) gives inadequate language to what we do not know and will never understand. And that is deeper than any word, any symbol, theory, movement, or religion.

Appendix II
Cataclysmic Change and the Fundamental Transformation of Consciousness

There are events affecting entire societies . . . that provide threats to the reality previously taken for granted. Such situations may occur as the result of natural catastrophe, war or social upheaval. At such times religious legitimations [that serve to help a society regain its balance] almost always come to the front.

Peter Berger[3]

People don't change until they have to.

Many of the great sacred stories emerged from a critical turning point in the lives and cultures in which they originated. They spoke to a *fundamental reorientation* for their Time. Here are some examples that demonstrate the creative potential inherent in the collision between old and new ways. They show us how human consciousness evolves as people adapt to cataclysmic cosmic, global, or social change.

Fundamental Awakening
As the Result of Cosmic Change

A story so ancient, it was never written can be found in the excavations of a Neolithic village high on a cliff in northern Scotland. These ruins tell about a Time when human beings left their hunter-gatherer ways. Most probably forced by an ice age beyond their control,[4] persons on four continents stopped walking as a way of life and settled in one place for the first time in history.

Without a written story, we have to use our imagination as we touch the rough stone walls and peer down into partitioned spaces filled with granite benches, sleeping alcoves, and a central hearth blackened from their fires. When we look at the piles of archaic oyster shells where they ate by the edge of a cold North Sea, we can only guess at the profound disruption that preceded this settled way of life. There must have been massive conflicts in people's hearts between the old beliefs and stories they'd relied on in the past—and what they had to do differently to adapt to new circumstance. *Who they thought they were, what was true,* and *what a man or woman was supposed to do*—all of these certainties were challenged. Surely, there were many who persevered in the old ways, even when food became scarce and the byways their ancestors had traveled were nearly impassable. It probably took a long time before a few of them heard some new inner suggestion and tried to heed it. Most probably didn't. But with glaciers encroaching on every side, those few who did, risked everything for the unknown.

Theirs was an immense transformation. Instead of following the seasons, the animals' paths, the ripening fruits on the trees, they learned to build shelter, and then to plant seed, tame animals, and store their food. Out of the long human awakening that ensued, there emerged a new kind of people: Neolithic families who had settled.

They had changed their minds.

What an upheaval of identity it must have been for each hunter-gatherer to see himself—not as someone who carried everything he needed on his back—but as a person who lived in a house of stone!

Fundamental Awakening As the Result of Global Change

The same process of transformation was recorded many thousands of years later in the teachings of the Buddha. His was an era of global changes that caused enormous cultural dislocation in India. Monarchs from other continents had taken control of the country's small villages and replaced them with huge domains. The inhabitants of these new domains were used to being guided by village elders who knew them; now they were shocked to find themselves subjects of unknown kings who ruled their lives from distant lands. These tribal people had not yet come to experience themselves as individuals; theirs was a group identity—a *participation mystique*.[*] Seeing their plight, the Buddha gave them both a practice and a philosophy to help them face the chaos in their lives. But the impact of the changes was traumatic:

> Each person had to bear the knowledge that the old props of community were gone and that the awareness of being an individual brought both freedom and pain.[5]

By showing them how to stay with their pain and walk a spiritual path, the Buddha offered a Way to help them reorient their lives.

Those of his followers who were willing to change their perceptions learned to see and hear differently. Eventually, they saw themselves, not as a collective body, but as individual persons. Like the hunter-gatherers who, instead of walking, stayed— they came to experience a fundamental change of mind and an entirely different kind of identity.

[*] See Chapter 4

Fundamental Awakening and Its Relationship to Social Change

Ellen Grace O'Brian reminds us that whoever dares the unknown and awakens makes a difference:

> The influence of a single transformed life is beyond calculation; it ripples out and touches the lives of countless others. [6]

This same message about transformation from an old order to the new is epitomized by the lives and teachings of the Buddha, Moses, Jesus, Paul, and Martin Luther King. It also characterizes the words of scientists such as Nobel physicist, Max Planck. Each speaks to the radical revolution of perspective needed *in the culture* by addressing what needed to change *in the individual*:

> All things change. (The Buddha)

> Thou shalt not covet. (Moses)

> You have heard 'an eye for an eye, a tooth for a tooth,'
> but I say, 'love your enemies.' (Jesus)

> Love bears all things. (Paul)

> Black is beautiful. (Martin Luther King)

> When you change the way you look at things,
> the things you look at change. (Max Planck)

Each makes clear that the kind of social action and social change needed is rooted in a change of mind.

Fundamental Awakening in Our Time

We belong to life, and at this evolutionary juncture, we can trust that life knows how to engage us creatively. Our work is to be present, to listen, and to step forward when it taps the potential deep within us. Then, whatever social, global, or environmental changes lie ahead, we will be participants in life's creative unfolding and the gradual awakening of Love.

Endnotes for Appendices

1   Neil Douglas-Klotz, *The Hidden Gospel—Decoding the Spiritual Message of the Aramaic Jesus*, Wheaton IL: Quest Books, Theosophical Publishing House, 2001, 18-19. Douglas-Klotz holds a doctorate in Religious Studies (in particular, hermeneutics, the science of interpretation), and Psychology.

2   *Ibid.,* 130.

3   Peter L. Berger, *The Sacred Canopy—Elements of a Sociological Theory of Religion,* New York: Anchor Books/Doubleday, 44.

4   Brian Swimme, Introduction, *The Powers of the Cosmos* (DVD), 2004.

5   Pankaj Mishra, *An End to Suffering—The Buddha in the World,* New York: Farrar, Strauss and Giroux, 2004. Italics mine.

6   Rev. Ellen Grace O'Brian, Center for Spiritual Enlightenment, 'Daily Inspirations,' *http://www.info@csecenter.org*

Gratitude

"Talking with people who agree with you," said Bill Moyers, *"is like jogging in a cul de sac."*[1]

The moment I started to write this book, life offered new opportunities to dialog at length with men and women with widely divergent points of view. I had rich conversations with scientists and engineers, doctors and psychologists; academics, company presidents, consultants, and school teachers. I talked with atheists and agnostics, and questioned clergy, some of whom had remained in their traditions, and others who had left. Among them, were a Buddhist nun, a rabbi, a Sufi sheik, and priests from Anglican, Roman Catholic, and Episcopal traditions, as well as pastors from Presbyterian, Congregational, and Unity churches. I learned from laypersons in all the major religions, some of whom were Pentecostal, others who were mainstream, and still others who'd questioned and set aside much of what they'd been taught. How grateful I am to all of them!

I had no sooner begun the book than I received a letter from Tennessee: **Frankie Brogan** wrote to say that she'd just finished *The Dancing Animal Woman* and described herself as an 81-year old woman and an author (*The Snare of the Fowler*). She also said she was an Episcopalian and had been on a spiritual quest all her life.

It was just a month after my writing group of fifteen years had disbanded, and as our correspondence flowered, I asked rather hesitantly if she might like to review the manuscript as I wrote it. She responded enthusiastically, and for two years, gave the most loving care to the early drafts coming into such tenuous existence. I learned a lot from Frankie, and in our interaction, she taught me about a more charismatic spirituality. I also found how important it is to hear just where two points of view may be different and hopefully, how to speak in a way that can sometimes span the gap.

I applied what I learned from Frankie to my interactions with other people as they stepped into my life and offered their unique skills. Each gift of self was exactly what I needed at the time. They are listed in the order they 'arrived':

Colin Oliver, a gifted British poet and educator, had read *The Dancing Animal Woman* years earlier, and in turn, sent a book of his poetry inscribed, "You held a mirror to my face . . . " Colin had been lifelong friend of the late philosopher Douglas Harding (*On Having No Head*), and they had deeply influenced one another's journeys and philosophies. He reviewed each of the early chapters, contributing warmth, wisdom, and encouragement as well as comments from his own rich life experience. His published books of poetry include *Ploughing at Nightfall* and *High River*.

Bill Veltrop offered to help shape the book in its early stages and gave freely of his time. He asked critical questions of intent, desired outcome, and organization. A large-systems change agent, his skillful questioning came from an evolutionary perspective. Bill maintains a practice of Kriya Yoga and his website reflects his mastery of co-creative interaction. See *http://www.theinfinitegames.org*

Jim Blackburn, an Episcopal priest and scholar from Maryland, also teaches courses in the community on the mystics, T. S. Eliot's poetry, Dante's Divine Comedy, and a comparative study of Christianity, Judaism, and Islam. He read portions of the manuscript and was particularly helpful in translating Hebrew texts.

Pat Sullivan is the author of *Work with Meaning, Work with Joy,* a speaker, and a consultant on the nature of ethical work from the perspective of all faiths. She gave the manuscript its first critical reading, and helped me begin to integrate and structure it. Now a Unity church member, her comments came from her own long struggle with traditional religions.

Stephanie Brown, PhD, generously offered much-needed suggestions about structure. A psychotherapist, researcher, and internationally recognized expert on the trauma and the treatment of addictions, the most recent of her ten books include *A Place Called Self* and *Stages of Family Recovery*. See *http://www. stephaniebrownphd.com*

Marv Hiles, a former pastor in the Presbyterian Church, is a spiritual director, retreat leader, and writer, who with his wife **Nancy Hiles** created the *Daybook*. They now coauthor *The Way Through* and other publications, some of which are online. Both of them offered valuable commentary. The wise voices they gathered in the *Daybook* have been my guides for thirty years. A limited edition of *An Almanac For the Soul*, a compilation of *Daybook* entries from 1976-2000, is to be published in 2008.

Elaina Hyde-Mills is a Canadian Anglican priest, hospital chaplain, and poet. Elaina's comments—particularly on how portions of the manuscript affected her own inner process—were invaluable.

Bill Kueppers, PhD, took a deep personal interest in the content of the book and for more than two years, gave freely of his time and wisdom. A former teacher and later, a corporate consultant, he provided significant editorial help. Bill's professional focus is the development of authenticity. He holds a doctorate in transpersonal psychology, is a spiritual director, and an experienced group facilitator. He brought his heart and a long inquiry into the Roman Catholic tradition to our rich dialog, and offered insightful questions, suggestions, and many valuable resources. His companionship on the last leg of this writing journey made all the difference. See his website *http:// www.radicalauthenticity.com*

I have learned much from colleagues and friends, as well as from the many participants in *Mining Your Life for Meaning* groups offered locally (which include a writing practice). I am very grateful for the generosity of **"Maria"** and **"Bruce,"** whose more extensive contributions remain anonymous, and for all those who permitted me to use excerpts from their unpublished writing. In the order they appear in this book:

Marilyn Veltrop holds a PhD in transpersonal psychology and guides individuals and groups on the spiritual journey.

Shirley Holley has been a licensed family therapist for many years. She writes both poetry and creative nonfiction.

Harriet Wright is a dancer, a poet, and a creative artist in several arenas.

Joan Blackmon is a businesswoman with her own company and is also a trained spiritual director.

Mark Goodman-Morris, DMin, is a Presbyterian pastor. A trained spiritual director, he is also a poet and sometimes, mime.

Susan Neville, MBA, is a consultant who facilitates leadership groups at the Stanford Graduate School of Business.

I needed people like these: people with talent, with wonderful minds and big hearts who encouraged and reminded me to trust the inclinations of my soul. They were honest. They told me the truth, shared their stories, and revealed their own humanity—their flaws, their joy, and their pain. As they did, they also shed light on my own quest.

I also received skilled help from the following people:

Sharon Hamrick, librarian at the Institute for Transpersonal Psychology in Palo Alto, CA, gave generously of her time to research the sources of several elusive quotations.

Denise Moynahan, an illustrator and author of children's books (most recently, *The Great Cavern of the Winds: Tales from Backbone Mountain*), made the pen and ink drawing of the triple foundation in Greece. She also proofread the text. I am very grateful to my sister. See *http://www.denisemoynahan.com*

Editor, **Sheila Ellison**, is the author of nine books including *The Courage to be a Single Mother* and *365 Days of Creative Play*. She is the founder of two Internet support communities for women, and is currently working on her first novel, teaching writing, and gratefully raising six children! Sheila maintains a daily spiritual practice of walking the labyrinth. She contributed objectivity, skill, and insight, and it was a delight working with her. See *http://www.CompleteMom.com*

In the mega-world of publishing, everyone should be lucky enough to be in dialog with a publisher like **Larry Bramble.** Besides his considerable gifts of artistic conception, layout, and design, Larry took a personal interest in this book from its inception. He read several versions as it evolved and made significant suggestions about its content, style, and organization. Most important, Larry brings the wisdom of his own spiritual odyssey to the table. It has been a privilege to work with him.

I am particularly grateful to two persons whose work has illuminated my way: Teilhard de Chardin's biographer **Ursula King, PhD**, and cosmologist **Brian Swimme, PhD.** Both of these scholars also helped to clarify some of the material.

How very generous, how gracious are those who willingly took time from their full lives to write endorsements for this book. I am deeply indebted to **Thomas Berry, SJ, Don Bisson, FMS, Marigold Farmer, Richard Farmer, Tai Chi Master, Carol Lee Flinders, PhD, Ursula King, PhD, Bill Kueppers, PhD, the Rev. Ellen Grace O'Brian, Brian Swimme, PhD, JeremyTaylor, DMin, and Llewellyn Vaughan-Lee, PhD.**

Without **Joyce Schmidt, PhD, Richard Moss, MD,** and **Brenda Morgan, PhD,** there would have been no journey. Each one knows why I have dedicated the book to them. Each has offered a priceless gift.

I first met **George Comstock** at an interview for a consulting project at his company, and as we neared the end of our conversation, he asked what else I hoped to do in my life. The reply was out of my mouth before I even thought about it: "Someday, I'd like to write a book." His face softened and he looked a little wistful; then added in almost a whisper, "I've always wanted to be there for someone who was writing a book!" George hired me for the consulting project, and several months later, asked me out . . .

Last summer, after almost 30 years of marriage, I asked if he remembered making that statement, because this book would never have seen the light of day without him. "Oh, Anne," he replied, and his voice cracked, "it was one of my life's dreams!" What an amazing gift! I was surprised by his answer but I shouldn't have been. George has freed me from many of the routine tasks of running our household for the last five years. He's been my sounding board and has helped to articulate ideas when the struggle with words seemed almost impossible. He's read and reread every chapter and offered critical commentary, as well as guidance on matters of science, history, literature, and grammar. George has been my friend, soul mate, and partner. Most of all, he's just kept loving me—and I wrote the book for him.

Endnote for Gratitude

1   From a lecture at De Anza College, Cupertino CA, 2005.

Observations From Many Perspectives

A work of great beauty, a clarion call! I know of no one else who has tackled our vital need for awakening to the transforming powers of love as thoroughly as she has. This pioneering work strikes the right note for which many people are waiting. Let us hope that it will be widely read.

URSULA KING, PhD
Teilhard de Chardin's biographer, author of *Spirit of Fire: The Life and Vision of Teilhard de Chardin* and *Spirituality and Society in the New Millennium*

It is always a joy to see love taken out of the small enclosure of personal relationships where our Western culture has trapped it, into the real arena of the heart which includes all of creation. Through Anne Hillman's voice, we can feel the deeper currents of this primal power that both makes and unmakes us, and that leads us to the depth of being and beyond.

LLEWELLYN VAUGHAN-LEE, PhD
Sufi teacher and author, *Working with Oneness* and *Traveling the Path of Love*
http.//www.goldensufi.org

Fire, indeed! Led by visionaries like Pierre Teilhard de Chardin, we are piecing together a radiant new/old vision of human be-ing itself, and *Awakening the Energies of Love* will add real momentum to that holy work.

CAROL LEE FLINDERS, PhD
Lecturer and author, *Enduring Lives: Portraits of Women* and *Faith in Action* and *Enduring Grace: Living Portraits of Seven Women Mystics*
http://www.tworock.org

If you are interested in the deeper implications of dreams and dreaming, do not miss this book! Anne Hillman's examples and understandings as she traces several paths of awakening are most illuminating.

JEREMY TAYLOR, DMin
Unitarian Universalist tradition, author of *Dream Work* and *The Living Labyrinth*
http://www.jeremytaylor.com

The difference between a martial artist and someone focused on self defense is love. For the martial artist, to receive a blow is an opportunity to say "yes" and ultimately, to love—not fear—the attacker. Anne Hillman understands this and with a story teller's beauty, writes of this journey from one to the other.

RICHARD FARMER
Tai Chi Master. Founder and Principle Instructor of the
International Rising Dragon Tai Chi School
http://www.soulmoves.co.uk

Awakening the Energies of Love is not intended to give an academic rush. But if you read it with an open spirit so that you can sense what comes through its pages, you will be buoyed up—an updraft that is real, immediate, and quite abiding.

BILL KUEPPERS, PhD
Transpersonal psychology, Roman Catholic tradition, Educator
http://www.radicalauthenticity.com

Anne Hillman is like a master gardener who first prepares the ground so that what already lies deep and waiting to grow is given the opportunity to thrive.

MARIGOLD FARMER
International conference and retreat organizer
Teacher, Alexander Technique
http://www.soulmoves.co.uk

About the Author

 Anne Hillman mentors groups and individuals who seek a mature spirituality. An author and educator, her writing and experiential learning groups are an invitation to step into a creative framework larger than those our cultures tend to offer. Educated at Smith College, she was originally a classical musician, singer and choral conductor, and later received a Masters degree in Adult Learning and Organization Development from Boston University. She became a consultant and for twenty years helped a broad spectrum of organizations tap new levels of group functioning and creativity in times of rapid change. Since 1978, she has explored the internal aspects of social change—an inquiry into the kinds of interior development that can contribute to fundamental changes in a culture. She is the author of *The Dancing Animal Woman—A Celebration of Life*. Her articles have appeared in national journals and in newspapers and her poetry in several anthologies. She is certified by the graduate Institute in Creation Spirituality founded by Matthew Fox, and in Ontological Studies by Richard Moss, MD. Anne lives in Northern California with her husband.